"OM Shri Ganeshaya Namah"

*The sage should study the scriptures in his search
for knowledge; but then he should leave them, like the
chaff that is left behind, when the grains
of rice have been winnowed.*

AMRTABINDU UPANISHAD

Shiva

THE WILD GOD OF POWER AND ECSTASY

Wolf-Dieter Storl, Ph.D.

Inner Traditions
Rochester, Vermont

Inner Traditions
One Park Street
Rochester, Vermont 05767
www.InnerTraditions.com

Library of Congress Cataloging-in-Publication Data

Storl, Wolf-Dieter.
  Shiva : the wild God of power and ecstasy / Wolf-Dieter Storl.
    p. cm.
  Includes bibliographical references and index.
  ISBN 1-59477-014-X
  1. Siva (Hindu deity) 2. Gods, Hindu. 3. Hinduism. I. Title.
  BL1218.S8 2004
  294.5'2113—dc22

                         2004010959

Printed and bound in Canada by Transcontinental Printing

10 9 8 7 6 5 4 3 2

Text design and layout by Mary Anne Hurhula
This book was typeset in Sabon, with Belwe as a display typeface

CONTENTS

Shiva

INTRODUCTION

With the stick raised high, Illusion herds the worlds.
Lord white as jasmine [Shiva]
no one can overcome your illusion.

MAHADEVIYAKKA,
SOUTH INDIAN POETESS, TENTH CENTURY

Shiva! For his devotees, he is the entire universe and the core of all beings. Who but a fool, be he ever so wise, would dare take on the task of writing about him? Has the writer not heard the old Indian tale of the goddess of learning who, despite having mountains of ink powder, the sea as an inkwell, the World Tree as her writing pen, and the surface of the earth as her paper, failed to describe the splendor of Mahadev, the Great God? Still, neither the writer nor the reader need despair, for Shiva is the devotee of his devotees, the lover of his lovers, and though he is all-encompassing and all-transcendent, he reveals himself to his worshippers—for he is the very Self of each and every one.

In south India, when worshipping Shiva, one must first of all purify the body with water as one enters the temple, or holy site, where he customarily reveals his numinous presence. One brings him flowers, sweet smelling incense, and other beautiful things representing one's heart and soul, and dedicates them to Mahadev. One also offers a ripe coconut, which the attendant priest dashes against a hard stone surface, spilling the milk in front of the idol, or the *lingam,* which is Shiva's sign. The hard-shelled nut represents none other than our skull, this citadel of our hardened out little ego. Willingly one sacrifices this accursed limited ego-nature to the all-encompassing greater Self. The ego dwarf, reducing the universe to his own diminished dimensions by means of his

1

clever, cutting intellect, is never capable of grasping the wider mystery. Shiva, therefore, in an act of mercy, seizes it, smashes it to bits, drinks out its life fluid, and lets us find at-one-ment with him, our true Self. It is no wonder that the ego-centered individual has always shunned and feared this seeming destroyer. And no wonder, then, that Shiva is often seen as the diabolos, or devil.

The stories told in this book are common Indian lore. Grandmothers tell them to the children, peasant storytellers or wandering sadhus recite them in the evening to eager listeners. They are told, not just to entertain, but to teach, to make a point, or to illustrate some insight into the mysteries of life. My sources were mainly such oral tellings. There are however a number of good books, published in English that also address these tales and legends. Many are found in the various Puranas ("tales of ancient times"), such as the *Shiva Purana*. Helpful to the curious reader might be *Cradle Tales of Hinduism* by Sister Nivedita, *Hindu Myths* ("Penguin Classics" translated by Wendy O'Flaherty), *Classical Hindu Mythology* (Cornelia Dimmit and J. A. B. van Buitenen, eds.), *Hindu Mythology, Vedic and Puranic* by W. J. Wilkins, and *A Classical Dictionary of Hindu Mythology and Religion* by John Dowson. All of these source books will be listed in the bibliography.

I went to India in the role of an ethnologist, as a visiting scholar at Benaras Hindu University, where I planned to record various aspects of cultural and social phenomena. Faced with the heat, health problems, and most of all, the magic of this fascinating land, my cool scholarly detachment could not prevail. It was as if I myself were seized by Hara, the seizer, and sacrificed to my higher Self. My paradigms of reality vaporized, my coconut was smashed, and the grace of a wider vision *(darshana)* was accorded. When I left Bharata (as the Indians call India), this holiest of lands, where the veil covering the supernatural worlds is gossamer thin and the gods still reveal themselves to humankind, I had no photographs, no tape recordings, and few notes. These things seemed too profane, too limited. I myself was the page upon which He had written His name. And now that sufficient time has passed since I came back into the "world," I feel at last able to tell something about Mahadev—who is, dear reader, also your innermost Self.

1

JOURNEY TO THE SOURCE OF TIME

———— ᴄ\ɔ ————

You have no form,
even though with the help of Maya,
you take on myriads of forms.
You have no beginning,
though you are the beginning of all.
It is you who creates, upholds and dissolves the worlds.
MAHANIRVANA TANTRA

Without number, like the stars, and endlessly colorful are the gods and demons of India. Equally manifold are the stories, myths, and tales told about them. In our quest for Shiva, however, these others concern us but marginally. With Shiva we reach beyond polytheism's glitter and glow. With him, we enter realms deep in our innermost nature and simultaneously penetrate the profundities of ancient history. There, as the light of our spirit beams into the abysmal chasm, we vaguely discern the outlines of a most powerful archetype. Carl Gustav Jung would surely have agreed that we are confronted by one of the most original configurations of the Eurasian collective unconscious. But let us not go astray and judge that we are dealing merely with an entity of depth psychology. We are confronting a power that still rocks our lives, that sends its impulses from unfathomable depths beyond our rational consciousness, that forms our reality and sends its lifeblood pulsing through the outer world of nature as well as through the inner world of soul and spirit. The archetype works on the outside world and on the inside—and beyond both.

The mystery we are approaching is the image of the human being itself. At the beginning of time, the image appeared as in a flash of lightning, by which a surprised primate saw himself for the first time and, in that instant, was torn from the dream consciousness of his animal state. This image of light, stunning that first human soul, has remained engraved in the human memory ever since. Undefinable and inapprehensible, the image was, nonetheless, given thousands of names, decorated with endless attributes, and honored in myriad rites and rituals. This first image became the king of all other archetypes, powers, and dominions—the Lord of Gods. This image, this primal Archetype, is the key to the unspeakable mystery of humankind.

> *Christ, by highest heav'n adored,*
> *Christ, the everlasting Lord,*
> *Come, Desire of nations, come,*
> *Fix in us Thy humble home.*
> *Veiled in flesh, the Godhead see;*
> *Hail, th' incarnate Deity*
> *Pleased as man with men to dwell;*
> *Jesus, our Emmanuel.*[1]

With songs such as this celebrating the Light of the world, which shows us the way to liberation, the Western world paid homage to this mystery, at least until the dawn of the present age, which Indians call, with some justification, the Dark Age (Kali Yuga). Indeed it has become dark, for by now we barely understand the symbols, images, rituals, names, and expressions of this primal Archetype. When we are not occupied with trivia and mindless consumerism, then anxiety, depression, or dullness clouds our perception of the source of our being.

In the ancient land of India, the memory and experience of the Archetype is closer at hand. Anyone who has spent some time there will have felt it. In carefully maintained cult and ritual, its expression continues through countless folktales, legends, plays, and festivals. Perhaps we can light our own torches anew on the well-kept fire of India's vision of God and once again illumine the way into our own depths, past the poison-spewing dragon, down through the realms of the gnomes, the elves, and the spirits of the ancestral dead, until we reach the treasure chamber of our own soul where the jewel of the self rests hidden. This self, the Hindus call Shiva, the Gracious One.

India's gift to the rest of humanity is her uncompromising tenacity in keeping memories alive and retaining—as in a living museum—all past states through which humanity has traversed. Hindu culture and the Indian soul remind one of the layers of sedimentary rocks of the towering Himalayas. In stratified geological deposits, each rich in characteristic lead fossils, all the sequences of past life remain recorded as they unfolded in ancient seas. South Asian society, with its many racial and occupational castes, represents, in a similar way, a layer cake of cultural evolution.

At the bottom of the social ladder are the thirty to sixty million hunters and gatherers, the *adavasi,* or tribal peoples, who even today pursue the oldest calling of humankind in the mountains and remaining jungles, while conjuring spirits and dancing shamanic dances. Beyond these primitive tribals, one comes across swidden and hoe agriculturists who worship the Great Mother, much as the megalithic Europeans did once upon a time. The cult of the Great Goddess was one of fertility and involved bloody rituals and headhunting. Prisoners of war, exemplary youths, or sacrificial animals, preferably bulls, were ritually hacked to pieces and buried in the soil, much as were planted the seeds and tubers. In this way, peasants replenished the Goddess's energy so that the earth would continue to yield rich crops. Even today, one might find a short notice on the third or fourth page of a provincial newspaper telling of an irate constable and his men who had to arrest a number of villagers. The charge: child-sacrifice, dismemberment of the body, and burial of the pieces in various fields to assure a good harvest.

The dominant cultural stratum, however, is that of the Indo-European tribes of nomadic cattle herders who fell upon the subcontinent some four to five thousand years ago. These new Aryan settlers—who have since dominated and formed Indian culture decisively—were a proud, patriarchal warrior folk who called themselves the "noble ones" *(arya).* They brought with them horses and the horse sacrifice, the worship of fire and the sun, holy cows, and a language that is akin to the European tongues. The Aryan priests, the Brahmins—like their cousins, the Celtic druids and the Roman flamins—learned endlessly long magical spells and sacred verses by rote. The wisdom contained therein eventually found its way into the

"Holy cows" are still worshipped today

written record of the holy Vedas. That the ancient chants might lose their magical potency due to incorrect pronunciation was as constant a worry to the Aryan priests as that their blood might become diluted by mixture with the subjugated races of planters and hunters. In order to forestall race miscegenation, a system of castes *(varna)* was imposed. In order to keep the sacred language pure, the sage Patanjali set up a carefully wrought system of the rules of Sanskrit grammar and phonetics.

Aryan dominion was not seriously threatened until the twelfth century, when Muslim zealots, drawn partially by the lure of the immense riches of the land beyond the Indus, launched their invasions. They brought with them the culture of medieval Islam, whose sounds, sights, and smells we can admire to this day, preserved in nearly original purity in the Muslim ghettos of India's towns and cities.

There are other rare specimens purely preserved in the cultural sediments of India. There are the Zarathustrian fire worshippers—the Parsees of Gujarat and Bombay, who had fled the Muslim ravages of Persia. There are the Jews of Cochin, who came as merchants and as refugees when the Romans destroyed Jerusalem. There are the Portuguese whose Baroque Christianity, greasy pork sausages, bullfights, sweet wine, and leisurely Mediterranean lifestyle still color the local culture of Goa. Then, of course, there are the British, whose two-hundred-year domination has left a legacy of dutiful train officials (the trains still run on time in India!), stodgy postmasters with handlebar moustaches, plucky Indian Army officers, a collegiate passion for cricket, clubs, teatime, remnants of gingerbread architecture and, last but not least, a rather queer-sounding Hindu English. There are moments in Calcutta or Bombay when the whole Victorian world rises in front of one's eyes in uncanny purity.

Thus every invasion, every epoch has left its nonvanishing trace in the fullness of India, well preserved in the formaldehyde of a system of castes, subcastes, and occupational niches *(jati)*. What a storehouse of treasures for the student of ethnography and cultural history! Like a peacock's fan, the spectrum spreads before one's eyes:

the Old Stone Age; the Neolithic, matriarchal planters; the patriarchal peasantry (the majority); the medieval towns and guilds; the men
and women of the Enlightenment; Victorian capitalism; and an ultra-
modern world of show biz and high tech.

Each era and each culture has had a part in forming the current cult and
iconography of the Archetype, which is the subject of our treatise. The
shamanistic hunters provided the core, in the form of the trance-dancing
horned god who is the lord of the animals and the guardian of the souls:
Pashupati. The matriarchal planters gave him the Great Goddess as a
companion and as the personification of his magical, illusive power:
Shakti. They also associated him with the fertilizing phallus, serpents,
and bulls. The Aryan bards, in turn, lauded him as the all-consuming
fire god, Agni, the intoxicating brew (*soma*) and, above all, as the howling storm god, Rudra, with his host of the spirits of the dead, ghosts,
and goblins.

Perhaps it was through the Persian prophet Zarathustra* and his
coercive vision of the one God of Gods that the image of Shiva grew
in the direction of Mahadev, the Great God, for whom all other divinities become mere appendages, reflections, or masks.[2] Like a great
sponge, he soaks up all of their characteristics and makes them his
own. Varuna (the Uranus of the Greeks), the ancient Aryan god of
heaven and guardian of the cosmic law, is pushed into the lesser role
of ruler of the waters and misty air, while his function as the keeper of
the universal right and ritual *(rita)* and as master of the magic we call
existence, is taken over by Shiva. Agni, the god of fire and sacrifice,
becomes the mere backdrop, the wheel of flame in which Shiva dances
his dance of creation and destruction. The sun god Surya, who trav-
erses the heavens daily in his horse-drawn chariot like an Aryan warrior crossing the battlefield, has a similar fate. Even though his name
is called upon daily by the worshipper in the holiest of Sanskrit
mantras (Gayatri Mantra), his light diminishes next to that of Shiva.
Even the Brahmins, those fearsome priests of Vedic times—once considered to be almighty due to their mastery of all spells and due to the
belief that the gods and the worlds were born from within their

---

*Zarathustra = Greek Zoroaster

Surya, the Vedic sun god

minds—even they were humbled by the Great God. We shall see how the seemingly omnipotent Brahmin, in the person of Daksha, the chief of sacrificial priests and creator of many gods, is reduced to a pitiable goat by Lord Shiva, and how Daksha's lovely daughter, the image of the divine human soul, leaves her strict father to take her place at Shiva's side.

Periodically, when the Central Asian steppes became too dry for their grazing animals, wild nomads would sweep into northwestern India: the Scythians (Sakas), Huns (Hunas), and Mongolians (Kusanas). Brought along by these horse people were elements of north and central Asian shamanism, which were absorbed into the Indian Shiva cult. Grandiose names like Ishvara (lord), Mahesvara (great lord), or Paramesvara (highest lord), all titles with which the lords and kings of the nomads decorated themselves, became the names of the great God. Many characteristics indicate that Odin (Anglo-Saxon, Old English *Wodan, Woden, Wotan*), the magic-wielding lord of the winds and protector of the Nordic warriors, sprang from the same imagination as this shamanistic Shiva. Odin, too, seems to have had his origin in the steppes and forests of Asia. Engraved discs *(bractea)* of hammered gold, showing this shamanistic god on his horse, are found all over Siberia and Central Asia.[3]

Perhaps Shiva owes his reputed hemp addiction to the influence of the Scythians. These notoriously wild horsemen had the custom of celebrating their wakes for the dead in sweat lodges in which hemp leaves were strewn over red-hot stones. The resultant fumes helped the mourning kinsmen "lift off" and, for a time, accompany the departed over the threshold of the dead.[4] To this day, the devotees of Shiva, the wandering saints *(sadhus)* and little fathers *(babas)*, who often take on shamanistic functions, inhale the smoke of this plant to enter the realm of the spirits of the dead. Even though they use clay funnels *(chilam)* instead of sweat lodges, the principle is the same.

Women play a major role in Hindu culture and Hindu lore. This

A sadhu

stands in contrast to the more patri-archal ethos of Muslim culture or even to the western Christian cul-ture. It is no problem at all to Hindus to worship God in form of a Woman, as a divine lover, as a companion, as a universal maternal being (Durga, Kali, Chamunda, and Shakti are very popular). Hindu women have a lot of social clout: they are active in pol-itics and professions, and in the indi-vidual extended households, the elder women, the "matajis," domi-nate the entire family and also dominate the daughters-in-law.

However, as the title suggests, this book deals with only one aspect of Hindu culture, namely, the cult of Shiva. Because it is not my intent to write an all-encompassing book on Hinduism, I don't have space to fully elucidate these feminine aspects other than to mention that Shiva himself can be and is worshipped as a female deity (Shivā) or as male and female at the same time (Uma-Shankar; Ardhanarishvara, Shiva-Shakti). However, the Shaivites, especially the sadhus, with whom I spent some time, generally image this god in his male form. They do this, fully aware, that he can only *be,* by the grace of Shakti, the female ground of being.

The ancient Greeks, who, after the escapades of Alexander the Great, established the Seleucid Empire and the Greco-Bactrian king-doms in the East, also salted the stew. "These conquerors equated Indra with their own Zeus, Shiva with Dionysos, Krishna with Hercules and the goddess Padma (Lotos) with Artemis."[5] The legends of the Greek Dionysians tell of a time when the god of wine and orgiastic religion arrived from the East riding a white bull; others tell of his two-year sojourn in India. Some scholars are convinced that the Indian Shiva and the Mediterranean Dionysus are more than casually related.[6]

The temple architecture as it exists in India to this day seems to be a gift of the Bactrian Greeks. The Vedic Aryans had worshipped their gods out-of-doors, putting their sacrificial beasts to the knife on low platforms laid out with fragrant herbs and sacred *darbhah* grass (*Desmostachya bipinnata,* L.). Wandering Shiva sadhus still perform their rituals in the open air. However, after the Greek incursion, rectangular

A typical Hindu temple

stone temples similar to those found in the Mediterranean world made their appearance.

The heart of the temple is a little shrine *(garbhagrha)*, which (when dedicated to Shiva) contains a phallic stone shaft, the *lingam,* as a sign of the presence of the Great God. Above this holy of holies rises a tower *(sikhara),* richly decorated with gods and heavenly singers, symbolizing Mount Meru, the center of the universe, piercing all the heavenly spheres. The assembly hall *(mandapa)* faces the shrine, its roof carried by a forest of stone columns. Just in front of the hall is a small vestibule. The temple is considered to be the sacred body of the god. The gateway *(gopuram)* is his feet, the shrine is the heart and the tower is his neck and head, which ends in a tuft of hair *(sikha),* just as it does with the devotee.[7]

Since our Western churches have their origin in Greek architecture, the similarity should not surprise us. Here, too, we find the vestibule, the assembly hall, the tower, and the *sanctum sanctorum.* Though the shrine on the altar does not contain God in the form of a lingam, it does contain the core symbol of the Christian faith, the monstrance, the chalice of the Lord's Body, the Host (Latin *hostia* = sacrificial animal).

Besides building the first stone temples, Greek sculptors fashioned the first lifelike images of Buddhas and bodhisattvas meditating in lotus postures as we still find them displayed all over south and east Asia. It was not long before Shiva, in his appearance as the peaceful Shankar, was sculpted in a similar manner, sitting in the absolute tranquillity of deep meditation on his tiger skin.

Perhaps it was the contact with the so-called Syrian Christians of Kerala (the little flock of Christians that the apostle Thomas had supposedly converted) that gave Shaivism in south India a totally new turn. It was the *bhakti* movement, preached by Tamil saints, that conceived of their dancing lord as the God of Love, similar to Christ. In complete self-abandon and devotion, they sing that God's ocean of love is not found in some external object but in the devotee's heart. The holy bard Basavanna, the founder of the Lingayat sect (whose members wear a little Shiva lingam encased in silver around their necks, much as Catholics wear a cross), sings the following verse:

> *The rich will make temples for Shiva.*
> *What shall I, a poor man, do?*
> *My legs are pillars,*
> *The body, the shrine,*
> *The head, a cupola of gold.*
> *Listen, O Lord of the Meeting Rivers,*
> *Things standing shall fall*
> *But the moving ever shall stay.* [8]

The indwelling of the blessed Lord cannot be gained through pious works but flows continually out of his fountain of immeasurable grace toward the human soul. Our relationship to God is not like that of a baby monkey that needs to muster its strength to cling onto its mother; rather it is like that of a kitten that the mother cat carefully carries in its jaws to safety. Shiva, thus, is a savior who seizes the human being much like "a peasant who grabs his cow by the horns when it is about to sink into the quagmire."[9] Like Christ, who took upon himself the bitter cup of perdition, so Shiva drank the poison of the world, which the activity of the gods and titans churned from the depths of the primal ocean. To his *bhaktas*, his loving devotees, he is a caring mother and a good shepherd. Basavanna sings:

> *. . . the Lord of the Meeting Rivers*
> *stays with me*
> *every step of the way*
> *and looks after me.*

As we see, every cultural stream is a river feeding the ocean of Shiva. He takes the images and imaginations of every age as his decoration. The process has not ended. This powerful Archetype is by no means fading as the materialistic, hyper-rationalistic mania of our civilization reaches ever-new heights. On the contrary, our thoughts and achievements become his adorning tinsel. Bhagwan Shree Rajneesh (Osho), for example, reinterpreted the palate of Western psychotherapy and transpersonal psychology in partially Shaivite terms.[10] Various swamis (spiritual teachers), from Shri Chimoy to Gopi Krishna, insist doggedly that their teachings and methods for achieving Shiva consciousness are solidly "scientific." There are Indian scholars *(pundits)* who, having realized the power inherent in a historical interpretation of the world process, go as far as claiming that Shiva is a historical figure who some five thousand years ago invented tools, speech, fire, music, and all other prerequisites of human civilization, and fathered humankind with his three wives: with Gauri the white race, with Durga the yellow race, and with Parvati the black race. Such immodest scholars have even ranged themselves with atomic energy. Taking Nehru's slogan ("Let your factories be temples and your temples be factories") as a starting point, they easily interpret the rounded cement core of the nuclear plant as the expression of the Shiva lingam and the horrible energy potential it contains as the expression of his Shakti power.

Even for us Westerners, the naked god with matted hair and a trident in his hand is not just a curiosity of cultural or religious history. He stalks, unrecognized, the alleyways of our megalopolises and roams the minds of some of their inhabitants. A chance glimpse of him irrevocably fascinates and sets to vibrating long-neglected strings in our innermost soul. Long-forgotten reminiscences of ancient, Indo-European and pre-Indo-European shamanism, vague memories of a time when humankind was wild and free, will suddenly shimmer through all the layers of our cultural conditioning. No timid prayer or hasty striking the sign of the cross, no government authority or weighty scientific fact-finding will banish him. Though long pronounced dead by the rational Enlightenment, or at least banished to the garden of lunacy, accessible to a few poets, lovers, and madmen, the Archetype will raise its head and make the ground tremble. The tiled walls of the laboratory already show ominous cracks: wars on terrorism, star wars, financial jitters, environmental collapse. A wild, uncanny god smiles through these fissures and beckons us to cast our eye into dimensions that make us sway and steal our breath.

Of course, one had been aware of this "oriental idol" for some time. Ever since the British berserkers in the guise of cool colonial administrators and businessmen took on India, scholars have been busy studying and defining this phenomenon. But it was not until the 1960s that the floodgates were opened wide, when masses of flower children, hippies, adventurers, and refugees from a dismal, materialistic consumer society followed the call of the Pied Piper of the Orient. Cheap jet travel and the newly completed overland route made it possible.

Once again a New World was discovered, a world whose king is Shiva. Once again there was culture shock on both sides. At first, the flower children were received by the Indian peasants like gods. They were fed, sheltered, and worshipped. Many a young hippie couple was treated like Shiva and Parvati who, as every Indian knows, occasionally take on human form to travel the land in order to test the strength of devotion. Some of the young seekers never made it back. Dysentery, hepatitis, cruel fevers, sheer exhaustion, and drugs took their toll. Most, however, returned transformed to the cities of the West. They reappeared dressed in afghan velvets, shining silks, colorful paisleys that smelled of musk, patchouli, and other exotic fragrances. Hair freely flowing and eyes filled with a gentle glow, and ornamented with necklaces, bracelets, ankle bracelets, nose-rings and earrings, they told tales of wonder and delight. None who went came back unchanged. Even if they managed the jump back into the everyday routine of job and family, somewhere along the line their "minds had been blown." Like seeds cast into fertile ground, Shiva, Kali, and Krishna came back with them, taking root in the wasteland, sending shoots here and there through the cement and plastic.

Since then, the first wave of India freaks, dropouts, *ganja* devotees and guru seekers has ebbed away. The established powers spared no effort to stay the cultural erosion and end this seeming heyday of fools. But though the external tide of the India craze has receded, the inner

Indianized Western hippies and Westernized Indians in Goa

tide is flooding on. Everywhere people are practicing meditation and yoga. They do it to stay fit, lose weight, find themselves, give easy births and, in the executive suite, to cope with the stress of competitive business. It should be known that Shiva is Mahayogi, the lord of yoga.

Drugs, especially the smoking of marihuana, have become firmly integrated aspects of the youth subculture and the music scene. It should be known that Shiva is Aushadhishvara, the lord of herbs and drugs. Knowingly, he winks his eye at the hippy and the ganja-smoking Rastafarian who, with dreadlocks and easygoing lifestyle, looks like an African version of the Shiva sadhu.

Tantra (Nepalese print)

In a society where men and women are at war with each other and sex is used as a weapon, it is no wonder that tantra and sex-yoga are increasingly popular. Shiva appears as the master of tantric technique and teaches frustrated couples how to be eternally in love (as he is with Parvati) and how sex can be a pathway to enlightenment.

Is it any wonder that a repressed, over-civilized humankind, thoroughly out of harmony with its basic nature, is fascinated by a figure such as Tarzan, Lord of the Apes? The fantasies of Edgar Rice Borroughs have been translated into fifty-eight languages with a total of over fifty million copies in print. The natural man, he who can talk to the animals and make unfettered love to his companion, Jane, has appeared in film after film since 1918. In him we meet again the archetype of Shiva as Pashupati, lord of the animals. With his mistress, the goddess Parvati, or at times alone, clad only in a tiger skin, unkempt, and unburdened by civilization, he roams the wilderness and jungles and hears the stories of all creatures.

"Psssst!" he whispers to the man in the pinstripe suit. "How do things stand with the environment? Can you hear what the plants and animals are telling you?"

2

FIRE AND ICE

If it rains fire
you have to be as water;

if it is a deluge of water
you have to be as the wind;

if it is the Great Flood
you have to be as the sky;

and if it is the Very Last Flood of all the worlds
you have to give up self
and become the Lord.

ALLAMA PRABHU,
MEDIEVAL SOUTH INDIAN POET, TENTH CENTURY

Whereas animals possess consciousness, human beings are gifted with reflective self-consciousness. Long, long ago in some dim past, while foraging for food in the savannas of Africa, the awesome realization of the Self must have suddenly flashed into the soul of some apelike primate ancestor. Legions of anthropologists and prehistorians have attempted to locate this threshold of humanity and reconstruct a picture of this past by patiently taking clues from bone fragments and pollen analyses, charcoal scrapings and bits of chipped rock. No flights of fancy here, but hard, objective data and clear thinking to match it.

Occultists and "spiritual scientists," on the other hand, approach the problem with entirely different methods. Using meditation and trance, they try to sink consciously into the deeper layers of the mind, like geologists taking bore probes to find what picture images lay buried there in the racial memory. Their tools are "spiritual organs" (for example, the "third eye"), developed by rigorous spiritual exercises and supported by an ascetic lifestyle that often involves vegetarian diets, fasting, and abstinence from alcohol. Thus sensitized, they can fathom their own transpersonal depths or manage to read in the so-called Akashic chronicle. The basic assumption is that every thought, word, or event creates vibrations that leave their impression in the ether *(akasha)*, much as light rays do on photographic film. The initiate whose spiritual eye is open would be able to perceive these subtle impressions in his or her soul and in the ethereal mantle of the earth.

Obviously, the hard-core scientist and the occultist researcher relate to each other as dogs do to cats. But this should not bother us. In our attempt to elucidate the Shiva archetype, we shall utilize the results of both schools. The one side deals with the phenomena more from the outside, the other more from the inside.

Prometheus chained to a rock

In Greek myth, it was Prometheus (the forethinker) who took pity upon the human animal and brought her fire and, thereby, culture. Fire was the prerogative of the gods and its theft angered the deities tremendously. Which evildoer would thus dare disrupt the cosmic order? Father Zeus, the only divinity it behooves to carry the thunderbolt, had this rebel who dared to steal the fire chained to a cliff in the Caucasian mountains, where an eagle feeds daily on his liver. There Prometheus must remain until, on some distant day, Hercules will free him from his suffering.

The scientific anthropologist is not especially interested in such mythological imagery. Instead, she will point out the bits of wood coal found at L'Escale in southern France, radiocarbon-dated at nearly eight hundred thousand years ago. There, at the dawn of the last series of Ice Ages, rather apish-looking hominoids *(Homo erectus)* had built distinct hearths. Some five hundred thousand years ago, another Homo erectus, the Peking man, roasted the meat of bears, buffalo, and boars, as well as other Peking men, on hearths in the Choukoutien Caves. It is now estimated that humanity came into control of fire some million years ago. One of the primate horde must have been possessed by sufficient courage to lift a burning fire brand, perhaps where a brushfire had set a bush aflame or where lightning struck a solitary tree. Such a flash of lightning kindled not only an elemental fire—it kindled the human spirit. It was truly a moment of

Homo erectus *tending the fire*

heroism when that individual overcame the animal fear of fire and reached for the flaming torch. No animal can do this. At that very moment, the first of humankind stood on earth—a sovereign!

With that horrendous deed, everything changed. Nothing remained the same. Even if the act of kindling remained a secret for ages, the next time lightning struck a tree the sacred element could be caught again, carried along, fed, and kept alive. Culture (Latin *cultus* = the careful tending), the essential criterion of humanity and symbol of human freedom from the compelling guardianship of the gods and instincts, took its beginning. The carriers of the flame wielded power. They had power over predatory beasts. In the ambers they could fire-harden the tips of their wooden spears. Raw meat and tough tubers could be cooked soft. With fire, early humans could enter the cold forests and steppes of the north, despite ice and winter storms.

But it was not just the human animal that dared grasp for the fire: the Fire seized the human being. The Spirit, equated in most cultures with fire or fiery air, incarnated in the human primate. The Fire Spirit from the external macrocosm of Nature took up residence in the human microcosm. As this happened, the inner divine light became so strong that the first fire catcher no longer feared the external flame.

Thus, the old myths of Prometheus, who angered the gods, and of other light-bringers, such as Lucifer (Latin *lux* = light, *ferre* = to carry), the disobedient angel who fell from heaven, indicate archaic memories. In the form of a shimmering serpent appearing at the tree, this Spirit "deceived" the feminine receptive soul, leading the innocent half-animal astray and initiating it into the mystery of good and evil. In that act, the serpent tore the original oneness apart, splitting it into the dichotomies of inside/outside, microcosm/macrocosm, man/woman, I/other. Adam loses his rib and must leave the original paradise where death, toil, and suffering are unknown.

This moment of the rending of the universe must have been the moment when the spark of speech moved the tongue for the first time. (In India the *muni* sage, who has bridged the chasm and regained the pristine unity, stops speaking and commenting. With a mysterious hush of a smile on his lips, he sits in silence.) In this twinkling of an eye, when Fire sundered us from the rest of creation, all naming, denoting, designating, and objectifying began. The incarnating Luciferian spirit cast its harsh light upon the now "external" Nature. Its intelligence created the "world." Gods and demons appeared in myriad forms and screamed to be named. *Maya*, the grand illusion, which the wise of India try to flee, started her seductive dance. At the same time, religion, the yearning of the suffering soul for the original harmonious oneness, entered the scene. One must come to terms with these gods and demons. Their anger must be appeased. One offered them prayers, respect, and tribute in blood and sacrifice.

That first bold reach for the flame burned itself deep into human memory. It is recalled in the dreams, myths, legends, and rituals of all peoples. The sacred fire plays a central role in most rites. It is the focus of attention—*focus* being the Roman word for all private and public sacred fires. The hearth is the center of the house, just as the sun, the celestial fire, is the heart of the heavens. In the blood sacrifice, the red embers and the warm red liquor of life find communion. Fire and blood are a bridge to the other world and provide blessing (Old English *bledsian* = to bless with a daub of blood).

The cooking fire is the flaming mouth of Agni (related to Latin *ignis* = fire, ignition), Shiva in his fiery form. Indian mothers to this day flick bits of butter or flour into the stove, calling each god by name to accept the offering. Fire is also the door through which mortals enter the spirit world: those who have lost their worldly attachment enter the fire's light as it diffuses into the eternal, indivisible Brahman.* Other souls, still attached to the endless cycle of life and death, enter the smoke of the fire, rise to the rain clouds, reenter the

---

Brahman refers to the all-pervading numinous power that permeates the Universe. The concept is not to be confused with Brahma, the creator god, nor with the Brahmins (or Brahmans), the caste of priests who have the power to wield and manipulate Brahman.

soil with the rain, are absorbed by the crop plants, become food, enter the blood, transform into sperm and egg, and commence with a new incarnation.

On the other hand, heroes can be born of fire. Draupadi, the wife of the five Pandavas (the heroes of the *Mahabharata*) was born, along with her twin brother, when a libation was poured on the sacrificial fire. Karttikeya, Shiva's son and savior of the world, was born of fire, as were Romulus and Remus, the first Romans, when a virgin was made to conceive by a male organ of generation that sprang

Agni, the god of fire

out of the sacrificial fire. It is a common belief among European peasants that when a woman's apron is scorched by flying cinders, she is about to conceive.[1] Everywhere, mantras, oaths, and binding spells are spoken into the living flame, be it to bind a man and a woman into wedlock, be it to swear loyalty or revenge.* Such is the power of this element.

Whether it was actually a flash of lightning that led humankind on its odyssey of self-discovery, we cannot, of course, know as a scientific fact. But the theme crops up again and again. Even modern fantasies are fueled by the idea of the generative force of the thunderbolt. Benjamin Franklin, who drew lightning from the sky with his kite and inaugurated the age of electricity, stirred the imagination of his time. A few years later, in her classic novel, *Frankenstein, or the modern Prometheus* (1818), Mary W. Shelley gave a prophetic vision of the mad attempt of science (represented by Dr. Frankenstein) to create a new superman. This new being, constructed of choice limbs and organs derived from the freshly deceased, is brought to life by the electrical discharge of a lightning storm.

This archetypal picture of life derived from heavenly fire spooks in the brains of sober, modern scientists as well. One still assumes that it was the influx of cosmic radiation combining with electrical arcs (lightning) discharged into the Precambrian sea that caused the "dilute

---

*The Rütli Oath, that marks the birth of the Swiss nation, was spoken into the bonfire of the first of August, a day that formerly celebrated the Celtic fire god Lugh or Lugus. The biblical story of Pentecost, when fiery tongues descended upon the faithful, causing them to "speak in tongues," illustrates also the connection between fire and speech.

The holy fire is the focus of the Indian wedding

organic soup" of amino acids, proteins, and other polymers to weld together to form the first living molecules capable of reproduction.*

The god associated with fire in the old Nordic and Germanic sagas is the trickster, Loki (his name being related to Swedish *laga*, Old High German *Loug*, Old English *Lieg* = a shooting flame). He is the cunning, magical being who can change his form at will, whose scandalmongering tongue outrages the gods and whose offspring include Hel (goddess of the underworld), the world serpent, and the wolf of doom. His father is Farbauti, the lightning bolt, and his mother is Laufey, the verdant oak. Having killed the sun god, Baldur, he tries to flee the wrath of the gods by constantly changing his form. Thor catches him anyway and he is chained, like Prometheus, to a rock where a snake's venom continuously drips on him. Were it not for his faithful wife, who catches the acrid drops in a bowl, the pain would be too much to bear. When she turns to empty the bowl and the bane burns him, he writhes in pain, causing the earth to tremble.

The Slavs tell of Perun, a heaven god associated with the thunderbolt and fertility. And the Baltic tribes worshipped a Perkun, whose lightning bolt strikes out of high heavens. It is interesting in our context that the names of these deities refer to the oak tree (Latin *quercus*, Old Latin *perquos* = oak).[2] Surely our conjecture is not too far off when we guess that the initial kindling of the human spirit took place when lightning, like a cosmic serpent, struck a towering deciduous tree next to some hapless Homo erectus, for everywhere folklore combines the elements of fire/lightning/heaven/god/trickster (serpent)/tree in an archetypal symbolic complex.

*S. L. Miller's now classic experiment (1953) of synthesizing amino acids by reconstructing an early atmosphere of hydrogen, helium, methane, and ammonia, along with saltwater and electrical charges, lends support to the "dilute organic soup" hypothesis.

In later times the tribal king—as a representative of the heaven god—held court under such a tree.* Often a cone-shaped rock (*menhir*) was set in the same place, as a symbol of the heavenly thunderstone. Under its protection, the *Thing* or *Ting*, the assembly of the free and noble, was held at astrologically auspicious times (usually at full moon), to decide what shall be and what shall not be, what is right and what is wrong. Here at the thingstead, duels were fought and ordeals were held, sacrificial

A pipal (fig) tree

fires kindled and oaths sworn, for this was the First Tree. Its roots reached into the underworld where the dragon dwells and its crown pierced the heavens. It is the same archetypal tree that is the shaman's ladder. Under a tree such as this, Siddhartha, the son of a king, meditated until he became illuminated and became the Buddha, the Enlightened One. We shall soon see what all this has to do with Shiva.

⁘ THE ROCK ⁘

Monkeys occasionally pick up stones to throw at predators or to crack the shells of tasty nuts. At the dawn of humanity, however, it was no longer a frightened or hungry animal that haphazardly picked up a stone, but a being possessed by a newly incarnate spirit who then formed the object in accordance with an inner imagination to serve her as a tool or weapon. At that point in time, regular toolmaking traditions appeared that help the prehistorian to trace cultural development and migration routes. The so-called firestones, the flints and cherts that, when struck, flake off into razor-sharp blades, were the preferred raw material. The accompanying sparks and smell of sulfur are to this day the sign of the Promethean, or demonic.

Is not the hard rock, which can kindle a fire, like the male organ, which when stone hard, engenders the spark of life in the maternal

---

*The tribal council held under a mighty tree is, according to historians of religion (Eliade, Campbell), nearly universal. Here, however I refer primarily to Indo-European or, specifically, northwestern European tradition.

womb? The association of stone, fire making, and fertility is so basic that it has left its trace in language. The word *child* (German *Kind*, from Old German *kenda* = generated) is related to the verb "to kindle" and can be traced to its Indo-European root *gen*, "to bear, kindle, generate." (We recognize it in such words as Sanskrit *Janati* = he begets; Greek *Genea* = birth, race; and Latin *generatio* = kindle, generate.) The flint chopper or hand tool with which the hearth fire can be kindled, thus readily becomes the symbol of the phallus through which the fire of life is passed from generation to generation. In turn, it is associated with the thundering god of the heavens, whose fire-semen lights up the sky and impregnates the Earth Mother, just as it generates ideas in the minds of human beings.

The lightning bolt (or thunderstone) is the scepter of numerous gods who bring life and fertility as well as deal in death. The worship of a hammer god (Thor) and "thunderer" is recorded for the culture of northwestern Europe already some three to four thousand years ago in the Bronze Age rock engravings of Scandinavia. His stone hammer *(mjollnir)* played an important role in all rituals.* Marriages were solemnized by laying such a hammer in the lap of the bride! Sacrificial victims were slain with it. At the thingstead, rapping thrice with the hammer made a transaction or judgment legal and binding—as it still does at our courts and auctions today. In heathen times, northern Europeans wore a miniature Thor's hammer around their neck as an amulet, much as the Lingayats of south India carry a Shiva lingam.

Just like Thor (the Thunar of the Anglo-Saxons), Indra, the old Vedic thunder god, sports a mighty thunderbolt *(vajra)*, with which he smashes the skulls of demons and blesses the earth with fertilizing rain. The vajra (lightning, thunderbolt, jewel, diamond, phallus) is to this day the focus of the esoteric sects of Vajrayana or the Diamond Vehicle of Buddhism. It rests as a jewel in the lotus *(padma)*, as the phallus, or lingam, in the vagina, and as enlightenment (Buddha) in the heart.

The dual nature of this magical stone is readily apparent. It is the generator of life and fertility, as well as the dealer of death and the kindler of the final conflagration. As a weapon of war and hunt,

---

*The word *hammer*, interestingly enough, is derived from the Indo-European *akmen*, which signifies a "stone fallen from heaven." Related are the Sanskrit *ashmen* (stone, heaven), Greek *akmon* (anvil, meteor stone, heaven), and Slavic *kamen* (stone).

the hand ax, or spear point, brings the quarry to fall, assuring food for the clan; and it brings the destruction of the enemy, thus restoring peace. As a phallus, it wounds the virgin but makes continued life possible. As a grinding stone, it destroys nuts and grains in order to prepare the life-sustaining meal. The act of grinding destroys the grain but, at the same time, multiplies it by fragmenting it. In a similar way, in the original act of creation, the Cosmic Giant (Sanskrit Purusha, Norwegian Ymir, Hebrew Adam Kadmon) was sacrificed and multiplied by dismemberment. The great sacrifice, involving the stone knife, thus stood at the beginning of the world. Creation is multiplicity derived from the destruction of the original unity.

To early humankind, the heat generated by the campfire, by the sexual act, by the effort of the hunt or battle, by dance or hard work, was the expression of one and the same source, the cosmic fire spirit. As the Indians view it, the ascetic, or sadhu, is holy because of the accumulated, unspent heat *(tapas)* generated by his or her ascetic practices. Because of this inner ardor, the sage can burn up sins and reduce old works *(karma)* to ashes. At the same time, he or she can brood out new worlds, just like the hen broods out its eggs.* Because of their fiery nature, the Indian fakir and the Siberian shaman can walk over red hot coals, pick up glowing iron, plunge their arms into boiling water, sit naked in the snow, or burn their potent imaginings into souls that are not as hot.

In this context, the word *shaman* is quite revealing. Once, Pali-speaking Buddhist monks, the *samana*, carried the concept to the forests and taigas of the north. It is derived from the Sanskrit *shramana*, referring to an ascetic, one who makes an ardent effort (from Sanskrit *shram* = to exercise, to heat up). The ashram (Sanskrit *asrama*) is thus such a place where a heated effort is undertaken. Shiva is the master of all ascetics, fakirs, and shramanas. He contains all the heat of the universe in his lingam. At the end of time, this heat will conflagrate all of creation, just as it will generate it anew.

Archaic societies all over the world set up boulders, menhirs, megaliths, and styles as centers of religious activity. They can be interpreted as oversized hand axes, thunderbolts, and (yes, old Sigmund Freud was right) phalluses. They were the gateways to the other world. The dead

---

*Indeed Brahma, the Creator, was the original golden egg (Hiranyagarbha), which he divided with his own heat, separating it into two parts, which now form heaven and earth.

were buried near them and the unborn hovered there in order to incarnate anew. Often they were smeared with sacrificial blood, later with blood red ocher (hematite). In India one still finds cylindrical *bir* or *bhairan* stones—painted a bright vermilion—in which local divinities manifest themselves. The Shiva lingams, conical stones representing God, are no longer covered with blood or cinnabar red, but washed with milk, coconut juice, or Ganges water. The priests *(pujaris)* who attend the lingam, nonetheless, dab red powder on the foreheads of the devotees. In a similar manner, the ancient Germanic and Celtic priests blessed the worshippers by dabbing sacrificial blood onto the middle of their brows.

❦ WATER ❦

The heat of the flame brings about its dialectical opposite: It melts ice to water; it smelts metal out of the rock. The flow of semen ends the heated passion of the sensual embrace; the gushing of the quarry's blood ends the heat of the chase; the moist cool of the moon's night ends the fiery rule of the sun's day. Out of such opposites life arises.

In the Nordic creation myth, which has similarities to the myths of the Vedic Indians, the first being, the giant Ymir, is created out of the mingling of ice and fire. Simultaneously the first animal, the Cow, arises, whose milk nourishes the primordial being. Ymir's grandsons, Odin, Willi, and We (Loki), create the world by sacrificing and dismembering the grandfather giant. His skin becomes the earth, his hair the trees, his blood the rivers and seas, his skull the heavenly vault, and the gray blob of his brains, the clouds.

*The river goddess
Sarasvati*

In the Celtic creation myth, also, the cosmos is created out of water and fire. The Roman ethnographer Strabo notes the fear of the otherwise fearless Celts that someday the world will fall apart again into these two opposite elements.

Water, the feminine counterpart to the masculine fire, heals, cleans, and gives birth to life's seeds. Supernatural beings of feminine gender are apt to manifest at springs, waterfalls, rivers, lakes, and seas. River goddesses, such as the great white goddess Dana, who gave her name to many Eurasian rivers (Danube, Don, Dee), nymphs, nixes, and swan maidens, all have their counterpart in India. Foremost among these are the river goddess Ganga, who flows from Shiva's locks, and the river goddess Sarasvati, the queen of muses, who rides a white swan.

Many holy rituals of humankind aim to symbolically recreate the original unity of the primordial elements of fire and water (or ice). Whoever has been enflamed by the fire of the Spirit will seek baptism in sanctified waters. In India, it is a daily ritual to greet the rising sun with a bath in the river. As part of the observance, one cups one's hands and offers water to the rising celestial fire. Elsewhere, libations of holy water, mead, or blood are poured into the sacred fire. In the sex act, which—as in Tantra—is often seen as a sacred act, heat and moisture find creative combination.

A fever is the collision of the two primal elements in the microcosm of the body, bathing its victim in sweat and shaking him between waves of heat and cold. A violent fever, which rips the individual out of his mundane routine and catapults him into madness, is part of the "initiation illness" of the traditional shaman. In his or her delirium, the initiate into shamanism enters the world of the spirits and the dead. If the initiate lacks magical strength, he or she will remain in this other world, that is, die.

The creation of artificial fevers by means of the sweat lodge is one of the oldest shamanistic techniques. Going back to Paleolithic times, it can be found from Scandinavia (sauna) to the tip of South America. Shamans sit naked as the day they were born, while water ladled onto red-hot rocks produces billows of blistering steam. When the temperature becomes so fierce that they can stand it no longer, they plunge into an ice-cold river, lake, or snow bank. In this way, they purify their bodies and souls so that they can talk to the gods and cure illnesses.

It should not be surprising that Shiva, who combines all opposites in his being, is also the lord of fever. The naked sadhus, who have given themselves totally to their Lord,

A siddhi baba, descendant of shamans

are clearly descendents of this ancient shamanistic tradition. Though
they do not build sweatlodges, they expose themselves to extreme heat
and cold in order to increase their magical power *(siddhi)*. In the hottest
summer heat, one might see them sitting between "five fires" (a fire to
the left, the right, in front, behind; and the sun above). In the winter
they meditate for days in icy cold mountain streams. Some wander in
the fall into the snowbound Himalayan valleys only to appear, to the
utter amazement of ordinary mortals, with the spring melt.

⚛ KASHI ⚛

It might strike the reader as odd to delve so deeply into the beginnings
of human culture. Yet that is necessary if we want to understand
Shiva. Though this enigmatic god did not scribble his name on the
walls of the Paleolithic hunters' caves in the manner of "Kilroy was
here," nonetheless we sense his presence at the very dawn of history.
In Shiva's iconography and mythology we find all the traits of the first
gods. Shiva is all, but predominately, he is the lord of the fire. Myth
lets him appear at the beginning of creation as a gigantic pillar of fire,
out of which the world sprung and within which the universe is still,
to this day, contained.

Many Hindus believe that it was in Benares (Varanasi) where the
column of light, the flash of divine lightning, first manifested. This is
the city that natives lovingly and full of gentle devotion call Kashi, "the
shining one." It is said that those whose eyes are purified and
unclouded by worldly illusions can still see the fire lingam *(jyotirlingam)* in this auspicious city by the Ganges. Benares is also called
Mahashmashana, "the great funeral pyre," for here souls are freed
from worldly fetters and their sins are burned away. In the mystical
geography of India, Benares is the blazing "third eye" of Shiva, whose
rays will one day incinerate the creation.

Day and night, one can see the funeral pyres burning on the river-
bank of this most unusual city, the one at Manikarnika Ghat, the other
at Harichandra Ghat. Legend has it that the fire used to cremate the
dead has never been rekindled since it was taken from the first fire on
earth. At the last rite, it is always the eldest son of the deceased whose
duty it is to light the pyre on which the corpse lies, shrouded in silk, garlanded with flowers and drenched in butter. A *dom*, a funeral attendant

A Shiva temple in Benares (Kashi)

from the caste of the untouchables, hands him the burning bunch of sacred *kusha* grass,* which has been lit on the ancient fire. His head shorn and dressed in the white of mourning clothes, the chief mourner circumambulates the pyre five times in a counterclockwise direction. (In rituals for the living, the circumambulation of the fire or of a sacred shrine is always clockwise, but since this is a ritual for the dead, whose world is the inverse mirror of the world of the living, the order is reversed.) The five rounds represent the five elements (earth, water, fire, air, and space, or ether), which form the sheaths of the mortal body and which are now dissolved and reabsorbed by the macrocosm. If the skull does not burst of its own accord in the incandescence, the oldest son or one of the dom attendants cracks it with a tap from a strong bamboo pole. This is necessary so that the soul *(jiva)* might be able to leave the corpse *(shava)* in the form of a miniature Shiva, complete with matted hair, trident in hand, three-eyed and naked. The departing soul, dancing as Shiva, is accompanied by demons and goblins, which personify the sins and transgressions of the deceased. In a final act, one of the

---

Desmostachya bipinnata L.; Eragrostis cynosuroides, a kind of Bermuda grass

dom attendants rakes the ashes and sprinkles them into the holy waters of the Ganges. In this fashion, the final sacrifice is completed.

The doms became the guardians of the sacred fire a long time ago, when they saved it from defilement by fanatical Muslims, bent on destroying all vestiges of heathenism in the name of Allah. They hid the embers and nurtured them secretly for many years. Because of this deed, these untouchables are still the guardians of the holy flame and have the right to demand a few rupees for their service at each funeral. But recently their privilege was threatened by Rajiv Gandhi, the Western-educated prime minister. Embarrassed by the primitive, superstitious image that this city of Shiva presents to the modern Western tourist, Rajiv Gandhi decided to clean it up. When he visited the holy city in the spring of 1985, he placed the cornerstone for a new, ultra-modern, "sanitary" electrical crematorium that fits so neatly with the newly asphalted streets, the glaring mercury vapor lights, and the cattle guards that keep the holy cows from soiling the scenic riverfront. Shiva's city was to have a new face, befitting the twentieth century. Many Hindus believe that it was this sacrilege that led to the untimely death of the prime minister when in the year 1991 the "Tamil Tigers" set off a bomb blast.

ᘒ KARTTIKEYA'S STRANGE BIRTH ᘒ

Fragments of the earliest beliefs of humanity are found in all cultural and religious traditions, but seldom are they as transparent as in India. The countless stories told about Shiva focus on singular aspects of the all-encompassing archetype. Let us now enjoy one such story, which has a firm place in the oral tradition and was told to me in several versions. It tells of the birth of Karttikeya, the savior of the world, born of the love of Shiva and the Goddess. Here, once again, the dynamic interplay of the polar opposites water and fire are brought into focus:

For no less than ten thousand years, Shiva and Parvati embraced in the pleasure of carnal love, forgetting the cares of the universe. The heavenly hosts, oppressed by an egomaniacal demon named Taraka, became ever more disheartened. At this rate, they asked themselves, when would the hero be born who could vanquish the monster under whose whims all of creation suffered? Finally they could stand it no longer. In their council, they decided to send Agni, the fire god, to remind the cosmic lovers that sex does not exist for pleasure only, but also for the creation of progeny.

In the guise of a turtledove, the fire god flew to their love nest, hidden high in the mountains. The sudden fluttering of the bird interrupted their lovemaking and caused Shiva to spill his seed. It spurted through the air and entered the open beak of the dove. Parvati angrily cursed the noisy intruder and the gods who sent him: "May the wombs of the other goddesses be as fruitless as mine!" Shiva's seed was so hot that it nearly burned the fire god to a crisp. Agni's

Karttikeya

senses nearly failed him as he tumbled back to Brahmloka, the hall of Brahma. On the way, he met the river goddess Ganga. "Woe is me!" he cried. "How difficult is this seed of Shiva to bear! But if I let it fall, it will burn up all three worlds, heaven, earth, and the underworld!" Proud Ganga believed that her glacier-fed waters would be cold enough to cool down the hot seed. "Give it to me! I shall be able to take it on!" she proclaimed to Agni, whose body hair, skin, and eyes had taken on a golden glow due to the contact with the semen.

Alas, Ganga had overestimated herself. After ten thousand years, she was but a shadow of her earlier self. Brahma, the Creator, seeing her in such distress, asked her: "Most lovely maiden, with rounded hips and a full bosom, what has drained thee of thy vigor?" After she told the grandfather of the gods what had happened, he searched his mind and finally counseled her to leave the burning seed in the bed of reeds by the river's shore. "In ten thousand years hence, a little child will be born in those rushes, a child who shines brighter than the morning sun."

And that is exactly what happened. During this time, all the rushes, the trees, the animals, as well as the human beings that lived in the area, all took on a golden hue, and the reeds glistened and glittered like hammered gold. Then suddenly one day, an infant lay there and cried with the voice of thunder. It just happened that the six sisters, the Pleiades (Krittikas), played on that same shore. They were delighted to find the babe. Each wanted to cuddle it and offer it her breast. To please them, little Karttikeya grew six heads so he could suckle each one of them at the same time. Thus, Shiva's son, the vanquisher of demons, was born. His mothers include all the elements: Parvati (earth), Agni (fire),* Ganga (water), and the Pleiades (air and cosmic space).

---

*In the Hindu construction of reality, the genders are not as fixed as in the current Western worldview. The Hindu gods can appear in male or female forms, as does Shiva himself. Gods can give birth and goddesses can impregnate their devotees. Brahma gives birth to children from his brow, Vishnu often appears as the beautiful enchantress Mohini, so that gods and demons fall in love with him. Thus, there is no discrepancy in the male Agni being a "mother."

3

THE SHAMAN AND HIS BLACK DOG

———— ᴄᴡᴐ ————

Look here, don't leave me!
If you leave me,
I'll insult You saying,
"O Madman who wears the fierce elephant's skin!
O Madman who wears the tiger's skin!
O Madman who ate the poison!
O Madman surrounded by the fire of
the town's crematorium!
O Madman who has me as His slave!"

MANIKKAVACAKAR,
TAMIL POET, TENTH CENTURY

After having climbed down from the trees sometime during the early Pliocene, the hominoid hordes metamorphosed into Paleolithic hunters and gatherers armed with stone choppers and fire. They roamed the earth freely for an estimated three million years. The mere ten thousand years humans have spent as tillers of the soil, tied to small swidden plots, are but a very short time in comparison. Recorded history started a bare five thousand years ago. The three hundred years of industrial civilization—which so impresses and, at the same time, oppresses our contemporaries—what are they in the face of this immense journey? This brave new world might just be a bubble on the stream of time that could pop at any moment!

Considering the eons spent at the bosom of Nature, which formed,

31

molded, and imprinted the body, soul, and spirit of humankind, what weight has this thin veil of civilization? Too deeply lodged in our racial memory, our collective unconscious, are the impressions of our ancient life as hunters and gatherers. Our cults, folk stories, beliefs, dream images, and language are full of its traces. Every child repeats the long development in its games of hide and seek, tag, tracking, building huts and hideaways. The bow and arrow were once a way of life; hopscotch, clapping rhymes, guessing of riddles, running the hoop, and playing ball were serious magic. With almost religious seriousness, children repeat the cultural history of humankind, just as in the biological development of the embryo all the stages of evolution are recapitulated.

Can we not, each and every one of us, sense the savage in our soul? Underneath the mask of the well- or ill-mannered urbanite, behind the façade of the suave, domesticated men and women, one discovers the old hunters still sitting at the campfire. Shamans with horns on their headbands, dressed in the skins of predatory beasts, ornamented with glittering chips of mica and bird's feathers, invite to the dance, to the flight into the magic mountain. Their chants and drumming still spellbind, as the thin veil of our conditional reality melts and another world opens to our inner vision. Look at this shaman in your soul! She is half man, half woman, possessing the powers of both. Her magic allows her to bear heat and cold, hunger and thirst beyond measure. His single-mindedness allows him to pick up poisonous snakes and dance with them. Her third eye lets her look far into the past, far into the distance and even into the future. Its rays can stop a charging enemy or fleeing game, or calm a raging bear.

ᴥ THE OLD HUNTSMAN ᴥ

In all the old shamanistic cultures, animals dominated the concepts and imaginations. To this day, hunting tribes are likely to give animal names to their children. Furs, pelts, claws, fangs, and feathers—preferably of ferocious predators such as wolves, wildcats, bears, eagles or ravens—are the favorite body decorations of the hunter, warrior, or medicine person. Talking animals appear to them in dreams and visions, teach them the secrets of nature, guide them as familiars or guardians, and give them the priceless gifts of courage, endurance, or keenness of senses. (The familiars of medieval witches, the owls, cats, and toads, are remnants of this ancient form of conceptualization.) The clans and lineages of these societies trace their ancestry to a totem animal that mothered/fathered them in a far off dreamtime. To this day they remain brothers and sisters to such an animal species. These totemic animals are celebrated at certain times of the year in what anthropologists call rites of increase.

Such rituals, once universal, involve ecstatic dances during which the hunters, dressed in horn and hide, turn into animal spirits themselves. They dance their lives in minute detail: the rutting, the coupling, the calving, the searching for fresh pastures, and finally,

Dancing Siberian shaman

their deaths at the hands of the hunter. Such dances are carried out in a state of pure empathy and complete identification. In the process, the prey is already killed in spirit before the hunter brings the actual body of the animal down with his spears and arrows. After the ritual, the animal has but to be gathered up, for its guardian, the "lord of the animals" or the "animal mother," has already released it unto death. The guardians of the animal souls live deep in the belly of the mountains, accessible only by a few hidden caves; or they live on the bottom of holy lakes. Only with the permission of the lord of the animals may the hunter hunt. In order to avoid disaster and misfortune, the path to this god has to be found so that the taboos and proscriptions might not be violated.

It is by means of rhythmic, repetitive dancing and drumming, fasting, or self-inflicted pain (asceticism), along with the use of mind-altering plant drugs such as mushrooms, nightshades, or hemp, that the ancient hunters achieved contact with the animal spirits and their guardians. By flooding the nervous system with more stimuli than the mundane mind can cope with or, on the contrary, by starving the senses, by concentrating on one single point or one monotonous sound, the archaic hunters were able to lift off and fly away into the other world. An individual who mastered these techniques better than anyone else, naturally became extremely valuable to the group. He or she became the shaman, the ritual leader and speaker for the tribe vis-à-vis the spirits and gods.

The roots of such practices reach deep into the Old Stone Age. Cave paintings and rock etchings are their witness. In the caverns of Trois-Frères in the Pyrenees, deep in the womb of Mother Earth, one finds, for example, next to paintings of numerous bison, mammoth, and other

*"Hunting Accident," upper
Paleolithic cave painting
(Lascaux, France)*

game, the figure of a dancing magician, dressed in animal furs, with horns on his head. Some fifteen thousand years ago, this "great sorcerer" danced hunting dances similar to those recorded by nineteenth- and twentieth-century anthropologists among the few remaining hunting tribes of Asia, Africa, America, and Australia. An even older cave painting is the "Hunting Accident" in the Cave of Lascaux (Dordogne). A man with an erect penis and a staff with a bird perched on it is shown lying in front of a wounded bison bull. It is probably not a hunting accident at all, but a shamanistic trance, which is commonly associated with an erection. The animal guardian appears in the form of the bull. The bird on the stick (it is more likely a string!) is a common representation of the flight of the soul (astral body) out of the physical body, which lies corpselike and rigid, as is common in deep trance.

When confronted with the image of Shiva, an anthropologist will most likely think of a super-shaman. As Nataraja, Shiva appears as the king of dancers with a drum in one hand and a fire in the other. The drum is the universal mark of the shaman. With it, he can whip up a rhythm that sends him off into ecstatic dance or, on the other hand, he can beat so slowly that his heartbeat slows right along and trance (self-hypnosis) becomes possible. In both cases, the soul is pushed beyond the normal confines of consciousness.

Shiva, the universal shaman, is equally the master of ecstatic dance and of deep, deathlike trance. In the latter state, he can sit motionless in the deepest cold and snow or in the blazing heat of summer noon and wander in inner worlds. Like many a shaman, Rudra (as he is called in the Vedas) transcends everyday reason and logic. Thus, to timid souls, he has an awesome aura of the uncanny and incalculable. He is a mad god, a wild and wily wanderer of the wilderness. As Ardhanari, "Half-Woman," he is androgynous like many a shaman who wears women's garb and considers himself to be the bride of some god.

In the *Yajur Veda Shri Rudram*,[1] an ancient account in which the Aryans stored their memories, Shiva-Rudra is called the lord of fire and water, of trees and herbs (life), of waking and sleeping (states of con-

*Dancing Shiva with a
shaman's hand drum*

*Nataraja, the king
of dancers*

sciousness), and of the high and low (spirits). He is addressed as the wanderer, hunter, healer, holy man, dweller-in-caves, master thief, and smith. (The smith with his fire, smoke, and hammering noise, is recognized as a magician and as a reflection of the god of thunder and lightning in all old cultures.) The image of the tribal shaman, as it appeared in early humanity, shines through most of these appellations.

In the first verse (Anuvaka I, Rik 1), the *Yajur Veda Shri Rudram* lauds him: "Oh, Lord Rudra, unto your anger let there be my salutations, also unto your arrows, salutations, salutations unto your bow." Subsequently, he is hailed as the healer who has might over scorpions, serpents, tigers, and invisible enemies, such as the host of demons *(rakshasas)* and evil spirits (I, 6). He is described as the one with a thousand eyes: shamans often decorate themselves with magic, all-seeing eyes. Siberians sew hundreds of tiny metal mirrors (a thousand eyes) onto their coats in which the spirits can see themselves, or with which the shaman can see the spirits. Other verses describe Rudra as the wanderer in the wilds and the lord of animals (II, 2), the carrier of the ax (II, 6) and the lord of forests and trees (II, 8,9). Shamans are traditionally in "vibrational" contact with all the plants and animals of their home region. Knowing where each species grows and where the beasts have their hideouts, they are responsible to all. (These

*Shiva as Ardhanari,
the half-woman god*

days, it is often only the children who know these things.) Rudra is called the lord of thieves and swindlers (III, 3,4,5), much like Hermes, the Greek god of healing, or like Odin, the magician. Shamans are swindlers because they are masters of legerdemain, pantomime, and tale telling, and the creators of "other realities."

Rudra's special relation to the canine breed is readily acknowledged: "Salutations to ye who are in the form of the hunters and the leaders of dogs" (IV, 16); and "Salutations to ye who are in the form of dogs and the lord of such dogs" (IV, 17). In further verses he is greeted as the drummer and the drum, as the magician who kills from afar, and as the one who is in the clouds and lightning. He is hailed as the one with matted locks, which he piles upon the top of his head like a crown. It is often the case that shamans let neither scissors nor razor touch their hair, for each fiber is an antenna into the spirit world. Besides long hair, tribal magicians often wear unusual headgear studded with feathers, gems, and the signs of the sun, moon, and stars. These are precursors of the pointed hats of magicians, like Merlin or the witches, or the crowns of kings. Shiva's tower of felted hair, stiffened with the juice of the banyan tree, decorated with snakes, flowers, nuts (*rudraksha* or ustram beads*), and with the waxing crescent moon, is such a crown or magician's hat. The moon, representative not only of the rhythms of growth and decay, but also of imagination and the mind, is a common feature of the shaman's costume. As a wearer of the moon, he is lord of the flow of the tides in the outer world of nature, as well as the inner world of dream, fantasy, and inspiration. Like all shamans, Shiva is dressed in the skins of wild animals he has slain (tiger, elephant, and gazelle)—that is, when he does not appear in a state of "sacred nakedness."

ঙ় PASHUPATI, LORD OF THE ANIMALS ৼ

Of the "thousand and eight" names of Shiva, Pashupati (Sanskrit *pasu* = animal, *pati* = lord), "lord of the animals" is one of the most common. In later times, this title was applied mainly to his function as guardian patron of the yeoman's cattle and as keeper of the souls. All of them, animal and human, the quick and the dead, are in his hands. Freely he sends them into life and equally freely he deals them the blow of death. He is the good

---

*The nuts of the Himalayan tree *(Elaeocarpus ganitrus)*

Pashupati representation—pre-Aryan lord of the animals (Mohenjodaro seal)

Lord of the animals, Illyrian-Roman engraving (Bosnia)

Attributes of Shiva

bow and arrow (pinaka, ajagava)

dog (kukur)

axe (parasu)

sling or noose (pasa)

magic staff (yoga danda)

shepherd, as well as the wolf, which delights to chase them to their doom.

Sharva, "the hunter," is one of his names. In one folktale, Sharva-Shiva appears to the Aryan hero Arjuna (the archer we know from the *Bhagavad Gita*) in the form of a *kirata*. Kiratas are savage inhabitants of the jungles and impenetrable mountains of India. The epic *Ramayana* portrays them as were-tigers. As with the Nordic werewolves, the leopard men of Africa, or the cannibalistic windigo of Canada's Algonquian, the term must refer to feral human beings who live outside of the borders of normal, civilized society.

Shiva's scepter is the first of hunting weapons, the spear. The tip of the spear has been multiplied by the magical number three into a trident. The trident is so important in Shiva's iconography that it can stand for the god. In his two, four, eight, ten, or thirty-two hands, depending on which theophany we are considering, he carries the oldest and earliest weapons and tools of humankind: the ax *(parasu)*, the hand drum *(damaru)*, the staff *(danda)*, the bow and arrow *(pinaka* and *aja-gava)*, the simple spear *(pasupata)*, the sling or noose *(pasa)*, and the divining rod *(khatvanga)*; furthermore, he might be shown with a deer in his hand or a rosary, a discus, a skull, a lotus flower, or a sword.

In the Vedas, Rudra appears as an archer who, like the Greek Apollo, strikes human and beast with arrows

trident
(trishula)

bead necklace
(rudrakshamala)

fire (dhuni)

skull
(khatvanga)

of sickness, fever, and death, as well as with arrows of healing. The *Yajur Veda* contains songs beseeching him to direct his shower of missiles against enemies and wild animals and to spare one's own kin and kine. In a legend that we shall see later, an angry Shiva in the form of Sharva, the hunter, storms the sacrifice of the chief of the priests who has excluded the unsavory savage from participating in the holy rite. The frightened sacrificial beast lifts off, and taking the shape of a fleet-hoofed deer flees into the southern sky, but the merciless hunter and his dogs bring it down. To this day, Rudra and his hunting hounds are seen in the constellation of Orion and Sirius (the dog star), which begins to be visible in the waning half of the year. The Greeks also saw in that constellation the ranging hunter Orion, chasing the fluttering doves (the Pleiades) in front of him, followed by his dog Sirius.

How ancient this complex of symbols might be can be surmised by the fact that the Plains Indians also associated the same stars with the Great Hunt. In a riotous festival of buffoonery, the Cheyenne danced the lives of the animals in the Massaum celebration. Held just after midsummer, the ceremony recreated the time when the first shaman, Sweet Medicine, was taught the hunt and the animals were released from the womb of the sacred mountain. The Grandmother of Beings, in the form of a horned wolf (Sirius), and her husband, the Thunder Spirit, in the form of a red wolf (Aldebaran, the red eye of the bull in Taurus), sponsor the ceremony. They legitimize the right of the Indians to hunt by sending their daughter, the mistress of the animal spirits, to live with the shaman in the world of humans. Considering that the Paleolithic ancestors of the Indians crossed the land bridge that once connected Asia to North America some thirty thousand years ago, we have some indication of the antiquity of such associations.*[2]

---

*That tribal myths can indeed be very old is shown, for example, in the Ojibwa tales of a monstrous buffalo with legs like tree trunks, two long protruding teeth, and a nose with a hand on its end. It obviously refers to a mammoth elephant.

✥ THE NOOSE ✥

The snare and lasso are an essential part of the hunters' gear. With them they can trap their prey, tie it up, and transport it. The looped rope was once the symbol of Varuna, the ancient god of high heaven and the keeper of the universal law (Sanskrit *rita*). With it he binds all those who transgress against the Right and fetters them with illness, madness, or misfortune. Yama, the god of the dead, likewise binds his victims with a rope, as the hunter does his slain game. The old Nordic Odin, the Wodan of the Anglo-Saxons, lord of magicians, hunters, and fallen warriors, also carries a noose. Sacrificial victims dedicated to Odin were hung on tree limbs, as were all thieves and criminals, for this god is the master of the gallows. Continually Odin binds or frees his followers with the cords of passion, lust, and the fury of battle, with the lariat of mead and hallucinogenic mushrooms. He ensnares them with his masterful spells. Great Shiva, too, carries the noose (pasa) as one of his attributes. As the master yogi, he ties his devotees into the self-discipline of yoga, as the yeoman yokes his oxen to a cart.

Varuna with the noose

✥ THE BLACK DOG ✥

In his most terrifying form as Bhairava, Shiva is referred to as the one whose mount is a dog. It is a black dog, befitting the archetypal image of a god of shamans, hunters, and the shades.

Wild canines were the first animal companions of humanity, long before cattle, swine, fowl, sheep, or horses were domesticated. Hoping to relieve their ravenous hunger with cadaver remains, feces, and bones, they followed the Paleolithic big game hunters to the four corners of the world. They followed them into the Americas, perhaps already harnessed as pack carriers. They boarded the log rafts of the first aboriginals going to Australia. Early on, they became man's proverbial best friend: they sniffed out and tracked game; gave alarm when danger threatened; and in time of famine, when the lord of the animals was angry, the clan could eat them. Even to this day, the Prairie Indians, descendents of big game hunters, consider an unweaned, milk-fed whelp a delicacy. (As the Indian said to his cowboy guest who was ladling himself seconds of a scrumptious stew, "Dig deep, white man, many puppies on bottom.")

Dogs and their close relatives the jackals, coyotes, and wolves are predators and carrion eaters. It follows that they, along with ravens and vultures, became associated with gods of battle, destruction, and death. Indeed, one sees dogs and jackals lurking about the funeral *ghats* along the rivers of India, where they hope to snatch bits of charred corpses or bloated cadavers that the river washes ashore. For the natives, this poses no problem. It is Shiva himself, in the form of a wild dog, that is freeing the soul from its elemental shells. Indeed, if one regards it in a meditative way, putting all preconceived, programmed notions aside, one is awed by the gentle, nearly loving way in which these gnawing animals cause the mortal remains to disappear.

Often it is a black canine, like the mummy-guarding god Anubis of ancient Egypt, who guides the departed across the threshold to the "dark side of being." Even Saint Christopher, the "Christ bearer," who carries souls across the turbulent stream, was once, in pagan times, a dog-faced god and guardian between the earthly and the spiritual world much like Cereberus, the hellhound of the Greeks, or Garm, the Nordic guardian of the underworld, or the Mexican god Xolotl, who guides the dead across the nine streams of hell. Even now, the funerary rites of the Zarathustrian Parsees of India demand that a dog sniff the corpse so that evil spirits might flee before it is placed on top of the "tower of silence."

Odin, too, has ravens and wolves as his companions, and the warriors sworn to him are wolf men *(ulfhednir)* or bear hides *(berserkir)*. Shiva's retinue is also replete with such feral beings. The poet Goethe has reached deeply into the archetypal treasure chest when, in his *Faust,* he has the warlock and lord of the flames, Mephisto, appear in the form of a black poodle. Folk imagination, drawing on images imprinted in early ages, loves to surround magicians and sorcerers with black dogs. One such beast was reputed to have followed Agrippa of Nettesheim, the Renaissance magus, wherever he went.

⛧ THE GOD OF THE SHADES ⛧

On behalf of his tribe, the shaman tries to establish a good relationship with the lord of the animals, who lives far away, "inside of the mountain" or "deep in the forest," where he guards the souls. In order to travel there, the shaman must know how to overcome the strictures of ordinary consciousness by means of trance, ecstasy, or fury. On his spirit flight, he meets all kinds of supernatural beings, elemental beings, nature spirits, dwarves, demons, elves, and, of course, the shades of the dead. Every real shaman, like the witches of the days of yore and some of the spiritualist mediums of today, is steadily surrounded by a whole troop of such fantastic creatures.[3] Shiva, as god of the dead and of the shamans, is no exception. Drunken, madly dancing, frolicking ghouls, *bhutas* (those who died unexpectedly and who take on animal forms), *vetalas* (vampires), *pretas* (specters), *pisachas* (flesh-craving ghosts), wicked dwarfs, black elves, and whatever else one might expect at a witches' sabbath, surround Shiva Bhuteshvara, the lord of goblins, wherever he goes.

Techniques of inducing spirit flight, ecstasy (Latin *extasis* = to be out of it, beside oneself), trance (Latin *transire* = to go over), or what we now call altered states of consciousness (ASC)[4] are learned in torturous initiations that might include hanging for several days suspended upside down from a tree, being tied up, exposure to the raw elements, swallowing poisons, fasting, and withstanding deprivations of all kinds. In south Asia, it is Shiva Mahayogi, the patron of rigorous self-discipline, who makes the stepping into other dimensions of reality possible. In northern Europe it was Odin, the one-eyed god, who inspired to such asceticism. Like a bird of the gallows, the grizzly god hung nine days upside down on a tree to snatch from the depths the Runes of Wisdom. His eight-legged white steed is but a metaphor for a bier carried by four mourners, for, while the soul roams in other worlds, the body lies stiff and rigid, as in death. Such eight-legged shaman's horses are known throughout Siberia.[5] The Gonds, a tribal people of the Eastern Deccan, know also of the magic horse with eight legs, which is really the dead man's bier.[6]

In Indian lore, Shiva himself appears as an eight-legged sphinxlike creature with a long nose, claws, a horselike mane and tail, and wings. In this awesome guise as Sarabha, he kills the man-lion, Narasinha, who happens to be no lesser being than Lord Vishnu in his fourth "descent"

The shamanic god, Odin, on his eight-legged steed

(avatara). Whenever evil starts gaining the upper hand on the earth, Vishnu, the preserver of the universe, takes on a physical body in order to kill the demons that are threatening the rest of creation. This time the Preserver appeared as a were-lion. However, after ridding the world of the tyranny of an arrogant titan, he forgot his own divine origin, became attached to a wife and family, and in turn, became a world terror, hardly better than the offensive demon he slew. It was then that Shiva, as the eight-legged Sarabha, freed Vishnu of his illusion by killing him and letting him return to his proper place on the heavenly throne.

It becomes obvious that the entry into the "other dimension" is equivalent to an entry into the realm of the dead. It is, thus, understandable that Asian shamans often dress like skeletons, showing all the bones. During his initiation, the shaman travels the other world, where he is hunted by hungry demons, killed, and stripped of his worldly flesh. Like human hunters, the demons skin him, scrape his hide, and leave his blank bones behind. Subsequently, a "bird-mother" gathers these bones, carries them to her nest, and places them in their right order, so that he may come alive again. (This ancient Paleolithic custom of arranging the bones is a gesture of respect for the animals and is meant to insure their survival.) Some icons show Shiva, as well as Buddha, as a skeleton. His total asceticism has reduced him to mere bones. Tibetan folktales tell how Buddha became a skeleton because, in his compassion for hungry wild beasts and ogres, he let them feast on his flesh. Following the footsteps of Shiva, yogis attempt to imagine themselves as skeletons in their meditations, or to imagine how the goddess Kali devours their flesh and drinks their blood.

How a yogi proceeds to strip off her worldly attachment and return, reduced to mere bones, to the Lord, is shown in the south Indian story about Shiva's mother, the devotee *(bhakti)* Punitavati*:

By the grace of Shiva, this saint was born to a wealthy merchant who had no other children. The girl grew up pure of heart, loving to chant the names of the Lord and wearing holy ash on her forehead. As she was as beautiful and industrious as she was pious, she was soon married to a rich merchant named Paramadatta. The young couple delighted in feeding the wandering bhaktis

---

*This version of the story comes from Sri Swami Sivananda, *Lord Shiva and His Worship* (Shivanandanagar, Distt. Tehari-Garhwal U.P., India: The Divine Life Society, 1984), 226.

of Shiva—never forgetting the commandment of the Vedas, "Let the guest be a god unto you!"—and enjoyed listening to the chants praising God.

One day a sadhu came by and gave Paramadatta two ripe mangos. These in turn he gave to his wife to store while he went to town to do some business. In the meantime, a hungry beggar knocked at the door. As Punitavati was not yet finished cooking her pulses and rice, she served him one of the mangos with some milk. When her husband returned, weary from his work, he desired to snack on the mangos. Punitavati gave him the remaining one. It tasted so good that her husband immediately asked for the other one also. The pious wife did not know what to do other than to send a quick sigh of a prayer to heaven. Instantly, a ripe mango fell into her lap. When she served it to her husband, he found it to taste a thousand times better than the first one.

"This is incredible," he exclaimed. "It tastes like no other I have eaten! Is this the fruit the stranger gave us this morning?"

"No, my husband," she confessed, "I prayed for it and it fell from heaven."

"Then pray again! I must have another one," he commanded. And, upon her wish, more mangos fell from heaven that instant. As he was gorging himself on the delicious fruit, remorse suddenly struck him.

"Oh, my God, I have sinned! I have treated a devotee of Shiva as my servant. How can I consider her any longer my wife!" Tormented by inner anguish, he left home the following day, pretending to go on a business trip. He never returned but settled in another city and took another wife. Day after day, Punitavati anxiously awaited his return. Years passed. She became sadder and sadder. *Perhaps thugs have waylaid him,* she thought. One day, she heard rumor that her husband was seen in Madurai where he had children with another wife. Immediately she went off in search of him and found him.

Though at first Paramadatta was overjoyed, he fell at her feet pleading, "What, oh saint, do you want from me? I am a worldly man, vile and greedy. How can I be your husband? Pray forgive me, oh goddess!"

Tears flooding her eyes, she tried to touch his feet, replying, "My lord, it is for your sake only that I preserved my youth and beauty! But as you want me no longer, I shall seek Lord Shiva."

With that, she gave away all her worldly goods, her silks and jewels, worshipped the Brahmins, and then, through the power of yoga, shook off all her flesh from its frame. Reduced to a bleached skeleton, she walked ever northward toward Mount Kailash, the mountain throne of Shiva. As she approached the mountain in the middle of the Himalayas, she feared that touching the holy ground with her feet might be a sin. Again, using the power that her austerities had given her, she turned upside down and moved, like a baby in the birth canal, head down up the icy slopes.

The goddess Parvati was stunned and asked of Shiva, "My Lord, who is that, coming thus our way toward the center of the universe?"

"That pious woman, oh beloved, is my mother, for she feeds all of my devotees! Once I passed her house and gave her and her husband two sweet, ripe mangos."[7]

Rejection and fear of the spiritual world is actually the fear of death. In order to overcome this fear, shamanistic initiations often occur at night in graveyards and cemeteries. Such spooky rites are ancient. The midnight cemetery rites of European witchcraft are remnants of such initiations. Some tribes of Australian aboriginals let initiates lie tied up in a graveyard for several nights where wild animals come to sniff and lick them. Finally, a supernatural appears, who drills a hole into their skulls with a sharp stick and places magic quartz crystals inside while, at the same time, instructing them in the magical arts and healing.

India's holy men and women (sadhus and sadhvis) and the *sannyasi*, those who have renounced the world, are often initiated in a similar fashion at the burning ghats and graveyards, where Shiva and his ghouls and goblins love to dance. At times, the mysterious god himself appears to the initiate as a vampire, revenant, or specter, and acts as the initiator into spiritual wisdom, as he did in the famous Sanskrit tale, "The King and the Specter in the Corpse," by Somadeva.* In the ancient rite, the initiate puts aside his worldly vestments and is wrapped in an unstitched, orange cloth, symbolizing the flames of the fire. He has become as dead to the world and its elusive ways as the corpses that are being burned. As one of the living dead, he smears his skin with the ashes from the funeral pyre. The cremation ground becomes a fitting symbol of the illusions of existence, which the holy man has reduced to a pile of ashes by means of the heat generated through his arduous ascetic effort.

The burning ghats of Benares, Shiva's favorite city, are the most popular places for such midnight initiations. For tourists coming from societies that try to hide all the unpleasant sides of life, cremation grounds such as Manikarnika Ghat are a shock. The image of burning

---

*This story from the Sanskrit classic *Vetalapancavinsati* is recounted at the end of this section.

corpses (the smell of which might remind the American visitor of the Sunday afternoon barbecues in suburbia), vultures and jackals fighting over entrails and charred bits of flesh, is a "mind-blower." Carefully nurtured paradigms of "reality" tend to collapse. But, just as one is about to turn and flee, a friendly voice, cawing in Hindu English, will explain, "Don't be timid. Look carefully and discover the ephemeral nature of your existence. Cremation is education! Burning is learning! If you learn your lessons well, Shiva will grant you *siddhi* (magical) powers, perhaps even *moksha* (liberation)!"

The tourist who tries to capture it all on camera is stopped. A snapshot would fix and keep a tiny portion of the person from totally dissolving into the elements and would thus prevent the final and full dissolution. This would make the soul suffer and keep it from reaching its goal.

There is one sect of Shaivite anchorites who call themselves the fearless ones *(aghori)*. Not only might the Aghori carry the skulls of the dead as their begging bowls, they are also not above smearing themselves with their own excrements and devouring bits of charcoaled corpses. To the utter disbelief of the British, they followed the troops during the Sepoy Rebellion of 1857 in order to gobble up the casualties.[8] It was not brute hunger, apparently, that drove them, but ideology. With their behavior, they try to demonstrate that Shiva is all and everything: How can there be anything outside of God? Therefore, there is nothing horrible or terrible for someone who has overcome all separating illusions and nothing is impossible for those who have developed their siddhi powers.*

Here, now, is the story of The King and the Specter in the Corpse from the *Vetalapancavinsati*, which tells how the great god appeared to the famous king Vikramaditya, as a vetala inhabiting a corpse:

Among the visitors who came to the king's audience each day was an old mendicant, who offered him a fruit. The king accepted the gift each day but mindlessly tossed it aside. One day, after such an audience, one of the royal

---

*This theme crops up again in an anecdote told by Nirad C. Chaudhuri, to illustrate the avarice of the Bengalis. He knew of a young man, who, for the sake of obtaining five rupees, wagered a bet that he could eat a pile of "night soil." He won his five rupees. But from that moment on his life changed. People thronged to worship him, for anyone who could eat *feces* without regurgitating, must be a powerful *siddha*, a master of occult arts. Soon he even had disciples. Cf. Nirad C. Chaudhuri, *The Continent of Circe* (Bombay: Jaico Publishing House, 1983), 214.

apes escaped its keeper, snatched the fruit, bit it open, and, lo and behold, a jewel dropped out. When the king looked into his courtyard where he had thrown the fruits each day for many years, he discovered a pile of jewels.

His curiosity roused, he granted the monk a private audience. The monk, whose quiet patience had endured so long, asked the king for help in performing a magical ritual. How could the king, having received all these gifts, refuse? The monk told him to meet him that night in a cemetery, where he should cut a corpse from a tree and carry it into the magic circle where the monk would be chanting spells. That night, the king fearlessly walked amidst the charred bones and hoisted the body of an executed criminal onto his shoulders.

Suddenly, however, the corpse started to speak, for a specter had taken possession of it. It posed him a riddle. If he knew the answer, but did not tell, his head would shatter. Being knowledgeable, the king answered correctly, but no sooner had he done so than the corpse was hanging on the tree again. Again and again, he cut it down and carried it; again and again he was asked to solve a riddle; and again and again the corpse appeared back on the tree. The twenty-fifth riddle he could not answer. At this point, the spirit in the corpse said, "Now you may take me to the magic circle. But beware. The monk is not who he seems to be, but an evil sorcerer. He will set the corpse into his magic circle and will ask you to fall down and worship it. With his sword, he will then cut your head off, in order to make you his slave and to bind me into the corpse. Tell him that you do not know how to prostrate yourself and have him show you how. Then you decapitate him instead. That will free me, and it will make you the master of spirits."

Done as told, the brave king became the master of the spirits. The specter in the corpse was none other than Shiva, giving him his initiations into the occult arts.

☸ BHAIRAVA ☙

The Aghori are attracted by Shiva's most horrible manifestation, that of the blood-drenched Bhairava (or Bhairab), of whom Aldous Huxley wrote somewhere that his toys are the galaxies, his playground the infinite space, and that the span between one finger and the next stretches thousands of millions of light-years. A common icon shows Bhairava naked but for a loin covering of skulls, as black as night and with three eyes that bulge out angrily. In one of his six hands, he holds an arm ripped out of someone's socket; in another, he holds a decapitated head;

with another hand he swings his sword; and with a fourth he bears the trident. In his fifth hand, he holds a cup or a skullcap at heart level, as if he were communicating, "Even if the whole world is torn apart by my rage, here, in the heart, you shall find peace!" The sixth hand underscores the statement with an open-palmed gesture of blessing (the *abhaya* mudra) indicating, "Fear not!"

As Shiva's most terrible manifestation, Bhairava can take many different appearances or forms. These forms have been experienced and named by yogis and yoginis in states of deep meditation. This sort of imaging is typical in south Asian mythology, and is found in Buddhism as well. Various Dhyana-Buddhas can spring forth from Buddha, depending on the level of consciousness and depth of meditation. All in all, the terrible god Bhairava has some sixty-four materializations, coupled to sixty-four *yoginis*, magical female consorts. Kapali, for example, is the frightening form Shiva took on when, in a fit of anger, he sliced one of Brahma's five heads off and was forced to wander the world as an outlaw. The best known of his theophanies are these eight forms:

1. Kapali, "the carrier of the skull"
2. Asitanga, "having black limbs"
3. Samhara, "destruction"
4. Ruru, "the dog"
5. Chanda, "the wild one"
6. Krodhana, "the angry one"
7. Unmatta, "the insane one"
8. Kala, "the black one"

Without female power (shakti) even Bhairava would be totally helpless. In his energetic female form he is the godesss Bhairavi. Bhairavi plays an important role in Tantric ritual. The eight female shaktis of Bhairava have the same names as the forms listed above, except that their names are spelled with feminine endings.

In the wild, mountainous country of Nepal, where it occasionally happens that a whole village, with houses and fields, is swept into yawning chasms as the monsoon rains pour down, and where continual tribal warfare and wild animals often made life precarious, Bharaiva is vividly alive in the folk imagination, and tales such as the following are frequently told by the glow of the evening hearth. This story was told to me in various versions by Nepalese storytellers:

Once upon a time, a rich merchant's son set out to see the world. The path he walked followed alongside a mountain stream. He casually noticed a tree branch drifting down the churning river. All of a sudden, the branch took the shape of a giant serpent, which swam up to a bathing woman. Before she could even scream, the beast bit her, and she died in convulsions. Then the reptile took on the shape of a floating branch again.

"I must be tired," the young man thought, rubbing his disbelieving eyes and continuing his journey. After a little while, the drifting tree limb once again changed its form. This time it turned into an ogre, which climbed ashore, swallowed three of the fattest water buffalo grazing there, and returned to the river to continue floating as an ordinary branch. The young merchant was now frightened out of his wits but, at the same time, immensely curious. Suddenly, just as they were passing a herd of pasturing sheep, the branch changed into a flesh-eating pisacha. In an instant it devoured the whole herd, including the shepherd.

The sound of a waterfall thundering into a deep canyon interrupted the uneasy musing of the young traveler. Terrified and yet fascinated, he watched as the uncanny limb next turned into a wandering monk, smeared with ashes and wearing orange clothes. He took heart, let his steps catch up with the sadhu, and addressed him.

"I beg you kindly to forgive my inquisitiveness, but what I have witnessed is a sheer impossibility! Who are you?"

The sadhu stared at him. "If you really want to know, close your eyes for a moment and you shall see!"

He did as he was told. When he lifted his lids, he was dazzled by a blinding light. Then he saw none other than Bhairav in his terrible glory towering in front of him. The poor lad nearly died of fright but, again, he mustered his courage and asked, "Great Lord, forgive my curiosity, but as I am traveling in far and distant lands, please tell me the outcome of my journey."

"A rope, in the form of a noose, will be placed around your neck and you shall be hung!" At that, the apparition was gone. No one was there, neither a god, nor a sadhu, nor a branch. The merchant's son shook his head. "It must be that I am fatigued. That's all. Anyway, I am decent and have never committed a crime, so why should my life end on the gallows?"

After many years traveling in foreign lands, he felt he had learned enough and started on his long homeward journey. One day, while walking through a dense forest, near a spring he came across a woman who was sobbing and weeping bitterly. Having compassion, he asked her, "Can I help you?"

"Kind sir, I am all alone in the world. I have no family left, no home, no money, and nothing to eat. My last possession is this diamond, which I could trade for food, but I am too weak to even move from this spot. Could you help me? Would you take this jewel to the next city and trade it for some rice, beans, and bread?"

The young man promised to help, took the gem, and hurried to the city. He could not have known that it had been robbed from the king's treasury a few days earlier. Guards seized him immediately and dragged him before the magistrate, who condemned him to death by hanging. Nobody believed his innocence, for when they looked for the woman at the spring, there was absolutely no one to be found. As the executioner placed the noose around his neck, the rope whispered to him, "You might have forgotten the prophecy—but now it shall be fulfilled!"

With that, the young man knew that his fate was sealed. He saw it was useless to fight against God's inscrutable ways and went peacefully into death.

⚶ RUDRA AND ODIN ⚶

Comparing Rudra, "the howler," to Odin (Woden, Wotan), "the frenzied," we meet similar archetypal configurations that most likely have a common Eurasian origin. Rudra, the wild hunter, sweeping down the mountainsides with his storm and wind spirits (the Maruts), is really not much different from Odin and his "wild hunt" of fallen warriors, sorcerers, and wind spirits. To this day, in central and northern Europe, country folk associate the November storms with the passing of Wotan's hosts. They rattle at the doors and shutters and must be fed so that they might turn into "grateful dead" and not horrible specters. The wild reveling of delirious crowds, high on drugs and possessed by ghouls and goblins, celebrating Shiva's Night (Shivratri) in India, in February, is in essence not different from the many fool's festivals, carnivals, masked dances, and Mardi Gras that have survived even into Christianity in Europe and which are celebrated in the ritual calendar from late fall into early spring.

When the horned god and his train of witches, warlocks, unbaptized dead, and hanged criminals passed the thatched farmsteads of Lower Saxony during the twelve nights of the winter solstice, the prudent peasant made sure that all windows and doors remained locked, that no beam of light, be it ever so small, would draw one of the spooky hounds that accompanies the wild hunt. When the one-eyed hunter passes, he wants to hear no creaking cart wheels, no grinding millstones, neither the spinning wheel humming, nor the spindle turning. Woe to the household where this injunction is ignored! Wotan will send one of his dogs. For a whole year it will sit by the hearth if one does not sacrifice a cow, or at least a calf.[9]

The custom that no wheel may turn during a holy time or at a holy place has its parallel in Kathmandu Valley, Nepal. Here, out of respect for Shiva (who is worshipped here mainly as Pashupati, the lord of the animals, or as Bhairava), all the loads must be carried on the back. The wagons, carts, and cars one sees rolling through the streets belong exclusively to outsiders who are not natives of the valley.[10]

In the world of the ancient northern Europeans, the eight-spoked Wheel of the Year ground to a halt each winter solstice.* It was the sacred moment of the "mother-night" (the *modra niht* of the Anglo-Saxons), when the earth is fertilized by the germs of life descending from the starry, crystalline cosmos. Then, at the end of the sacred period, Freyr, the fertility God, whose symbol is the phallus and in whose honor the yule boar was slaughtered and eaten, sets the wheel in motion once again. The absence of turning wheels during this most sacred of seasons can be seen as a ritual return to the pristine condition of long ago, long before wheels of any kind had been invented, long before wagons, spinning wheels, gins, and mills had disturbed nature. That was the time when the primordial shaman gods and goddesses and their animal ghost companions ruled unchallenged.

Shiva's abode, high up in the eternal snow and ice of Mount Kailash, represents this very original state of peace and quiescence. It is the motionless polar star around which the heavens revolve, the resting hub of the cycles of time, of the dance of creation and destruction. Even now there are holy men or women, naked as the day they were born, or dressed in the fiery red of the pyre's flame, who try to reach this mystical center where *samsara,* the wheel of birth and death, turns not. Through meditation and asceticism, they try to bring it to a standstill.

---

*The spokes of this wheel making up the old Indo-European ritual calendar are: the solstices, the equinoxes, and the midpoints between them, namely, the full moon days of February, May, August, and November.

⋙ THE TREACHEROUS GOD ⋘

The oldest Vedic writings depict Rudra as dangerous, wild, and treacherous. He shares these traits with many shamanistic gods that roamed the earth since Paleolithic times, be it Loki, cunning Lugh of the Celts, or one of the countless, elusive divine tricksters such as Great Hare or Coyote of American Indian tribes. No laws of reason can fathom him, nor can the spells of priests quell or control him. One avoids speaking his terrible name and calls him instead, Shiva (the gracious), Sambhu (the kind), or Shankar (the peaceful) in the humble hope that such euphemisms might flatter and cause him to act in the preferred manner.

"Fiery-eyed evildoer," "transvestite," "confuser," "instigator," "double-natured one," and "deceiver" are some of the epithets heaped upon Odin, for it is known that he has lured faithful followers into doom and destruction.[11] The same accusations could be leveled at Rudra. Even his spouse is upset by what she perceives as his treachery toward his devotees. The story of Rudra's "treachery" toward his devotee Ravanna is derived from the *Ramayana*, and is as common in India as Judeo-Christian Bible-stories that are told again and again. This version of the story was related to me orally by Virendra Singh of Varanasi:

The ten-headed king of the demons, Ravanna, captures the divine Queen Sita and carries her off to distant Sri Lanka where he wants to make her his wife. Sita's husband is none other than King Rama, an avatar of Vishnu. Rama sets out to free his queen with his brother and an army of allied monkeys but experiences one setback after another. The campaign is void of success because Ravanna is an ardent devotee of Shiva. He has gained Shiva's favor through severe austerities and daily worship. Countless summers he sat in the blazing heat between fires, countless winters he stood motionless in icy waters, focusing his mind on his Lord; and during the monsoons, he practiced headstands by day and by night.

King Rama and the other gods, frustrated in their effort to topple the demon, finally proceed to Shiva's mountainous throne to beg that he drop his devotee. Apparently without a second thought, Shiva grants their wish, saying, "On the seventh day of the big battle, he shall fall!"

Upon hearing this, Shiva's better half, Parvati, becomes angry, "How, pray tell, can you drop such a fervent devotee just like that? Have you no conscience? But, of course, your mind is decayed from all the hemp you smoke!

What is to be expected from one who dwells in ashes and dances on funeral pyres?"

Shiva does not take this tongue-lashing sitting down—so the folktales of India tell us. "Ha, you are but a stupid woman who does not know a thing! Anyway, who are you to point a finger at me? Haven't you been killing giants and then intoxicating yourself with their blood? And what about wearing a garland of skulls? What normal woman would do such an atrocious thing?"

Thus they argued violently for such a long time that the gods became afraid and had to calm their tempers with soothing songs and the pleasant smell of incense. Ravanna's end came as foretold. On the seventh day, the titan with ten heads was killed on the battlefield. But there was nothing unjust about his death. All the fruits of his asceticism happened to have been used up just at that moment when the magic arrow, released from Rama's bow, struck him down.

4

GOD'S VIRILE MEMBER

—————— ⚭ ——————

Whoever lives his life without honoring the Lingam
is truly poor, sinful and without luck.
To honor this giver of joy is worth more
Than good works, fasting, pilgrimages, sacrifices
and other virtues.

SHIVA PURANA

O Son of Kunti,
All creatures are born out of the infinite womb,
but I am the father,
I bestow the seed.

BHAGAVAD GITA

It is a common misconception that India is a quiet, meditative, phlegmatic country of silent gurus, gentle cows, and long-suffering peasant masses. Upon landing, this impression evaporates immediately. Freshly arrived tourists generally try to flee the noise and confusion by hiding away in their air-conditioned hotel rooms, if they do not go as far as booking the next flight out of this jungle of apparent confusion.

India's streets are a psychedelic journey without LSD. They are a constant hustle and bustle, a clanging and clattering of sounds, sights, and smells, crowded with thronging folk, with vendors, rickshaws, cows, dogs, children, and vintage cars. On top of all this, every step of the way one is confronted by a multitude of gods and goddesses. For those coming from iconoclastic societies, it is a trial. They try in vain to hang onto their rationalistic or monotheistic straws afloat in the raging sea of idolatry.

Deer-eyed, wide-hipped, buxom, multi-armed goddesses sit enthroned on bright pink lotuses or ride on some animal and smile down from the posters and placards plastering the walls. A vermilion red, pot-bellied, elephant-headed god sits above every doorway as a guardian. At merchants' stands, perfumed smoke wafts upward toward the glossy prints of the goddess of fortune out of whose hands gold coins shower upon her devotees. There is hardly a wall or a niche without a gentle-eyed, blue Krishna, playing his flute while leaning on a white cow; or Durga riding her tiger while beheading a demon; or Sarasvati riding her swan while playing a lute; or the long-tailed monkey god Hanuman, who opens his chest in a sacred-heart gesture showing that God (appearing as Sita and Rama) lives in his soul. A favorite picture shows chubby baby Krishna snitching butter from his mother's pot; another shows the same god as the driver in a hero's war chariot just before the great battle that took place in ancient times and, according to the *Bhagavad Gita,* still continues to take place in each human soul. And then there are the countless local gods and spirits depicted plastically and gaudily. Ancient magic rituals conducted by priests, as well as the faith of the believers, have animated all these images so strongly that even a Westerner might have *darshana,* "a glimpse of the inner reality."

As if that were not enough, the gods have colonized the movies. Screen idols play the stories of sages and the legends of the gods with great pathos, in the biggest film industry in the world, the output exceeding that of Hollywood. The film stars themselves are worshipped as gods.

To the Western mind, using the divinity to guarantee the quality of one's products seems blasphemous: remember what an uproar the "Jesus jeans" of the Levi-Strauss Company caused! Not so in India. "Shankar," "Krishna," "Durga," "Devi" are common for brand names or business names. "Uma-Shankar" produces textiles. "Krishna" sells automobiles. Even India's most popular rock group from Calcutta, with charming Cecelia as the lead singer, is decked out with a name of divinity: "SHIVA." The band's name was deliberately chosen as a symbol of rebellion against restrictive traditions and a sign of the yearning of

India's young bourgeoisie for the "freedom" they imagine exists in a modern consumer society.

Shiva as a rock star

The overland trucks and lorries, honking nonstop in order to blast a path through the cows, peasants, and oxcarts that stuff the streets, look like veritable temples on wheels. Mudguards and hoods, fenders and trunks are painted with eyes so that the machines might see. The insides as well as the outsides of the drivers' cabins sport colorful Shankars (he gives calmness), Durgas (she gives power), Hanumans (the flying monkey god gives speed), and other gods. Barrel-chested, bearded, turbaned Sikhs, veterans of the Indian Army Motor Corps, who like to steady their nerves while driving by guzzling whiskey, paint their trunks with images of their guru, Nanak Singh. Muslims like to paint the mosques of Mecca or the Ka'aba on their vehicles, while Christian drivers from Kerala display outrageously gaudy Jesuses, Marys, and Josephs on theirs.

Not only idols and graven images crash one's gates of perception. The senses are also assaulted by a barrage of signs and symbols such as the swastika. For the Indians, it is a sun symbol, a sign of good luck (Sanskrit *svasti* = well-being). It is the discus *(chakra)* of Vishnu in whose center he himself dwells, as the preserver of the universe. The four arms represent the four worlds—that of the gods, the human beings, the animals, and the demons—that eternally orbit the cosmic center. It is also the fiery wheel of the universe in whose center Shiva dances. For Westerners it has, of course, other associations. Young Germans nervously reach for their cigarettes when they see it. It reminds them of the hooked cross under whose banner their grandfathers ran amok all over Europe. An American teacher asked me nervously, "Are the Nazis trying to take over here?"

Equally common is the *pranava* (ॐ), the Sanskrit symbol of the OM or AUM, the first sound vibrating out of the creative void. Chanting this syllable rhythmically drives all evil spirits away and wears down the results of past deeds (karma) that still affect the present. The OM is the first syllable of all the holy mantras and powerful chants, such as the *Om Namah Shivaya* or the *Om Shiva Mahesvara Mahadev* by which God is invoked, or the *Om Mani Padme Hum* of the Buddhists. Lucky are the mortals whose last utterance is OM, for they will obtain liberation no matter how wickedly they have lived.

Yet another omnipresent symbol gracing the national flag, the money, and the walls of buildings is the World Wheel (Dharmachakra) with its eight spokes. An ancient Indo-European symbol, it was once honored in heathen northern Europe as the spinning wheel, upon which the three goddesses of fate, the Norns, spun out the destiny of all existing

Panava—
the primordial
sound: OM

beings. In India, it is associated with Vishnu or it is taken as the wheel of the eternal, divine law. For the old "congress men," the supporters of Mahatma Gandhi's movement of nonviolent resistance, it, too, represents the spinning wheel, as a basis of local autonomy and self-sufficiency for India's five hundred thousand villages. For Buddhists, it represents the *dharmachakra,* the noble eightfold path (right view, right aim, right speech, right action, right living, right effort, right mindfulness, right concentration). It is the wheel that the seeker Siddhartha, the onetime Shaivite sadhu, set in motion some 2,500 years ago when he preached his first sermon in a deer park near Benares after he had become the Buddha, the Enlightened One.

Thus an endless flood of symbols overwhelms us. Added to the religious icons and emblems are the jingle-jangle of commercial trademarks, the signs of sects, and the hieroglyphs of a dozen or so political parties. The cow, lotus, spinning wheel, swastika, hand, tree, and the sheaf and sickle (replacing the hammer and sickle), along with the bearded face of "Prajupati" Karl Marx, vie for the attention of the illiterate voter. But none of these signs and symbols is as powerful as the one marked by grace, simplicity, and quiet dignity: the Shiva lingam. Like a mountain in the plains, it towers above all the others.

ॐ LINGAM YONI ॐ

The Shiva lingam (or linga) commonly has the appearance of a simple, smoothly polished, cylindrical or egg-shaped stone. It stands upright, placed into the oval, flat receptacle that is called a yoni (Sanskrit *yoni* = vulva). Its plainness can be taken to indicate the underlying fullness of divine excellence, the undifferentiated origin and indivisible unity of Being. The concept is similar to that which ancient Greek philosophers once called *pleroma*. The lingam contains all there ever was, is, and will be. There is nothing outside of it. It is the fount of life and the gateway into death.

The lingam and its base, the yoni

For the orthodox Christian, the bread and wine of the Eucharist are truly the body and blood of God. It is not a mere symbol. In the same manner, the Hindu sees the lingam as no mere symbol. It is Shiva! This bit of polished rock is the tiny point *(bindu)* out of which springs divine manifestation. It is the ford *(thirtha)* over the treacherously turbulent streams of incarnation. It is the bridge connecting the ephemeral with the eternal, the conditioned with the absolute, the hidden with the manifest.*

Stone worship such as this is not as unusual as it might seem at first glance. Since prehistoric times, menhirs,† dolmens, monoliths, stones that fell from heaven or rose out of the earth have been sanctified as dwellings of spirits, sources of fertility, or doorways to other worlds. Often they are seen as the center, or navel, of the universe, such as the Muslim Ka'aba in Mecca, the Greek Omphalos, the tomb of the sacred python at Delphi, or the Rock of Ages of the Christians. They are houses of God, as are the Semitic *beth-els* (like Bethlehem). All over the world, barren women visit such sacred rocks to become fertile. And do we not still carry "pet rocks" in our pockets, place tombstones for the dead, and honor our heroes with marble or granite, sculpted to aid our enfeebled imaginations? The Shiva lingam expresses such archetypal sentiments. Out of the lingam, when worshipped, honored, and loved, Shiva can manifest as the personal Lord and God (Ishvara) of the worshipper. Which form he takes in doing so depends entirely upon the mental and spiritual predisposition of the individual devotee, for what he images as his "Self."

The lingam is at the same time, of course, a phallus, an organ of generation, containing all the seeds of being within it. It is imagined as resting in the everlasting embrace of the yoni, the vulva of the Great Goddess. In the rapture of this union, all beings are generated and, at

---

*For those who worship Vishnu in place of Shiva, the *salagrama*, a black fossil of a prehistoric ammonite or seashell, plays the same role as the lingam.

†*Menhir* (Breton *men* = stone, *hir* = long), a single upright monolith of prehistoric times

Worshipping the lingam/yoni

the same time, all dichotomies and disharmonies are dissolved. Ajit Mookerjee, expressing a basic Hindu conception, states, "Bliss *(ananda)* lets the Cosmos appear, bliss sustains it and bliss absorbs it again!" [1]

How the lingam came to be worshipped is told in a tale from the *Padma Puranas:*

In ancient times, the holy seers (rishis) held council in order to find out, beyond a shadow of a doubt, which of the countless gods were equal to the Brahmins and thus worthy of worship and sacrifice. After long deliberations about the merits of diverse celestials, only Brahma, Vishnu, and Shiva remained as contenders. But, as for these three, the rishis could come to no final consensus. Therefore, they delegated one of their wisest, Bhrigu, son of the firstborn of Humankind, to travel to each god's paradise and to test each of their characters respectively.

First, Brighu went to Mount Kailash. As he wound his way up the steep slopes, Nandi, Shiva's bull, suddenly blocked his path, "You cannot see my master," he snorted threateningly, "my lord and lady are enjoying the delight of intimate intercourse and should not be bothered! So, please wait!"

An eternity passed before wise Brighu lost patience. He stomped back down the path angrily, turning only to throw a curse at the two lovers, "Shiva, you are enmeshed in the darkness of your carnal desire. You gravely dishonor me by preferring the caresses of a woman to the company of a sage. Therefore, I curse you that you shall be worshipped only as a lingam and yoni! No decent, upright human beings shall sacrifice to you, but only social misfits and heretics, covered in ashes!"

When Brighu arrived at Brahma's hall, he fared no better. The creator of the universe sat basking in his radiant glory, enthroned among his creatures full of complacency and self-satisfaction, letting himself be worshipped and served. He did not even bother to acknowledge the irate sage at his doorstep.

Finally, Brighu searched out Vishnu and found him fast asleep, floating in the primal ocean on the cosmic serpent, much like a vacationer on a holiday. "Bah," grumbled the sage, as he delivered an angry kick at the breast of the sleeper, "this one is not worthy of worship, either!"

The swift kick awakened Vishnu. As good manners demand, he quickly touched the visitor's feet, rubbing them humbly while speaking salubrious words of welcome. Brighu was sufficiently flattered. On his return to the other rishis, he reported that only Vishnu is worthy of the honors accorded to a Brahmin. (That this was a misjudgment, as far as Shiva was concerned, we shall find out later.)

The proposition that the lingam holds within it all the beings and all the worlds is best illustrated by the following story of what happened to Sukra, Brighu's son:

Sukra's path among the celestials is seen, to this day, as the movement of the planet Venus in the night sky. He inherited enough wisdom from his father to become the teacher (guru) of the titans, and his advice was effective enough to leave the gods in dire straights. Indeed, the gods feared their doom and pleaded to Shiva to help them against Sukra's guile and trickery.

Shiva heard their prayers and let his bull, Nandi, charge the guru of the demons. Like a lion pouncing on a frail deer, Nandi brought him to fall while Shiva picked him up like a bread crumb, between forefinger and thumb, stuck him in his mouth, and swallowed him. As terrified Sukra slid into Shiva's stomach, he was overwhelmed. There, in front of his eyes, all the universes unfolded; all the heavens, seas, and underworlds became visible. There were the *adityas*, the twelve heavenly gods of the seasons, the *vasus*, those eight lords of the elements, who accompany the thunderbolt-carrying Indra, all the *ganas* (the heavenly hosts) and the *yakshas*, those nature spirits attending Kubera, the god of all the wealth hidden underneath the earth. Sukra witnessed degenerate, beastly human beings, the *kimpurusas* and the corpse-devouring pisachas, as well as the *apsarasas*, those most lovely heavenly nymphs and elflike dancers. He saw the *gandharvas*, those angelic, divine musicians who nourish themselves on the fragrance of flowers. All beings were there, the rishis and common folk, the creatures that live in the air and those that live on the ground, the cows, the ants, worms, trees, bushes, herbs, the creatures that swim and those that run, those that blink

Sukra, the guru of the demons

their eyes and those that do not, those on two legs, on four, six, eight, and those with a thousand legs.

The vision so overwhelmed him that he spontaneously burst into songs of praise. "Hail, Thee, fulfiller of wishes! Hail Hara, seizer of souls, carrier of all virtues, giver of life, protector of the world! Thou great ape, devourer of time, mover of all! Honor to Thee, three-eyed One! Oh, Bhava,* oh Shankara, oh husband of Uma, rider of clouds, dweller in the cave, lover of cremations, carrier of the trident, Lord of the Animals, master of the cows, ash-covered one, highest Lord, thine is the honor and the glory!"

On and on he sang, pleasing Shiva tremendously, causing him to smile. "Well, you moon of the Bhargavas, you have become my son! You may leave my belly, by way of my penis. For this reason, you shall be called Sukra (semen)!"

At this, Sukra popped back into the external world. He made his obeisance to the Lord, rejoined his army of titans and led them with renewed vigor against the gods.

This story clearly illustrates that Shiva is not only the God of gods, but of the demons as well. He embodies the primal oneness, before the world divided itself into the divine and demonic forces.

❧ THE LINGAM IS EVERYWHERE ❧

Countless lingams fill the universes! There are gigantic ones, such as the World Mountain or the heavenly vault, whose associated yoni is the earth or the sea. There are minute lingams, as small as the grains of sand. Every pebble in Kashi (Benares) is considered to be a lingam. There are those molded by the hands of humans, the rishis, or the gods, and those that formed themselves (svayambu lingam). There are those that last for eternity and those made for the moment, kneaded of rice or wheat dough at a festival, or made of mud or sand while bathing at the river-bank. There are renowned lingams and those that no stranger would notice, save for telltale grains of rice and a few wood apple leaves or marigolds indicating someone has worshipped.

Shiva lingams that have spontaneously arisen in nature are often strangely shaped, menhirlike blocks or rock outcroppings, such as the

*Sanskrit *bhava* = being

"Lingam of Light" at Kedernath in the Himalayas. Then again, they might be natural features such as stalagmites of ice or stone; an example is the mighty ice pillar in the caves of Amarnath in Kashmir's mountains, to which pilgrims climb steep, rocky paths to pay homage.

Lingam decorated with a wood apple leaf

The very first lingam, appearing at the beginning of time, was a mighty pillar of fire (jyotirlingam). This original, self-born fire lingam to this day is honored in twelve different places or different forms. It is worshipped as:

1. Lord of the Moon in Somnath, Gujarat
2. The mountain Shri on the Krishna River
3. The Great Lord of Death in the holy city of Ujjain
4. The Omkara, the sacred syllable OM, at various locations
5. Amareshvara, the God of Gods also at Ujjain
6. Lord of Physicians in Deogarh, Bengal
7. Rameshvara, on the small island between the mainland and Sri Lanka
8. Bhima Shankara in Dakini
9. Vishveshvara, Lord of the Universe in Benares
10. Tryambake, "Three Eyes" on the banks of the Gomati River
11. Lord Gautama
12. Kedarnath in the Himalayas

Lingam (menhir) (European Neolithic)

The fact that the one primordial Lingam of Light has manifested at several different places bothers the Indian sense of logic as little as the contention that each god may be worshipped as the one almighty God. In an infinite universe, the center can be everywhere.

In the first age of the world, the *krita yuga*, these lingams shone in indescribably pure light; in the second age, they turned to pure gold; in the third age, they became silver; but today, alas, they have become mere rock, and some have even been demolished by fanatical iconoclasts and disbelievers. Still, no matter what their external appearance, their power remains unbroken.

Lingam with a face
(ekmukha-lingam)

Lingam with faces
(Pashupathinath, Nepal)

There still are fiery lingams everywhere. The flame flickering in the hearth is a lingam and the stone plate that holds it is a yoni. The brass oil lamp, which Keralese kathakali dancers place on the stage and worship before each performance, indicates Shiva's presence in the form of a fire lingam. The fire of life's energy, burning in the body, can also be considered a lingam. The energy centers it penetrates (the chakras) are its yonis.

The lingam is, of course, also plainly and simply the erect male member. More than once has a shocked tourist fled aghast, after having stumbled across a grizzly yogi, meditatively engrossed in his *urdhava linga*, which he is worshipping as an expression of Shiva. Until recently, the Maharaja of Patila paraded through the streets at an annual festival dressed only in a diamond chest harness, displaying his upright member. This was no quirk on the part of a decadent, blue-blooded pervert. Far from it. It is, as Sir James Frazer has shown, the survival of an ancient ritual during which the king, this "bull among men," provides the visible guarantee that he is maintaining the fertility of his realm to which he is linked with body and soul. Other sovereigns do the same by fathering numerous progeny with many queens. It was common in prehistoric, sacred societies that old, impotent kings were killed by young, virile challengers, for only they could please the Great Goddess and induce her to bless human and beast with offspring and fields rich with harvests.

Ordinarily, the stone lingam is devoid of any embellishment since it is meant to be a bridge to the contemplation of God in his formless, "void" essence, without characteristics projected upon him. Yet sometimes a cobra, the sign of awakened shakti power, is shown winding its way up the shaft. Sometimes four or five faces are sculpted into the shaft, one for each direction and a final one looking toward the zenith. Each face represents an aspect of God: the first face beams out the forces of creation *(srishti)*; the second indicates preservation *(sthiti)* of what has been created; a third, terrible visage, invokes destruction *(samhara)*; and an equally sinister countenance betokens the concealment *(tirobhava)* between the cycles of creation and destruction. The fifth face, on top, addresses the devotee with its blessing *(anugraha)*. In Nepal, a smooth transition toward Buddhism lets the faces of meditating Buddhas appear on the shafts of the Shiva lingams.

ॐ How Arjuna Won His ॐ Magic Arrows

Arjuna is the noble archer we know from the "Song of the Lord" *(Bhagavad Gita)*.* During the long drawn-out war between rival kin groups, Arjuna realizes that he must have special magic arrows if the tide of battle is to turn in his favor. In order to obtain them, he makes a pilgrimage to a quiet, forested valley hidden in the Himalayas where he finds a cove of meditating yogis. To aid his meditation, he models a lingam out of clay and decorates it with fresh blossoms. Then, with undivided attention, he begins to chant the holy invocation *Om Namah Shivaya*. His meditation becomes so fervent that he heats up as though he were on fire. The trees around him turn yellow and lose their leaves; the grass smolders, causing the other meditators to wheeze and cough. His ardent effort bothers them so much that the holy men leave for

---

*The *Bhagavad Gita* is contained in the great Indian epic, the *Mahabharata*, written some time around 300 B.C. It tells of the wars between rival Aryan kin groups, the Kauravas and the Pandavas. The latter had been unjustly banned from rulership by the former. Lord Krishna, as an avatar of Vishnu, is neutral, but he lets the contenders choose between all his power and glory on one hand, or himself on the other hand. Arjuna, the hero of the Pandavas, chooses Krishna in person. Thus God becomes his charioteer. Before the big battle starts, however, Arjuna is hesitant to participate in what seems to be a meaningless slaughter, for he sees kinsmen and former teachers on the opposing side. Krishna exhorts him to act anyway, to do his duty as a warrior as correctly as possible and not to calculate the result. He teaches him that total surrender of one's deeds to God, doing right for the sake of right, not for the reward, leads to liberation. At the same time, Krishna reveals himself in all his power and glory, letting the hero glimpse the mysteries of God, Universe, and Soul.

Mount Kailash to beg the Lord that he might satisfy Arjuna's wishes, whatever they may be. This Shiva promises to do but first he would test the warrior's character to see if he is worthy of such a gift.

Shiva, then, takes on the appearance of a swarthy, muscular chieftain of the kiratas, those wild, widely feared mountaineers. Parvati, not wanting to miss the adventure, goes along as the kirata queen, and the clamoring host of ghosts and goblins change themselves into kirata wenches. Let us join them and see what happens:

At the very moment the kirata chief and his crowd of women enter the hallowed forest, a gigantic wild boar comes crashing through the thicket, grunting menacingly. The terrified hermits flee helter-skelter. Seeing through the swinish exterior, they recognize the demon (asura) Muka, coming once again to disrupt their contemplations. But no sooner has it appeared than two arrows whiz through the air, hitting the bristly beast simultaneously. Gurgling and hissing, the spirit of the nasty asura leaves the dying body of the boar. The kirata women clap their hands, shouting in chorus, "Bravo! Our great chieftain has slain the boar!"

"I beg your pardon," retorts Arjuna, sure of his skills. "It is I who killed the boar!"

The sinister headman fixes the young hero with a cold stare, saying, "Listen, stranger! These women speak the truth. Your arrow hit a boar that was already dead!"

Soon an argument flares up that becomes ever more heated until Arjuna, fired by righteous wrath, picks up his bow to strike down the impudent mountaineer. The arrow fails its mark, for the kirata shoots it in two as it flies through the air. Arjuna empties his quiver, but none of his arrows strike their target. Drawing his sword, he charges his dark-skinned opponent, but as he heaves to split his skull, the blade shatters as though it were made of plywood. At that, Arjuna loses all constraint. In blind fury, he uproots a tree with which to pound the enemy into the ground. The kirata grabs the trunk and flings it, along with Arjuna, into the air. The hero falls crashing to the ground next to the mud lingam. He is badly shaken but gathers himself enough to throw a prayer at the Shiva lingam. Immediately, fresh strength and new courage flood his limbs. Jumping to his feet, he shouts, "Kirata, your hour has come—"

He cannot finish the sentence, for, lo and behold, the flowers that had adorned the lingam now deck the long hair of the kirata! Awestruck, Arjuna realizes that his opponent is none other than the Lord! Trembling, he falls to his knees, as Shiva and Parvati take on their usual appearance as a sadhu and a noble lady. Holding their hands open in a gesture of blessing, they tell him, "Your courage and dedication have pleased us. You shall have the invincible arrows of the Lord of the Animals and victory shall be yours!"

⌘ HOW MARKANDEYA BECAME ⌘ AN IMMORTAL

The story of wise Markandeya, which was told to me orally in India, illustrates again the power derived from honoring the Shiva lingam:

Once upon a time, there lived a man and woman who, devoted to the service of the Lord, fed the poor and honored the cows. But their hearts were not as glad as they should have been, for they had no children. The man decided to do severe penance to propitiate Lord Shiva. And, indeed, after some time, the trident-bearing God appeared in the man's meditation.

"Lord, bless us with a son," the man prayed to the God.

"Tell me," Shiva asked, "do you want a son who will live a full life span but is lacking in virtue? Or, would you prefer a son who is wise and virtuous but will live for only sixteen years?"

"I will have a virtuous son, my Lord!" he answered without hesitating.

Soon thereafter, a babe, whom they called Markandeya, was nursing at his mother's breast. He turned out to be even-tempered, kind, and quick to learn. Already as a child he mastered the holy scriptures, which pleased the elders tremendously. One day—it was on the eve of his sixteenth birthday—Markandeya came back from the woods where he had gathered flowers for the evening worship and found his mother sobbing and his father's face frozen with grief. They tried to avoid telling him what was troubling them so, but they finally revealed to him his cruel fate. The boy put his arms around them and reassured them, "Please do not be sad! Shiva is the gracious one. He is master over death. Surely, I can ask him to spare me!"

Yama, the god of death

Having said that, he went to the seashore where he fashioned a Shiva lingam out of wet sand, decorated it with fragrant blossoms and, focusing his mind on it, began to pray. Toward nightfall, as his devotion became complete, he started tossing and dancing before the sign of the Lord. Suddenly a harsh, solemn voice interrupted him: "Get ready to die!"

There was Yama, the grim, black god of death, riding his black water buffalo, holding a bludgeon in one hand and a rope in the other.

"Oh, Lord of Death, please wait a moment, I have not yet finished my worship!" the youth replied.

"You are a fool! No one can escape me whose hour has come!" Yama roared, while slipping the noose over the boy's head. Markandeya tried to cling to the Shiva lingam, calling on the Lord for help. At that very moment, Shiva loomed out of the sand lingam and threw Yama to the ground. Death fell to his knees before his Lord and departed.

"Markandeya," said Shiva, "your unwavering faith has made you forever free from death. You are an immortal. Go in peace."

The sage Markandeya is said to be the author of the *Markandeya Purana*, a carefully wrought work of some nine thousand stanzas, in which birds, knowing right from wrong, tell bits of wisdom, anecdotes, and tales. After that work was finished, all trace of him was lost. If he has not of his own volition laid his physical body aside, he is probably still alive, perhaps meditating in a Himalayan cave, perhaps surfing in southern California.

☙ THE PHALLIC SYMBOL ❧

During the twelfth century, the sons of the Arabian Desert descended upon a fabulously rich and decadent India and put to torch and sword what in their eyes was lewd, impure, and idolatrous. As Islam spread, the era of great Indian erotic art, with its voluptuous images of copulating divinities, came to an end. Women began hiding their body curves, covering their breasts, and finally even pulling the sari over their faces. The very idea that the lingam referred to a vital and interesting part of the human anatomy was ever more repressed. "No, no," the Brahmins defensively protested, "the lingam is but a symbol, an indication of God, who is beyond and above any image. It is merely an object without concrete associations, used as a focus for meditation on the center of being, which is identical with your Allah!"

After centuries of religious outrage, the Muslims got somewhat used to their lingam-worshipping neighbors. But then came the Christian missionaries and, finally, the prudish Victorian scholars, always hot on the trail of the titillating nastiness of which the "savage and barbarian races" were capable. Again and again, the Brahmins had to explain that the lingam is not a phallic symbol but an imageless point *(bindu)* used by the meditant to concentrate the spirit, similar to the crystal ball of the fortune-teller. It is a sign of the pleroma, the void that contains all, the sound not yet heard, the quiet center surrounded by an ocean of movement, energy, and expression.

"The fact that a few degenerates or primitives, dark-skinned aboriginals *(dasas, adavasis)* worship the penis might be so, but it certainly does not apply to the Aryan caste Hindus," they hastened to add. Indeed, they were telling the truth, for the Aryan Vedas left no doubt about nauseating pre-Aryan customs of worshipping snakes and phalli. Phallic cults belong traditionally to matrifocal societies of planters in which a mighty Mother Goddess, together with an ever dying, ever resurrecting phallic son/lover, guards the recurrent cycle of vegetation, the sowing and harvesting of crops. The patriarchal herders of cattle, goats, and sheep, like the old Aryans or the Old Testament Hebrews, would have nothing to do with this; they would have little use for Mother lovers like an Attis, Adonis, or Tamuz. Even though the synthesis of the Aryan and the older Dravidian cults has long been accomplished, especially in the Shaivite and Tantric sects, the orthodox Hindus defend themselves vehemently to this day against insinuations that the regenerative organs are worshipped in the lingam and yoni. Gentle Hindu swamis, otherwise given to peaceful smiles, are apt to loose their temper on this issue. Swami Sri Sivananda, the founder of the Divine Life Society, is no exception. For him the lingam speaks an unmistakable language of silence. "Only pure, pious souls can understand this language. A curious, passionate, impure foreigner of little understanding or intelligence says sarcastically, 'Oh, the Hindus worship the phallus, or sex organ. They are ignorant people. They have no philosophy.' When a foreigner tries to learn Tamil or Hindustani languages, he first tries to pick up some vulgar words. This is his curious nature. Even so, the curious foreigner tries to find out some defects in the worship of symbol."[2]

The conflict between the rather puritan Aryan Brahmins and the followers of an indigenous, archaic ithyphallic god has been going on for a long time. The Sanskrit Puranas tell the following story:

Once upon a time, there dwelled a group of pious and devout hermits hidden deeply in the forests of the mountainous north. They lived together with their wives in chastity, spending their time praising and worshipping God. Their pride grew as their meditation became deeper and their vows more resolute. Then one day, a handsome, naked youth appeared among the pines, dancing ecstatically, holding his stiff member in his hands and making suggestive movements. It was Shiva. He had come to make his pious devotees laugh, to make them merry and happy. However, they were not only shocked but also thoroughly repulsed by such a lewd display.

The love-starved wives of the penitents could not help being fascinated by the beautiful ithyphallic man. Secretly their hearts beat double time at the thought of being ravished by him. Their husbands noticed this, and it poured the oil of jealousy into the fire of antipathy. Their outrage swelled to a terrible curse. "Your vile actions are unheard of! You violate the commandments of the Holy Vedas! May your phallus drop off!"

The curse of those who have practiced long and arduous austerities never fails its mark! Immediately Shiva's lingam fell from his body, catching on fire as it fell. It fell through all three worlds, heaven, earth, and underworld, wreaking flaming havoc. The entire creation threatened to conflagrate. Terrified gods and rishis hastened to Brahma, the wise Creator, to ask what could be done.

As always, the grandfather of all creation knew the right advice. "Shiva's penis must be quieted! Go to Parvati, the beautiful daughter of the mountain. Sing to this goddess the songs that old custom prescribes. Draw water from a sacred ford at the river. Then place the water jug, along with some kusha grass and barleycorns, into a magic circle (mandala) decorated with eight kinds of flower petals. Chant spells (mantras) over the water jar. Sing on, without stopping, until the goddess appears in the form of a vulva. The roaming fire-penis will find cooling relief in the vulva's moist embrace. Once it has come to rest, sprinkle it with more cool water and bind it faster with more spells. Honor the lingam with flowers, with the smoke of sandalwood, perfume, and sweet spices. Praise the Lord with songs and musical instruments, with bows and prostrations. Finally, to conclude the rite, call to the Lord, "Hail Thee, Lord of Gods, who bringeth peace and happiness to the world. Thou, Creator, Preserver, and Destroyer, have mercy. Rest Thou here, who are beyond the OM, who art the core of all. Be at peace, Great Lord, protect all the worlds."

The gods and seers completed this for the sake of the world's *dharma*. After the roaming fiery penis found rest in the yoni, both Shiva and Parvati were content. This was the first time that the lingam-*puja*, the worship of the lingam, was celebrated, as it is performed to this day in countless temples and homes. The swamis tell us that as long as people go on worshipping the lingam, peace and happiness will prevail in the three worlds.

⚜ THE PILLAR OF FIRE ⚜

The *Shiva Purana* tells us that the lingam was honored the very first time long before there were gods and rishis.[3] It was before creation began:

Vishnu, in whom the universe rests between cosmic manifestations, awakened from his sleep. He stretched, yawned, and looked with the light of one hundred thousand suns, which shone from his eyes, into the void of the primal chaos. Nothing existed but the glory of his being. But, suddenly, he became aware of someone else. There was a golden-hued god with five heads, surrounded by a radiant aura, shining like one hundred thousand suns. The holy Vedas sounded out of his luminous center.

"How is this possible?" puzzled the perplexed Vishnu, not realizing that the other one arose from his very own navel. "I am the only One. Who are you?"

The other replied like an echo, "I am the only One. Who are you?"

The world-egg had split in two. A terrific argument ensued between the two primal beings, as to who was the first and the mightiest. As the quarrel reached the point where they were about to strike blows at each other, a gigantic column of fire (jyotirlingam) struck in front of them with a deafening roar. Glowing like a million suns, it grew and grew, piercing the heavens above and the underworld below, losing itself in infinity. The two primal beings were stunned. When they finally caught themselves, they decided to find out what was behind this perplexing event. They agreed that whoever found the source of the fiery column would be the greater of the two. Thus, Vishnu took the form of a rooting boar, to find its roots by digging into the ground, while Brahma changed into a wild gander to fly upward, searching for its top.

The strong boar tunneled downward for thousands upon thousands of divine years but

Vishnu as a boar

*Brahma rides on a gander
or takes the form of a gander*

found no end. At some unfathomable depth, he happened upon Anant (Sanskrit *anant* = endless), the king of all serpents.

"Give up your quest," the endless snake advised the exhausted digger, "for the blazing pillar is a manifestation of Shiva, who has neither root nor crown." Vishnu conceded his defeat and surfaced.

In the meantime Brahma had flown upward for many eons without finding even a hint of a top. On the way through the high heavens, he met the original cow, Surabhi (or Kamadhenu), who advised him that the quest was futile, for the column had neither beginning nor end. Proud Brahma, Lord of the Vedas, wanted, at all costs, to win his contest with Vishnu. As he was a master of words and a powerful persuader, he managed to talk the dumb cow into bearing false witness on his behalf. Hesitatingly, she agreed to say that she saw the gander land on top of the mysterious column. He also talked three little plants, the century plant, the bandhuk, and the red-flowering hibiscus, which they met on their way, into supporting his deceitful claim. When he met Vishnu again, Brahma lost no time in boasting of his success. The flowers nodded their heads in agreement. So did the cow, but as she had a bad conscience, she denied it at the same time by shaking her tail. At that moment, Shiva Mahadev stepped out of the fiery lingam and put an end to the squabbling.

"Since thou hast spoken the truth," he declared, turning to Vishnu, "thou shalt be worshipped even as I am worshipped!"

Turning to the Creator, he said, "But, thou, Brahma, since thou hast lied, thou art not worthy of worship!"

The cow, of course, was forgiven for her weakness. But the three plants may not be used, even to this day, to decorate Shiva's lingam. Whoever absentmindedly does so is bound for hell. Having set things straight, the gracious Lord promised to let the infinite lingam of fire become so small that human beings might worship it also.

Opinions differ as to where this original fiery lingam, reduced to manageable size, is to be found on the earth. Most believe it to be in shiny Kashi (Benares). But the Nepalese insist it pierced the universe at no other place than the Kathmandu Valley, precisely in the holy district of the lord of the animals, Pasupathinath. The Tamils of southern India are sure it must have been at the holy mountain of Arunachala. Then again, it is said that everyone who earnestly searches for this lingam will find it, not in some far-off place, but very close to his home.

Ram and Lakshmi worshipping the lingam

The foregoing story is, no doubt, a favorite of the Shaivites, the followers of the three-eyed god. In their view, the holy trinity (Brahma the Creator; Vishnu the Sustainer; Shiva the Destroyer) is itself an expression of an all-encompassing Super-Shiva. The Vaishnavas, on the other hand, claim with equal unerring confidence that Vishnu is the one and only God of Gods, while all other gods, including the trident-bearer, are but partial aspects. Thus both Shiva and Vishnu are equally worshipped. Brahma, the hapless Creator, has no temples nor are offerings provided to him.

In the usual representations of the lingam yoni, all three aspects of the One are present. The base, or lower, square *(brahagraha)* represents the four-headed Brahma. The rounder middle part *(vishnubhaga)* represents the femininely receptive Vishnu, while the rounded shaft *(rudrabhaga)*, which juts out of the yoni, represents Shiva.

The divine trinity, the central principle multiplied by the sacred number three, is of early Indo-European vintage, coming also to expression in the triune Godhead of Christianity and in the three Goddesses of Fate of earlier heathen Europe. In India, the trinity has found a place in philosophical speculation and also in art, such as in the monumental sculptures of Elephanta. To the simple believer, that is all abstract; she generally tends to think of herself as a follower of Shiva or of Vishnu.

5

SHANKAR, THE YOGI ON THE MOUNTAIN

Being in Samadhi
in the state of supreme bliss
that arises from seedless yoga,

his knowledge free from constraint
he meditates constantly
within himself upon Himself.

UMAPATI SIVACARYA,
TAMIL POET, FOURTEENTH CENTURY

The ever so fine ethereal images witnessed by the seer, as he delves meditatively into the hidden springs of Being, become eventually transformed into the imagery of wise sayings, fairy tales, legends, songs, and dances. The seer's fellow human beings, who are enmeshed in their many daily cares and worries, in their work and duties, will be able to understand such images and allegories. They will be food for their souls and spirits. In return, they will free the seer from the obligation of labor, gladly filling his bowl with some cooked rice, and will address him respectfully as "babaji" (honorable father) or "swamiji" (honorable teacher).

The seer's images and words accompany the people through the day and into sleep, guide them through the seasons, through sickness and health and, finally one day, over the threshold of death. The most moving and most profound visions make up the spiritual treasure of a people. They are guarded with great care. Artists represent them and writers fix them on paper and embellish them. Whole troops of priests and teachers busy themselves to cultivate and propagate, display and worship such visionary images, for they are religion (Latin *re-ligare* = to tie back, to reconnect). They tie us back to the Source. They are upheld and honored in regular rituals.

Sacred, venerated images (icons) are an integral part of religious cultus. For the common people, they become keys unlocking the innermost chambers of one's soul. Religious icons have little to do with the whim and fancy of so-called creative artists. Rather, they are the careful rendering of a truly spiritual vision. The reproduction of the vision has to be correct to the minutest detail. It is far too sacred to allow for much speculation and extrapolation, which would render it impotent and lessen its magical effect on the psyche.

Present-day visitors to India, leaving their niche in consumer's paradise elsewhere for a few weeks, are first of all shocked at what they perceive as depressing poverty, filth, and crass superstitions that assault them. If they can overcome their mass-media conditioning and prejudices and open their eyes, they will see an immensely rich land. Indeed, they might suddenly feel, psychologically speaking, like poor beggars who have stumbled into the jeweled palace of a maharaja. They will find themselves in an ancient treasure house of the most colorful images, of inexhaustible folklore, endlessly rich in narrative, mysterious customs, and breathtaking song, dance, and opulent festivals. It is abundance beyond the measure of anyone's comprehension, constantly reminding the soul of its own hidden wealth and its birthright as a citizen of a spiritual universe.

The icons of Shiva that help to focus the mind and lead the soul in contemplation are many. But three of them are the most common. First, there is the icon of Shankara, the peaceful ascetic, sunk deeply into meditation, his body covered with ashes as he sits in a snowy mountainous landscape. Then, in contrast, there is Nataraja, dancing in the midst of a ring of fire, drumming the beat of life with his hand drum. A third icon shows Shiva and Parvati with their children in an idyllic scene placed in the mountains in the spring. We shall look more closely at these three images in the following section, for they hold the keys to the archetype.

❧ SHANKARA ❧

As the lord of the mountains (Girisha), Shiva-Shankar sits motionless in deep contemplation of the universe, which is his inner dream. The skin of his strong body is as white as the snows on the icy peaks of Mount Kailash, where he camps.* He is the embodiment of complete peace and quiet. All trace of passion, all desire to be actively involved in any outside interest has been extinguished like a fire that has burned down to a few pure white ashes. His athletic physique, however, lets us surmise that he could spring into action at any moment. He is not at all dead, but like the quiescence before the storm, a concentration of potential power.

His wild, unkempt mane is piled up high, its topknot held together

Shankar

by a hissing cobra. His devotees call him Dhurjati, or Jatadhari, "the one with matted, felted hair." A jet of water springs from the topknot, cascading to earth in a wide bow: It is the river Ganges, originating in heaven, personified by the goddess Ganga, who was called down by the sufferings and austerities of a holy rishi. Shiva is called Gangadhara, "carrier of Ganga," for he was willing to catch the goddess in his hair in order to cushion her fall. As she flows over the earth, she brings fertility and life. Passing the funeral ghats, she washes the ashes of the dead into the underworld before rising again into the heavens where she flows as the Milky Way, on whose banks the original seven rishis (the seven brightest stars of the Big Dipper) meditate. The goddess represents the cycle of life—and Shiva-Shankara, who wears her in his hair, is thus the master of this eternal round.

On the left side of his brow, Shankar sports the delicate silver crescent of the newborn moon. Scholars like to point out that the moon has a lot to do with the mind, with measuring and memory, with time and the tides.† In carrying the moon, Shiva is lord of all these lunar aspects.

---

*Shiva's external appearance is white, but his inside is darker than night. In that, he is the inverse of Vishnu (Krishna), whose skin is black, but his inside is white light.
†Etymologically, the Indo-European root *men* (= thinking, mentally active) or *menon* (moon) leads to a whole complex of semantics: Skt *man* (thinking, minding), L *mens* (mental activity), L *mentiri* (to make up, lie), L *mensis* (monthly period), L *memor* (memory), etc.

In Indian mythology, just as in European folklore, the moon's cup is filled with very precious liquid. It is the Water of Life, the soma of the gods, the drink of immortality (Sanskrit *amrita*), that the northerners called the Mead of Inspiration and the ancient Greeks called ambrosia. It is the liquor upon which the gods get drunk with ecstasy, and which lifts the poets and seers beyond everyday doldrums into the realms where eagles fly.

Soma, the name of the moon as well as of the divine nectar, is personified in Indian mythology as a handsome youth whose chariot is speeded along by ten milk-white horses. He is married to twenty-seven daughters of the demiurge and lord of priests, Daksha. Brahma installed Soma as the lord of plants (Oshadipati) who nourishes all seedlings with his refreshing dew; he also made him the master of elegant speech and poetry (Vacaspati). As a result of these gifts, Soma became so impressed with himself that he lost all sense of measure. His twenty-seven wives were not enough for him. He sought to spread his favor to other members of the fairer sex. He cast his eye especially upon Tara, (the star), the voluptuous wife of the old rishi Brihaspati (the planet Jupiter). Soma led her to his hideout, ravished her, and wanted to keep her as his own. Brihaspati was outraged. Even Brahma's patient admonishments could not move Soma to return the beautiful woman to her lawful husband. In the council of the gods the betrayed husband sought reparation. Indra (the king of the celestials) and his hosts set out to punish the rash youth's transgression against the laws of decency. The antigods (asuras), titans (daityas), giants (danavas) and howlers (rudras) took the side of the moon, finding it a welcome chance to put a little hell to the heavenly hosts.

A regular war of the stars ensued, which the "good guys" won, as usual. A hesitant Tara, who in the meantime had fallen in love with Soma, was returned to her lawfully wedded husband. She was pregnant. When the old patriarch Brahma asked her whose child she was carrying, she unabashedly admitted it to be Soma's and refused to have the "unclean" fruit of her passion aborted, as Brahma demanded. In due time, Budha (the planet Mercury) "the clever one," was born.

It was during this war that Shiva swallowed Sukra (Venus), the guru of the antigods, and released him again through his penis. But that story we know already. It was also during this conflict that Shiva, wielding his trident, whacked the moon into pieces and placed a sliver of it in his hair. For this reason, Shiva came to be called Chandrasekhara, "the moon-crested one," indicating that Mahadev is lord over Soma and the conqueror of lunar forces, such as the restless flow of mind and the merciless passing of time and tides.*

Shankar's other bodily decorations can be understood in a similar way. The poisonous cobras he wears as armbands, rings, necklaces, and hair decoration, signify that he has overcome the cold-blooded reptilian nature inside of himself. He does not fear their power. They do not crawl, stealthily hidden, through the darkest recesses of his psyche, as they do in so many people who seem, externally seen, to be so proper and decent. Much like the shaman with his badges and pendants, or the sailor or warrior with tattoos signaling having left fear behind, these vipers are the external insignia of inner self-mastery.

☙ THE TEARS OF RUDRA ❧

In the same way one must understand the acorn-sized, shriveled brown rudraksha beads, the seeds of the utrasum-bead tree *(Elaeocarpus ganitrus),* which, threaded upon a string, decorate Shankar's wrists, neck, biceps, and head gear. They, too, are trophies of victory. In his feminine appearance as the pitch black, bloodthirsty Kali, he lops off the heads of demons, lets them dry and shrink (much as the Jivaro headhunter's tsantsas, or shrunken heads), and strings them up as the beads of his rosary. With his garland of shrunken demon skulls, he is Kapamalin, "the carrier of a necklace of skulls."

Rudra's worshippers follow the footsteps of their Lord in an imitatio dei. The victors of the spiritual battles against the vices and weaknesses of their souls bedeck themselves with rudraksha beads, much like the red-

---

*In some iconic representations, the OM shines forth from the lunar crescent that decorates Shiva's brow. It is interpreted as follows: The primordial sound OM results from the union of Shiva with his Shakti. The OM becomes the seed (bindu), or the door through which the fecund void *(shunyata)* releases manifestation into existence, just as the black night sky suddenly lets the fine sliver of the new moon appear. In human beings, this point (bindu) is located between the brows, just below the middle of the forehead. Sometimes the bindu is shown split into two halves, like a pea. The vertical line thus formed represent the "I." The two halves, in turn, represent the "other," the dichotomous world, in which this "I" finds itself. Shiva and Shakti in union are likened to the dark of the moon, to unmanifested unity. The OM, as the first dawning of existence, is likened to the new crescent moon, while the whole split bindu represents the full moon. See Swami Swahananda, *Hindu Symbology and Other Essays* (Madras: Sri Ramakrishna Math, 1983), 6.

skins of the Wild West, who adorned themselves
with necklaces of the dried fingers and scalps of
their fallen opponents, or the Celtic warriors,
who hung the heads of decapitated enemies on
their horses' collar harnesses. Especially the sadhus, the wandering saints, like to wear them as
a visible sign of having overcome the demons of
egoism, hate, fear, desire, or any other evil. Only
someone who has been able to generate the spir-

Rudraksha beads

itual heat (tapas) of asceticism may wear them. Tourists might buy
rudraksha beads with money, but for them they will be useless.

When asked about the meaning of these beads, a fiery-eyed sadhu
who lived in the Nepalese jungle explained to me that all our wishes,
thoughts, words, and deeds are like the seeds of a plant sown into fertile ground. They might rest there in the dark, invisible and forgotten,
but sooner or later they will sprout, grow tall, flower, and finally shoot
to seed. Rather than sowing these seeds of suffering anew, one can
string them up and wear them as a sign that one's karma has ended.

The Hindus have made a regular esoteric science out of the
rudraksha seeds. It is as sophisticated as the wine cult of the French.
Pedantic scholars (pundits) whose passion for classification exceeds
that of the proverbially stodgy German professor, have classified and
differentiated the seeds according to size, color, weight, place of origin, and the number of rills, facets, or "mouths" *(mukhi)* each of the
nutlike seeds has. Theoretically, there are white, red, yellow, and black
mutants, each of which stands for one of the four races or castes
(varna): the priest-scholars (brahmins), the nobles *(kshatriya),* the
commoners *(vaishya)* and the servants *(shudra).* Admittedly, the uninitiated have a hard time distinguishing such fine nuances in the seeds.

The ordinary rudraksha seed has five facets.
But there are mutants that have anywhere from
one to thirty-two such rills, and these become
increasingly expensive by degree of rarity. The
least common is a true biological freak. It is a
banana-shaped, one-mouthed bead *(ekamukhi*
rudraksha). It is so expensive that it is set in
gold. Folklore has it that a tree does not bring
forth just one such rare bead, but always three
at a time. When ripened out, one of these shoots

Twin rudraksha—
a Gauri-Shankar
or Shiva-Shakti
rudraksha

*Rudraksha beads
with various
numbered "faces"*

directly into heaven, one sinks into the earth, and some chosen believer finds the third. The King of Nepal supposedly has several such one-mouthed beads in his treasure chest. Two such wonders are found in the temple of the lord of the animals (Pashupatinath) and are shown to the devotees but once a year, on the night of the dark moon in November. A single meeting (darshana) with a one-rilled rudraksha seed suffices to free the soul from all its sins.[1]

A two-faceted rudraksha seed is called "Shiva-Shakti" and promises its owner the fulfillment of all wishes. One with three furrows is named "Brahma-Vishnu-Mahesh," and it bestows intelligence and wealth. One with four mouths is taken as an epiphany of the four-headed creator god Brahma. It serves human beings in the attainment of the four goals of life: dharma, satisfying the spiritual law; kama, pleasure; artha, wealth; and moksha, salvation. Since Brahma is the god of intellect and speech, the wearing of such a bead will help in cases of poor memory, stupidity, or stuttering. The common five-rilled nut, the "Panchamukhi," implies the presence of Lord Shiva himself; whoever wears one will overcome all difficulties. This same bead also represents the former fifth head of Brahma, which the murderous Bhairava had sliced off. Such a bead can, therefore, be worn by those guilty of murder or manslaughter to atone their sin.

A bead that has six mouths belongs either to Karttikeya, the god of battle, or to his brother, Ganesha, the patron of scholars and merchants. The seven-rilled bead is identified with the seven rishis or the seven mothers of the gods (Saptamatrika) and provides its wearer with name and fame, honor and health. The eight-mouthed "Ashta Vasus" pearl promotes long life and prevents the owner from foolishly uttering untruths. A bead with nine mouths makes the wearer totally fearless, for it is a manifestation of Durga, the goddess on the lion. Not even death will frighten someone who carries it as an amulet. It is the gentle Krishna, god of herdsmen and lover of the souls, who appears in the ten-faced bead, protecting against negative planetary influences and assuring a long life and success in even the most difficult undertakings. A bead with eleven rills, worn in a woman's hair, will assure a long life for her husband; worn by a man in the topknot, it will turn him into a victorious conqueror, much like Indra, whose manifestation it is. The bead with twelve facets is identified with Vishnu, or with Surya, the sun god, whose chariot passes the twelve regions of the zodiac. Worn in the hair, it protects against illness and unemployment (legislators and government agencies take note!). All the powers of the Vishwadevas, the lesser gods, manifest in the thirteen-mouthed nut, providing good luck and fulfilling the wish for children. The extremely rare fourteen-faceted bead heals all ills with the power of Hanuman, the monkey god, or it provides the magic power (siddhi) of Rudra.*

At this point the reader may sense what a complicated "science" revolves around these shriveled brown nutlets. The whole of Hindu mythology is contained therein. We can but scratch the surface. Since all the gods and goddesses and their divine powers are present in the rudrakshas, it should not surprise us that they play a significant role in traditional Indian ayurvedic medicine. The doctor might prescribe, for instance, the wearing of a rudraksha-mala (rosary) to lower the blood pressure. (Anyone who knows the power of psychosomatic medicine will appreciate the effect.) A ten-faceted bead might be pulverized and taken in milk in case of influenza. For women's complaints, hysteria, or epilepsy, six-mouthed beads are ground up and taken in milk. For those suffering from cerebral problems, a four-mouthed bead is prepared in milk and taken once a day for twenty days.

It should not surprise us that the beads should be handled with utmost circumspection. They must be strung on an auspicious red, silver, or even golden thread, not any ordinary string. They must be dedicated by touching them to a Shiva lingam, by chanting mantras over them, bathing them in milk or Ganges water, and, finally, rubbing them with costly, scented oils so that the gods may take residence in them and unfold their demon-banning powers. Whoever deigns to wear such a mala (bead necklace)

---

*Hanuman, the monkey chief, became a god of healing during the battle of Sri Lanka, after he had been sent off to find a handful of healing herbs and came back with a whole mountain of medical plants. He is said to be the son of the wind and of a monkey woman. Shaivites, however, have turned him into a son of Shiva: Once, when Shiva caught a glimpse of the enchanting nymph Mohini, he shed his sperm. The seven rishis gathered the precious seed and put it into the ear of a monkey woman, who conceived and gave birth to Hanuman.

Nepalese saint with rudraksha malas

must abstain from eating meat, fish, eggs, onions, and garlic, all of which fire up the passions. If one does not obey these injunctions, not only will the beads lose their potency, they might actually turn into a negative harmful force for the wearer. Each day hymns should be sung to them and, occasionally, they should be bathed and oiled anew, for they are alive with a life of their own. There are even strict rules as to where and how one must wear them. The *Shiva Purana* decrees that three are to be worn in the topknot, six on each arm, and one hundred and one around the neck, eleven on each wrist, three on the holy thread, and five around the waist. Of course, there are a number of such systems but it would take us far beyond the scope of this book to list more. Commonly, one sees the rudraksha beads worn as a garland of one hundred and eight pearls (or much more seldom even one thousand and eight), which the meditant can use to count off holy syllables or the number of breaths. A rosary should be worn at all times, but if not, at least at the changes of the moon.

Rudraksha means, literally translated, "the tears of Rudra." How Rudra came into the world is told in the *Vishnu Purana*:

In the beginning of this age *(kalpa)* Brahma bore a son from his brow. The mind-born child was a three-eyed boy, red and blue of color, who immediately started crying in angry fits.

"Why are you howling like this?" his creator asked him.

"Because I don't know my name!" he screamed.

"Well, then," said Brahma, who could not think of anything better, "you shall be known as Rudra (Sanskrit *rud* = to cry or howl)." Having found out his name, the howler split into eleven persons, some dark and threatening, others light and friendly.

Rudra surrounded himself with wild wind spirits whose howling annoyed Indra, the king of heaven, so much that he yelled in exasperation, "*Ma rodih!* Don't howl!" And ever since, these furies have been known as the *maruts*. With his host of maruts, Rudra demolishes fields, forests, and mountains with storms of wind and fire and brings fever and the hacking cough to man and beast. However, if one succeeds in gaining his favor, the lord of these terrors can just as easily keep them at bay. The best way to do this is to put oneself into the yoke of conscious breath control *(pranayama)*; then, the uncontrollably raging Rudra will turn into the peaceful Shankar. The rudraksha beads will help in this effort. As the master of the air and wind, Rudra is, of course, also the master of life's breath, the lord of the eleven *pranas* (breaths). He can give and take away the breath of life; thus he is called the lord of those who breathe (the living) and those who do not breathe (the dead).

Whenever the demons start terrorizing creation, the pleas and prayers of the suffering gods, human beings, and animals rouse Shankar out of his deep meditation. Angry at being disturbed, he changes his breathing and turns himself into one of the wild Rudras in order to end the abuse. It is told that the rudraksha beads are but the tears of joy Shiva shed when, after having demolished such demons, the gods and all creatures celebrated him full of loving thankfulness.

❧ THE GOD CLOTHED IN AIR ❧

The silent god in the snow is a *digambara*, that is, he is stark naked, except when he wears, like Burroughs's Tarzan, the skin of a wild animal slung loosely around his loins.[2]

> Miserable fools alone laugh at the conduct of Lord Shiva who tasteth the bliss of his own self; they by whom this carcass of a body, food for the dog and the wolf, is mistaken for the soul and pampered by adorning it with clothes, ornaments, garlands and pastes; they do not understand, but scoff at the strange ways and behavior of Lord Shiva, who knoweth and tasteth the bliss of his own self. (*Bhagavantam*, 4,5,13)

Why should such an ascetic, who finds all he needs in his Self, need to bother wearing clothes or cutting and combing his hair? On India's streets and in holy places, one still encounters Shankar's friends, who dress themselves "in the winds," or "in the four directions," and whose hair is a wild mass of matted, bleached tangles. These are not

Tiger skin and elephant hide, symbols of Shiva

crazies, bums, or antisocials, as one might suspect. Quite a few of these naked babas had been, in their younger years, pillars of society, successful businessmen, lawyers, doctors. It is taboo to ask them about their lives, and if one asks anyway, they will refuse to talk about it, for they are dead to their past.

When he does not appear stark naked, Shankar might wear a tiger skin or an elephant hide. The latter belonged to Gajasura, a nasty demon who spent millions of years mortifying his flesh and torturing himself in order to gain spiritual power. At last Brahma deigned to listen to him and grant him his wish. What else would a demon wish for, but absolute power over the entire universe? As soon as his boon was granted, he humbled the king of the gods and drove the deities from their heavenly thrones. Then he went to Benares. There, in the form of a raging elephant demon, he delighted in molesting and ridiculing the rishis and silent munis, distracting them from their religious observances. Greatly disturbed, the saints hid behind the walls of the Golden Vishwanath Temple, which houses a self-manifested Shiva lingam. Just as the elephant was about to crash into this sacred ground, an angry Rudra jumped out of the lingam. He hoisted the elephant demon into the air with his trident and made him dance on the three prongs until he dropped dead of exhaustion. Rudra tore its skin off and wrapped it around his naked body. Garbed in the bloody hide as a sign of his victory over the demon of false pride, Shiva danced. Even now he dances this dance; swinging an elephant prod *(ankusha)* like a mahout, he shows his mastery over the overpowering elephant nature in man's soul.

Shiva sitting on a tiger skin

Many icons show Shankar meditating, sitting on a tiger skin. The head of the predatory feline is still attached and by no means dead. It fixes the devotee with a wide-awake, penetrating stare. The tiger, a man-killer, cruel and never satiated, kills just for the fun of it—at least, so it seems to the Indian peasant whose milk cow or even child has been mauled and killed by the jungle beast. As such, the tiger becomes a symbol of irrational hatred, insatiable hunger, and greed, which only Shiva can master. But it can also be taken as a picture of alert instincts that range the depths of the jungle of the soul, ready to pounce upon and devour the hapless ego that happens to venture into these realms. Shiva, our deeper Self, is not to be approached with the ego.

The Puranas tell that Shiva got ahold of the tiger's skin when he appeared as the ithyphallic youth to the rishis' wives in the pine forest. Using spells and the powers of concentration, the husbands vented their hatred in the form of a tiger, directing it to kill the stranger. Shiva skinned it effortlessly with the nail of his little finger and used it as his sitting blanket.

ॐ THE THIRD EYE ॐ

Tryambaka, "the three-eyed one," is another one of Shiva's many names, for he sports a third eye in the middle of his brow. Fortunately for the world, this organ remains closed, for it is an eye of cosmic fire. Were it to open, its fiery beam would annihilate everything in its way. Once, during love-play, Parvati teasingly held Shiva's eyes shut. The whole universe plunged into darkness, but at the same time, a third eye started to grow in the middle of his forehead. When he opened it, the world turned into a sea of fire. Parvati was stunned. After overcoming her shock, she started to sing and dance for her Lord. She did this in order that he might accompany her on his drum (damaru), knowing that its sound would create the world anew. Indeed, as the OM sounded from the damaru, everything was restored.

*The third eye—
a symbol of Shiva*

There had been another time also when Shiva, whose hair is the starry sky and whose two eyes are the sun and the moon, opened his eye of doom. Here is how that came about:

Lord Brahma, brooding over the depth of his abysmal being at the beginning of time, beheld a most handsome youth and brought him into existence. "You are Kama, the god of love," the Creator told him. "Your arrows shall excite passion in their victim's hearts and shall plunge all beings, from the tiniest bug to the mightiest god, into lust and heated desire!"

Kama (the Indian version of the Greek god Eros) immediately tested his power on his creator and, indeed, Brahma became obsessed with carnal desire for his creation, who stood there in front of him as his virginal daughter. Shiva, beholding Brahma who was shaking like an aspen and sweating from

*Insane Shiva with
Uma's corpse*

all pores, started laughing heartily, ridiculing the grandfather for his incestuous longings. Brahma remedied his daunted dignity by cursing the god of desire, "Though you have power over all, even over Shiva, one day the lord of fire will reduce you to cinders with his third eye!"

As foretold, Kama's arrow struck the heart of Shiva, the lone meditant. As a result, the Great God's contemplation took the form of a woman, and Shiva, who is the Self of the universe, forgot his Self. He became obsessed by a longing for the great Maya, the Mother of the Universe. Her beauty entangled him completely. When the Great Goddess was born as the youngest daughter of Daksha, the chief of the Prajapatis (the mind-born sons of Brahma and cocreators), Shiva took her as his lover and wife. Daksha, however, was not happy with his wild, unkempt son-in-law. Uma, as the goddess was called, could not bear the insults her father, Daksha, constantly leveled at her husband. It grieved her so that in an act of final desperation, she threw herself into her father's sacrificial fire and burned herself alive. When Shiva heard of Uma's suicide, he was shattered. Pain and anger drove him out of his mind. He made shambles of his father-in-law's sacrificial grounds, burning everything with his third eye. Then, clutching the charred remains of Uma to his chest, he danced a macabre dance with her, driven by mad rage. Again and again he kissed her lifeless body and washed it with his tears. The scene was so heart-rending that Vishnu, his friend, could stand it no longer. Out of compassion, he threw his discus, striking the corpse and dismembering it so that pieces of it fell here and there to the ground. At each place where a part of the goddess fell, a temple arose.*

In the meantime, Shiva, totally enmeshed in illusion, sank exhausted into the ashes that covered the barren ground. Then he wandered off as a madman with a crazed look in the eye and filthy, disheveled hair, driven by hunger and plagued by the elements. He finally came to rest in the rare air of the northern mountains and, sitting forsaken, sank ever deeper into stupor. His legs folded under him, his hands resting on his knees, and his eyes closed, he sat motion-

---

*Even now millions of pilgrims travel to these temples.

less like a rock. He did not notice the snakes and
scorpions that crawled over him, nor the vines
that grew up his limbs, for he was completely
self-absorbed, coming closer and closer to the
realization of his Self.

During all this time, a terrible titan named
Taraka was about to cash in on the fruits of his
formidable austerities. Nobody had ever tor-
tured himself like he had. How could Brahma
refuse him the boon of absolute mastery over
the three worlds? Nobody would be able to
topple him, for it was predicted that only a son
of Shiva would have this power. But how could
Shiva ever have a son? Shiva's wife was dead
and Shiva himself had become a fool, last seen
erring about in the wilderness. Untroubled by
any qualms, the new master of the universe took
pleasure in sadistically maltreating all creatures,

*Compassionate Vishnu
dismembering Uma's
corpse with his discus*

humans and gods included. It looked bad for the celestials; like deer, they
were hunted in the forest or living in mud huts like wretched beggars.

But as the wheel of time turned, Uma, Shiva's beloved, was reborn as
Parvati, daughter of the king of the Himalayas and his wife Mena, the finest
of heavenly nymphs. Little Parvati grew like the waxing springtime moon,
unexcelled in beauty and virtue. Absolutely no one would be able to resist her
loveliness! Surely, if Shiva would but get a glimpse of her, he would not be
able to resist her charms and soon the savior, the destroyer of the titan Taraka,
would be engendered and born. That was the prophecy and the sole hope
of the despairing gods. But Shiva was cold ashes; not even a spark was left
that could ignite the necessary fire of passion. What could be done?

The anxious gods assembled secretly. Grandfather Brahma, as always,
knew what could be done. He called upon the god of love. "Kama, your
hour has come! Awaken the entranced meditant. Shoot your arrow of fragrant springtime blossoms straight into his cold heart! Arouse his yearning for
the joys of lovemaking!"

Surrounded by colorful parrots, cuckoos, and humming birds, Kama
flew with the mild spring breeze up into the mountains to find Shiva.
Wherever he passed, the flowers burst into fragrant bloom and the air
sounded with glad music and bird's song. When he saw Shiva, he stealthily
approached the meditant. Carefully placing one of his flower arrows in his

*Kama, the Indian Cupid,
on his cuckoo*

sugar cane bow, he drew the string made of honeybees and took aim.

It so happened that, at that very moment, the lovely daughter of the mountain, Parvati, was about to lay some freshly picked flowers at the feet of her self-absorbed Lord. A flower that touched his foot brought him out of his trance and he beheld the maiden in front of him. As holy men are wont to do, he blessed her and foretold her the future: "God bless you, sweet maiden! May you find the husband you desire!"

Just as he was about to sink once again into deep meditation, Kama's arrow whizzed toward his heart. In a flash of anger at having been thus disturbed, the ashen meditant opened his third eye and turned the rash love god, who had dared interrupt his meditation, into a pile of ashes. Thus, Shiva became known as Smarahara, "the killer of Smara" (Kama).

The goddesses, and especially Rati, Kama's lovely female companion, cried in desperation: "What have you done! Without desire, the bull will forsake the cow, the horse the mare and the bees the flowers. There will be no homes, no families, for men and women will not love each other. Society will collapse and life will be devoid of its very essence. Desire may be the cause of suffering, but it is also the reason behind joy. What is life without it?"

Rati's lamentations moved Shiva; he saw the wisdom in her words. "I destroyed Kama's body, but not his spirit. Even so he will be able to shoot love's darts into everyone's heart."[3]

Shiva tried to sink again into the contemplation of the Self, but the image of that lovely damsel would not leave his mind. Some storytellers believe that it was at this point that Shiva, with the poison of erotic passion cruising in his veins, ran off into the pine forest where he became a satyr. Be that as it may, young Parvati still had a long time ahead of her until she could swoon in his arms. Shiva calmed down and continued his meditations. Her beauty could not budge him. Nothing she tried, no song, no dance nor tender look, could arouse his interest. Finally, she decided that, despite her tender youth and beauty, she too would become a meditant, covering her limbs with rough bark cloth and ashes and performing the hardest austerities.

Later on, we will get to that part of the story.
For now, let us try to understand this mysterious "third eye" a little better.

The "magic eye," either as a third eye on
the forehead or a single eye like that of Odin,
is a common theme in mythology. The old
Irish Celts tell of the primitive giant Balor,
whose evil eye wreaked havoc, fire, and death
wherever its glance might fall. During battle,
it was a formidable weapon, but its lid was so
heavy that it took four warriors to lift it.
Balor's cunning grandson, Lugh, a shamanistic god who himself has a magic eye, shot the

*Tibetan demon with
open third eye*

monster's eye out with his slingshot. The impact of Lugh's missile
was so powerful that it drove Balor's fiery eye through the back of his
skull, destroying all the giants behind him with its baneful glance. The
restlessly roving eye of Polyphemus, the Cyclops, which Odysseus
pokes out, is another such magic eye. This one-eyed Cyclops is, interestingly enough, a son of the trident-carrying god of the sea, Poseidon
(Latin Neptunus).

Rudolf Steiner, the Austrian philosopher of the occult, believes that
whenever one- or three-eyed characters appear in myth or fairy tale, reference is made to an ancient, atavistic mode of clairvoyant consciousness
that dominated the human soul before a strong, rational ego had developed. "It sent out ethereal sensors and perceived the environment in a
dreamlike manner. It was the 'eye' of Atlantian humanity of old."[4] In
mythical symbols, the blinding of the Cyclops by Odysseus tells of the
transition from a primitive, clairvoyant stage of human cognition to the
more rational mind of modern humanity. Odysseus, as the representative
of the modern Homo sapiens, no longer relies on dreamy, instinct-
bound, magical awareness, but on a down-to-earth consciousness, based
on clear external senses and logical reasoning. For human individuation
to occur, it was necessary to destroy this atavistic faculty.

Other occultists do not agree. On the contrary, they work hard,
using various techniques, to regain this old magic faculty. For them,
the third eye is symbolized by the horn of the unicorn, with which one
can bore into the secrets of the universe. It is the carbuncle, that dark
red precious stone that shines in the dark, lighting the way back to the
hidden, lofty citadel for the knights of the Holy Grail. It is deemed the

organ of spiritual generation, penetrating and impregnating receptive minds. Medieval alchemists assigned this (to external eyes) invisible organ to Jupiter, king of the gods. Located in the middle of the forehead, this Jupiter organ is the occult focal point of sovereignty and concentration of will. It is no coincidence that magicians and shamans often place the sun, moon, or an eye at this spot on their hats, or even that officers' caps sport shiny stars or "bull's eyes" at this place.

Yogis like to focus their concentration upon this center of ethereal energy in the middle of the forehead. It is thought of as a fiery whirl (chakra), so hot that it is often smeared with "cooling" sandalwood paste. After worship *(puja)*, the priest is likely to place a dab *(tilak)* of red powder on this point. Since the Hindus do not like to leave anything to chance, they do not put the tilak just anywhere on the forehead, but exactly there, where this third eye, this center of intellectual discrimination, is sensed to be. The more thoroughly one has cleaned up old karmic entanglements and the closer one has moved to God, the lower this point will be on the forehead. For someone who is already holy, that is, who has already achieved *samadhi* (union with the ultimate reality) in this life, this point will have sunk to between the eyebrows.

The myths of one-eyed Cyclops and brutish giants like Balor contain racial memories of archaic, chthonic states of being before Promethian self-consciousness made us truly human. Polyphemus, the cannibalistic cave dweller, is the son of the earth-shaking ocean god and, as such, bound up with dark, chaotic elements. He is crude and ruled by blind, unreflecting instinct, like a cold-blooded reptile.

Such myths reflect episodes of our immense journey through biological evolution. It is indeed true that ancestral fish and amphibians, which populated the seas and littoral swamps of the Mesozoic, were endowed with a light-sensitive organ (the pineal body), protruding from the forehead and connected with the midbrain. This extra eye responded to changing external light conditions, causing a camouflaging skin effect, as in chameleons. It also served to register increasing light intensities of waxing moons and of the springtime sun, inducing increased egg and sperm production at these times.[5] In the course of further evolution, this protrusion of the old reptile brain retreated deeper into the skull. Even so, it still reacts (registering the input from the eyes) to the changing rhythms of light and dark and helps maintain our "biological clock" and our sexual biorhythms. Some scientists suspect that the increasingly earlier sexual maturity of youngsters began with the development of artificial illumination, which, for the old reptile brain, amounts to a continual full moon. The covert link of sexuality to this third eye is mirrored in the myth of Shiva's third eye, which destroys the god of erotic love.

Shiva, as the god of the whole, has not destroyed his third, magic eye. Like other shamanistic deities, he has kept its awesome potential at his disposal. But, for the sake of his creatures, he mercifully keeps it shut. Only on that day when he desires to destroy the illusions that are the underpinnings of this world, will he open it and unleash an orgy of fiery destruction.

❧ THREE LINES OF ASH ☙

The number three, as we have noted, is the sign of wholeness and is associated with the highest divinity in all Indo-European cultures. Every curse or every spell must be repeated three times to work; every holy site, medical herb, or sacred stone must be circumambulated thrice to be beneficial. Even Christianity kept the symbolism in the Trinity of the Father, the Son, and the Holy Spirit, symbolized by an upward-pointing triangle with an all-seeing eye in the middle. The pyramid with an eye was adopted by the Freemasons as a sign of the new secular era, and it still graces the almighty dollar.

Saint Patrick reputedly explained the mystery of the Trinity to the old Irish heathens by use of a cloverleaf. It is doubtful that they were in need of such an explanation, for Celtic culture was replete with three-fold symbolism, from gods appearing in three aspects to a social order with a three-fold caste system of priests (druids), nobles, and commoners. The cloverleaf has its Indian counterpart in the trifoliate wood apple leaf (L *Aegle marmelos*, Sanskrit *shriphala*, Hindi *bilva* or *bel*), which is frequently placed on top of the Shiva lingam as an act of devotion.

Lord Shiva's three eyes are representative of all trinities, as are the eyes of the three peacock feathers that are stuck loosely into the dark hair of the flute-playing Krishna. They indicate:

Creation, preservation, destruction
Brahma, Vishnu, Shiva
Past, present, future
Father, mother, child
Heaven, earth, underworld

Time, space, consciousness
Sat, chit, ananda (being, consciousness, bliss)
A U M, the three sounds of the primordial syllable
Sattva, rajas, tamas (the light, the active, the dark), the gunas,
   or basic principles that permeate all

When one looks carefully at the icon of Shankar, one sees the Three emphasized by three horizontally drawn white stripes smeared across his forehead. Using the ashes left from the three supposedly invincible demon fortresses *(tripura)*, Shiva painted his brow like a victorious warrior. The demon who had built them had been granted the boon from Brahma that his castles could not be taken unless a single shot would penetrate all three at once. The monster felt safe and sound, for such an act seemed to be impossible. However, as the fruits of his austerities were used up, the fortresses (which represent simply the three impurities of soul: egoism, or *anava;* calculating, nonspontaneous action, or *karma;* and illusion, or *maya*) lined up like an astrological constellation and were zapped by the laser beam of Shiva's eye of fire. Since that time, it is said that Shiva's followers mark their foreheads with three horizontal stripes of holy ash *(vibhuti, bhasma)*. The upper arms, lower arms, and throat are decorated with ashen stripes to remind the believers to develop the power of the third eye or *ajna chakra,* to burn up the illusion that the Self and the absolute Brahman are something separate. When the three demonic strongholds in the soul have been turned to dust, then one will realize that one is identical with Shiva.

The *tripundra,* as the three white lines are called, are the mark of Shiva's disciples. The Vaishnavas, the devotees of Lord Vishnu, on the other hand, are recognized by a vertical V- or U-shaped mark *(urdhavapundra)* on the forehead with a red dot in the middle. It represents the footprint of Vishnu.

The ashes used are obtained from a consecrated fire or from a funeral pyre. The ash from Manikarnika, the main burning-ghat of Benares and Shiva's favorite dancing ground, is especially auspicious. The ashes left in a sanctified ganja pipe *(chilam),* this mini-Manikarnika that immolates the spirits of madness and illusion, can also be used. The sacred white powder can be made from cow dung as well, using a complicated alchemical ritual. As we know, in all Indo-European cultures, the cow is the epitome of what is sacred. For the Hindu, the cow embodies all the gods of the universe. Its five gifts—milk, butter, curd, urine, and dung—are food, medicine (including urine and dung), fuel (dried cow pies), and building material (dung mixed with daub is used to plaster the wattle), and ritual (butter is used to annoint the corpse in the cremation rites).

Three lines of holy ash— symbol of Shiva

A story from the *Bhasma Jabala Upanishad* tells of a holy man who took a pilgrimage to the mountain of salvation, Mount Kailash, where God appeared to him in the form of the *omkara* (the lingam as OM) and initiated him into the mystery of the sacred ash. With trembling knees, the yogi received this recipe: To make the holy ash out of dung, one must, first of all, pick an auspicious astrological time, making sure the planets, especially evil-eyed Saturn (Sani), are aspected favorably. The cow pie has to be scooped onto a plate made from the leaves of the palasa tree (*Butea monosperma*, "flame of the forest") exactly at sunrise and then dried in the sun. All the while, the venerable "Tryambakam Manra," the hymn to the three-eyed god, must be intoned. When it is dry, it is given into the fiery mouth of the god Agni. As it burns, an offering of one thousand and eight morsels of sesame seed, rice meal, and clarified butter is made into the fire. The butter *(ghee)* must be dripped slowly from a leaf, not poured, for that would constitute a sin. When the calcification is completed, the ash is sprinkled with Ganges water and kept in a jar of silver, gold, copper, or pottery. Finally, the alchemist is obligated to give a great feast to all the Brahmins of the area.

The right use of the thus obtained ashes demands of the devotee that he rise daily before sunrise, take his bath, and recite the Vedic Gayatri Mantra ("We meditate on that excellent light of the divine sun; may it illuminate our minds!"). Then he may, in the morning, at noon, and in the evening, using three fingers of his right hand, apply the ash to his body and drink a little ash dissolved in Ganges water. If whoever has vowed to do this fails to remember any aspect of the ritual even once, he is considered unclean and may neither recite the Gayatri as usual nor perform a sacrifice *(yajna)*. To purify himself again, he must fast the whole day and stand in water up to his neck, reciting the Gayatri Mantra one hundred and eight times in a row. If he fails to do so, Rudra's jackals and wolves will hunt him down and tear him to pieces.

Again, the ceremonial use of ashes is common in nearly all cultures. In the West, a festival of ashes is celebrated in Catholic communities on Ash Wednesday. In many areas Lenten fires are lit to conclude the time of feasting and merrymaking. On Ash Wednesday, the priest dubs ashes on the heads of the parishioners, uttering the mantralike biblical quote: "Dust thou art, and unto dust thou shalt return." This signals the beginning of the time of penance and fasting, reminding them of the brevity and illusionary nature of our existence. Since heathen times, ashes from the yule log and the Easter or midsummer fire have been valued as medicine for house and barn and as an antidote for witchcraft.

⊰ THE BLUE NECK ⊱

Covered as it is by stripes of ash, a winding cobra, and several rudraksha garlands, one might not notice at first glance that Shankar's neck is of bright blue color. How he came to be called Nilakanta, "the blue-necked one," is recounted in the frequently told story of the churning of the Ocean of Milk:

One day, an ill-clothed sage named Durvasas, who was an emanation of Shiva, was walking down a forest path when a heavenly nymph gave him a sweet-scented garland. Its fragrance was so intoxicating that he danced with delight. Just then, Indra, the king of the gods, rode by on his elephant. To please the mighty thunderer, the sage gave him the precious garland, which Indra put on his elephant's neck. The rude pachyderm became drunk from the sweet smell, seized the wreath with his trunk, threw it to the ground, and trampled it. The sage, thinking that his gift had been slighted, became very angry and cursed the god, telling him that his might would wane and that he would be defeated by the demons.

Not long after, the age-old battle flared up anew between the eternal antagonists, the gods and the demons. Things went from bad to worse for the hosts under the command of Indra. At the same time, Sukra (Venus), the guru of the demons, had found a powerful mantra, which, when chanted, raised the fallen asuras and daityas, demons and titans, back to life. As their ranks lightened, the gods soon found themselves hopelessly outnumbered. To stave off total disaster, old Brahma let the conches be sounded for an emergency council.

"Only the Water of Life, the nectar of immortality (amrita) hidden deep in the Ocean of Milk, can save us from total dis-

Vishnu as a turtle (kuma)

aster," he advised them, "but our strength does not suffice to churn it out. It would take the combined efforts of ours and those of the demonic hordes. Let us make a truce with our enemies and have them help us."

The truce was made. After some negotiating, the demon kings agreed to help, but only under the condition that they would receive half of the ambrosia, which gives eternal life. They then went to work churning the primordial waters, much as herdsmen churn milk to butter. They used Meru, the world-mountain, as the churning stick. Vishnu changed himself into a turtle and dove down to the bottom of the bottomless sea in order to serve as a pivot for the stick. Vasuki, the world serpent, also called Shesha or Ananta, lord of the underworlds, agreed to let himself be used as the rope that turns the buttering stick. Taking Vishnu's advice, Brahmins cast sacred herbs into the milk and chanted. Then, with the demons holding the tail end and the gods the head end of the endless serpent, they pulled to and fro, as in a tug-of-war, churning the liquid.

The first thing that appeared on the surface of the boiling, bubbling broth, was the mother of cows, Surabhi, who fulfils all wishes and blesses the world with milk, butter, curd, urine, and dung. Or, was it the poison of the world, the raunchy, acrid *halahala*, that first floated to the top? It is not clear which came first. In any case, the rank bane crept out of the vessel, threatening all of creation. Horrified, both gods and demons fled. Vishnu tried to stop the venom but could not. Its vapors turned his skin blacker than the night. Daunted, Brahma and Vishnu hastened to Mount Kailash to wake Shiva out of his meditation.

Calmly the great yogi cupped his hand and drank the halahala with one draught. No doubt, the poison—leftovers of which are found in poisonous spiders and snakes, and in the hearts of wicked men and women—would have

Churning the Ocean of Milk

Shiva drinks the poison of the world

done in the creation had not Shiva taken it upon himself. No one else could have done so! Parvati, worried about her lord, clasped her hands around his throat and pressed it shut. Thus, the poison got stuck in his neck, coloring it aquamarine blue.

The venom having been dealt with, the gods and demons went on churning. Wonderful things now appeared: the white horse, which both Indra and the demon king, Bali, coveted; and the elephant, Airavata, which Indra now rides. Up came Kaustubha, the precious gem now embellishing Vishnu's chest. Next appeared the tree of paradise, whose fragrant blossoms perfume the entire world and under whose flowering branches the heavenly nymphs dance their rounds. Then came the moon, which Shiva fastened to his hair as a shining diadem. Then, to everyone's wonder and awe, there was born from the ocean's froth, floating on a lotus bed

Indra on the elephant that arose out of the Ocean of Milk

> A maiden fair and tender-eyed,
> In the young flush of beauty's pride.
> She shone with pearl and golden sheen,
> And seals of glory stamped her queen.[6]

This foam-born goddess of love, beauty, and wealth was none other than Lakshmi, who became the beloved of Vishnu. Finally, there appeared the physician of the gods, Dhanvantari, who revealed ayurvedic medicine to the human race. In his hands he bore the cup of nectar that the gods and demons had worked so hard to obtain.

The gods, their attention being distracted by Lakshmi's radiant beauty, did not notice that the demons were about to grasp the cup and make off with it. Were it not for Vishnu's vigilance, they might have succeeded. Instantly, the great god turned himself into the loveliest of all heavenly nymphs, appearing as Mohini, the greatest seductress of all. It is said that Brahma was so struck by her dazzling beauty that he gave himself four heads in order to be able to watch her from every direction. The vile demons too, of course, became victims of Vishnu's power of illusion and chased after her, driven by desire, thus losing their rightful portion of the drink of immortality. (The theft of the heavenly nectar by the gods is a common motive recurring in all Indo-European mythologies.)

Even Shiva lost his senses at the sight of seductive Mohini. Even though an ash-covered ascetic, he became so excited that his seed spurted, raining silver and golden lingams all over the earth.

Lakshmi, the goddess of good luck

In a south Indian version of the story, Shiva chases the nymph, overpowers her, and begets a son with her, who is known as Hariharaputra (son of Hari = Vishnu and Hara = Shiva), or as Ayyappan. The extensive cult and large following of Ayyappan in Dravidian southern India can be seen as an attempt to overcome the continual rivalry of the two great gods, Vishnu and Shiva. It is a syncretism of Shaivism and Vaishnavism, each of which like to proclaim the supremacy of their particular god-vision. For example, the Hare Krishna sect, whose shaven-headed, saffron clothed members sang, danced, and begged in the metropolises of the West during the 1960s and '70s, see in Shiva but a minor, somewhat ill-mannered sidekick of Vishnu. In Ayyappan, this opposition is overcome.

The imagery of the churning of the primordial sea can be interpreted as a symbol for the process of meditation. Centered in the world-mountain (the backbone), which pivots on the back of the turtle (representing the oldest, reptilian level of consciousness in us), the meditant fathoms the oceanic depths of the unconscious mind. The gods and demons (the sympathies and antipathies) work together harmoniously to bring the wonderful spiritual gifts (siddhi) to the surface, that is, into the light of consciousness. These gifts are represented by such archetypal images as the wish-fulfilling cow, the tree of life, the dancing heavenly maidens (apsarasas), the magic white horse and elephant (vehicles of divine powers within the soul), the goddess of good fortune and beauty and, finally, the divine physician with his cup filled with the nectar of immortality. However, note that only when we accept Shiva—that unsavory outsider, living on the outer edge in the permanent ice of the north or in the hell fires of the south—can we enjoy these gifts. For he must be there to drink up the vile poisons of old karma that have settled on the bottom of our souls. Like Jesus in the Christian myth, so Shiva drinks the bitterness of the world (the cup of perdition) to the very last drop.

For educated Westerners, these stories are parables and images in depth psychology on the complexes and forces of the psyche. For the Hindu peasants, however, the stories are absolute reality. They do not separate the world into a subjective inner world and a real, objective external world (as defined by science). For them, all experiences are real and natural, and at the same time, illusory and supernatural. What our scholars, somewhat condescendingly, label myth, beliefs, and fairy tales, are for the ordinary Indians, "facts" that are seen and experienced. For them, the external reality is transparent. Every mountain, river, and city is evidence of some divine happening: "Shiva sat on these rocks." "This lake is one of Vishnu's footprints." "On this hill, the goddess killed a demon." Or, "In this city a great hero was born!"

Myth is timeless; it transcends time and space. Therefore, it is eternally present and can be experienced in a state of grace, when one has a darshana, an experience of the divine. The "once upon a time" is in the here and now and can be witnessed ever anew: the demons and gods are still churning the ocean of milk; Shankar, the peaceful ascetic, is even now meditating on Mount Kailash; Shiva-Nataraja is even now dancing in a ring of fire; right now, the world is being destroyed at the end of the dark age and reborn simultaneously from the navel of Vishnu into a new golden age. The battle of the gods and demons is raging and, after the gods have quaffed the nectar of eternal life, it turns in their favor. But then the penance and iron self-discipline of the demon king, Taraka, become so powerful that the dark forces triumph again and only a son of Shiva can restore the balance. Even now, the gods hold council as to how to mate the virginal daughter of the mountains to the ascetic on Mount Kailash and, thus, our story begins again where it has ended—and we, if we open our third eye, are the living witnesses of the cosmic drama, which is also our own story.

❦ SHIVA AND BUDDHA ❧

His legs folded under him, like a lotus, and steady of breath, Siddhartha Gotama, a Shaivite ascetic, sat under a mighty pipal tree (*Ficus religiosa*, the *bodhi* tree). Like Shankar, silent and unmoved he sat, absorbed in his own being, at the base of the cosmic tree, the *axis mundi*, which bridges the heavens, the earth, and the underworlds. He watched the fire of karma, the fateful chain of cause and effect, flicker and finally die out. Thus he reached *nirvana* (Sanskrit "to blow out") and became the Buddha, "the Enlightened One."

The cosmic tree, its three mighty roots piercing the netherworld and its crown touching the highest heaven, plays a central role in the mythology of nearly all people.[7] It is the navel and center of the world, the pillar that supports the heavens, the ladder upon which seers climb into other dimensions. To emphasize its supernatural nature, it is sometimes imagined as growing upside down from heaven,[8] as in the *Bhagavad Gita* (Song XV, verse 1) where it is stated:

> *The rishis know of the tree Asvattha,*
> *Rooted in heaven, its trunk growing earthwards,*
> *Its leaves, each one, bringing forth the Vedas.*
> *He who knows this, knows all.*

The icon of the meditating Shankar shows this world tree in its most archaic, runic form—as a trident. Its three roots are turned upward. Like Buddha, Shiva sits in deep samadhi, absorbed into himself. He, too, is "blown out" (nirvana). The ice and snow of the eternal Himalayan winter symbolize the ashes that are left after the flickering flame of illusions has been extinguished. Shankar is a picture of nirvana, or as the Hindus prefer to see it, of *satchidananda* (pure being, consciousness, bliss).

Between the cycles of active creation, Vishnu rests, self-absorbed in the pregnant world of his own being, sleeping on the back of the world serpent, sheltered by its thousand flared hoods. In much the same manner, the Buddha, sunk into samadhi, is sheltered from the cosmic storm by the thousand-headed king of serpents, Mucalinda. Like the Midgard serpent of the old Nordics, this wise, jewel-crowned ruler of the underworld has his realm underneath the three roots of the world tree. It is the same serpent that enthrones in Shankar's piled-up hair. Over it, the

Buddha under the bodhi tree

jet of Ganga's torrents shoot out like a fountain, reminding one of the torrential rains that would have inundated Buddha, had not Mucalinda sheltered him.

As the ascetic Gotama sat in meditation, just before he became the Enlightened One, Mara-Kama (death lust), the master of delusion, appeared in his inner vision and tempted him with all the riches and power of the world and all the joys provided by fair dancing maidens, in order to distract him. Like Shankar, who reduced Kama to a pile of cinders, Buddha pierced the tempter's illusion with the eye of spiritual insight. Not much different is the iconography of the Jains. The Tirthankara (maker of the ford across life's treacherous stream), having pierced the veil of illusion, is shown sitting in lotus posture underneath the cosmic tree, passionless, silent as a plant, his head protected by the wide-open hoods of a giant multiheaded snake.[9]

According to the tantric and yogic schools of philosophy, the cobra symbolizes the "serpent power" (kundalini), the energy potential centered in the lower regions of the body. When awakened by meditation and yoga, the energy starts winding its way up the backbone until it reaches the highest consciousness center, at the top of the cranium. When this happens, the energy becomes conscious; in other words, "enlightenment" occurs. The serpent's head flaring out above the meditant's crown is thus the iconographical rendering of spiritual illumination. This is what is symbolized by the shiny golden crowns of royalty—the right to rule. The god-kings of ancient Egypt wore a cobra with extended hood on the front of their crowns, evidencing their cosmic wisdom and divine power.[10] In myths throughout the world, serpents appear as guardians of the tree of life, the fountains of wisdom or youth, or of golden apples. The divine, impeccable human being who has dealt successfully with the serpent nature will come into possession of these treasures.

Like Shiva, Buddha, who walked India's dusty roads, is a homeless wanderer. Even though dressed in the saffron orange of a begging monk, his elongated earlobes indicate that he is a noble. Shankar too has long ear lobes (pulled down by heavy gold earrings), showing, among other things, the yogic faculty for clairaudience.

Some illustrations show Shiva holding a deer in his hands. This lithe, nervous animal represents the restless mind, ever ready to jump hither and thither. But here, it rests calmly, like the mind of a yogi. Likewise Buddha, preaching his first sermon about the cause and the overcoming of suffering while resting in the deer park (Sarnath) near Shiva's city of Benares, is shown surrounded by a herd of peacefully grazing deer. The Buddhist folktales, the "Jataka Tales," tell that Sarnath was once the forest in which Buddha had been the king of the deer in a former incarnation.*

The imago of Shiva-Shankar and the associated stories and legends are presumably older than those of historical personages, like Gotama Buddha or Mahavir, the founder of the Jains. Stone seals carved by the Bronze Age people, who built the cities of the old Indus civilization (Harappa, Mohenjo-Daro) some 4,500 years ago, show a naked, sometimes three-faced god, sitting with his legs crossed under him, heel to heel, toes pointing down, arms outstretched, and hands turned thumbs outward. This prehistoric yogi is surrounded by animals and under his seat are two deer (or gazelles), similar to the later icons of the preaching Buddha at Sarnath.[11] Apparently he has an upright phallus (unless it is a belt strap) and on his head is a pair of horns, looking like the crescent moon. The similarity to the Shankar icon is so pronounced that the archaeologist Sir John Marshal had no qualms about referring to a "proto-Shiva." It must be seen as the prototype of later imagery.

After Buddha had traveled up and down the Ganges Valley for many decades preaching his "noble path" *(arya dharma),* and after his selfless, dedicated monks had brought the message to the ears of many kings, it seemed as though all of India would convert to Buddhism. Mahavir's Jains were not quite as successful. But India is like a giant digestive apparatus, an immense compost that sooner or later turns all the ingredients into new humus, upon which the strangest and most elaborate fantasies of the human mind can sprout, bloom, and shoot to seed. Nothing is destroyed, but everything is metamorphosed.

---

*The owner of the Sarnath Forest, a maharaja who was a cruel and passionate hunter, had finally made an agreement with the king of the deer to take only one animal per day. One day, he ensnared a pregnant doe, who cried out: "Whom shall you kill, my kid or me?" Seeing that killing one would kill the other also, the deer king (the future Buddha) volunteered to give his own life instead. The maharaja was so moved by this act of compassion that henceforth he devoted himself to a life of nonkilling *(ahimsa).*

Historical facts quickly become myths, and simple, straightforward thoughts take root and grow like jungle vines, seemingly into infinity. Even now, Mahatma Gandhi and Indira Gandhi are turning into deities with all the trappings of cultlike devotion, just as the leader of the armed rebellion against British rule and commander of the Japanese-supported Indian National Army, Subhash Chandra Bose, is being worshipped as an incarnation of Ganesha, the elephant-headed son of Shiva. Even popular film stars like M. G. Ramachandran, Sivaji Ganesan, or Amitabh Bachan are raised to the rank of avatars of God in the minds of illiterate peasants and derive political power from their position. The politician N. T. Rama Rao, for example, who played the role of Krishna, is worshipped as an aspect of that deity. It would be nonsense to assume that Buddha and his teachings have escaped the mythomanic passion of the Indians. Indeed, it was not long before the Vaishnavas declared Buddha to be the ninth incarnation or avatar of Vishnu.* In his incarnation as Buddha, Vishnu appeared to mislead demons and wicked men and women. By teaching them to disregard the caste system, to ignore blood lines, to deny the existence of the gods and other such falsehoods, he assured their eventual destruction.

In the *Brahmanda Purana*, however, Buddha is expressly celebrated as a manifestation of Shiva.[12] It is said that in the first age (Krita Yuga), when the earth is a paradise, Shiva appears as a yogi. In the following age (Treta Yuga), he is embodied as Kratu, one of the "world creators" and keeper of the Vedic sacrifice. In the third age (Dvapara Yuga), he appears as the doomsday fire; and in our present age (Kali Yuga), so lacking in virtue, he manifested as Dharmaketu (Buddha).

In south India, Buddha went through the greatest metamorphosis, as we shall see in the following story:

Durga, the great goddess who rides a tiger and holds the weapons of all the gods, is in reality none other than Parvati, Shiva's faithful spouse. She destroyed the great buffalo-demon, Mahisasura, by beheading him. At

---

*Whenever evil threatens the continuity of the world, Vishnu, the Preserver, takes compassion and appears physically in order to restore Dharma. He has appeared as a fish (Matsyavatara), a turtle (Kurma), a boar (Varahavatara), a man-lion (Narasimha), a dwarf (Vamana), as Rama-with-the Ax, as King Rama, husband of Sita, as Krishna, as Buddha, and at the end of this era, he will appear as Kalki, the warrior with a blazing sword on a white horse.

that, Mahisi, the buffalo-demon's wife, swore revenge, cost what it may. For eons, she suffered the hardest austerities in order to gain merit. Finally, Brahma had to comply with her insatiable desire and grant her a boon. She wished that neither Shiva, nor Durga, nor Vishnu, the mightiest of all the gods, might be able to vanquish her in battle. To prevent the demoness from wrecking the universe, Vishnu took on the form of the enchantress, Mohini, and slept with Shiva. Together they produced a son called Ayyappan, who they abandoned in a jungle in Kerala just after he had been born. He happened to be found by a king and his entourage. Since the king had no children of his own, he was glad to bring the infant up as his own flesh and blood. As he grew up, the beautiful child performed many wonders. One day, for example, he brought a female leopard into the royal chambers, knowing its milk would cure the headaches of his foster mother. At the age of twelve, he met and quickly dispatched the demoness, Mahisi. At that time, he revealed his divinity to his father and asked him to build a temple on the exact spot where an arrow released from his bow struck the ground. That happened to be on top of the mountain Sabarimalai. To this day, each year hundreds of thousands of pilgrims dressed in black *lungis**walk barefoot to the temple on the mountain. For forty-one days they abstain from sex and obey strict taboos concerning eating, sleeping, and speaking.

Ayyappan (Hariharaputra), the son of Shiva and Vishnu, is also called Shastra or Dharmashastra, which means as much as "holy law." It is a name commonly applied by the Buddhists to Buddha, referring to his role as guardian of the Arya Dharma, the noble path. Ayyappan, whose name derives from the Dravidian mispronunciation of the Sankrit *arya*, rides a white elephant named Yogi. Since Buddha appeared to his mother as a white elephant, the conjecture that Ayyappan is none other than Buddha,

Durga destroying the demon Mahishasura

---

*Lungi = a piece of cotton cloth, tied around the waist

having been worked over by the mythomanic genius of the south Indians, seems likely. Ayyappan is the Enlightened One dissolved back into the ocean of Hinduism.[13]

The ubiquitous icon of Shankar and the worship of the lingam seem, thus, to go back partially to the old pre-Aryan civilizations now covered by the dry sands of the Indus Valley. As we can read in the Vedas, the cults of lingams, *nagas* (serpent deities), mother goddesses, and sex magic, did not find favor with the Aryan invaders. But the decree of the Brahmins did not have the power to banish images and beliefs from the minds of the non-Aryan masses, the lower castes and untouchables, and, slowly, they crept into and populated the Aryan universe. Gradually, emerging from the shadows, aspects of proto-Shiva transferred themselves onto Rudra, the Vedic god of storms and wild beasts. When the reform movements of the fifth century B.C., centering around Buddhism and Jainism, challenged the Brahmanic orthodoxy, what lay slumbering in the souls of the Indian masses rose to new life.

During the first century A.D., proto-Shiva's likeness came to new life in the hands of the Bactrian Greek sculptors, in the form of statues of the meditating Buddha. The icon of Shankar became popular somewhat later, in the fifth century, during the reign of the Gupta kings, when modern Hinduism emerged. The icon of Shiva as the dancer in the flames developed even later, when south Indian Tamils cast Nataraja in bronze in the eleventh century.

There is a brief but interesting biographical note concerning Siddhartha Gotama, the later Buddha: After he had left wife and family, he joined a group of sadhus who were devotees of Shiva. Even the name of his Shaivite guru is known. It was the wandering ascetic Makkhali Gosala (560–484 B.C.), of whom it is said, he practiced dance and divine drunkenness.[14]

⊰ THE TRIDENT AND THE ⊱ "BÂTON-DE-COMMANDEMENT"

Sitting straight-backed on his tiger skin, the meditating master of yogis rests his left hand loosely on his knee, sometimes fingering a rudraksha rosary. Stuck in the snow next to his right arm, the trident is in ready reach, while the elbow rests sovereignly upon a T- or Y-shaped armrest.

An ethnologist is immediately reminded by this armrest of the *bâton-de-commandement*, which is a symbol of sovereignty among Siberian shamans. Sometimes, these scepters are decorated with animals and magical runes, and an "eye" is drilled into the top so that it can see. Occasionally, it can be used as a drumstick for the shaman's drum, to call the spirits. The T-shaped instrument is ancient,

The "bâton-de-commandement"

having been found among the refuse left by the mammoth and bison hunters of the Old Stone Age. The late Paleolithic magicians who painted the walls of the Pyrenean caves would, presumably, not have been puzzled by such "armrests" that long-haired, ash-covered siddhi babas, who populate the "places of power" in the Indian landscape, carry around with them.

The trident *(trisul)* is also an ancient scepter of overlordship. Its antiquity is indicated by the fact that it is the symbol of the pagan god of the sea, Poseidon, as well as the "pitchfork" of the old Eurasian shamanistic god who sank into the (psychic) abyss to become the devil. Because of this association as a witch's or devil's attribute, the Church resisted for a long time the addition of the fork, alongside the spoon and knife, as an eating instrument.[15]

To this day, the natives of the Siberian taigas and steppes consider the trident as a symbol of the world tree. They fasten it to their boats and to the tent of the shaman or set it up to mark graves.[16]

Basically, the trident is a spear, whose power is multiplied three-fold. It is the oldest hafted weapon, the hunting implement par excellence, older than the javelin or the bow and arrow. The Neanderthals (living in the interglacial period of the Middle Paleolithic) already knew how to fasten razor-sharp, chipped hand axes onto slotted shafts, giving them power over even the biggest quarry, even over mastodons, rhinoceroses, bison, and cave bears. This tool, like no other, became a fetish, giving its yielder sovereignty, as though he carried the thunderbolt itself. It has ever since been the insignia of kings and lords. Nearly all tribes honored hallowed spears or "ceremonial lance blades," out of which the gods, ancestors, or spirits speak. The Nordics knew of the magic spear of Odin, whose shaft was made from the "World-Ash" itself. The Celts of Ireland knew of a "spear of light." Christian legend tells of the lance of the Roman legionnaire

Longius, who pierced the side of Jesus with it as he hung on the cross, gathering the blood in a cup which was to become the Holy Grail.

This lance of Longius became the spear of Amfortas, the guardian king of the Grail. It was wrested from him by the trickery of the evil magician Klingsor and not restored until Parsifal, "the pure fool" seized it again and closed the wound of Amfortas with its healing power. The Habsburg emperors made this blade their own symbol of power, believing themselves invincible and destined to rule the world as long as they kept it in their treasury in the Hofburg Fortress in Vienna. At the end of the Second World War, this spear of destiny fell temporarily into the hands of the Americans.[17] It has since been returned to Austria.

The trident is, of course, the cosmic tree of the shamans. At the same time, it is a symbol of the human microcosm. The symbol is applicable on the physical as well as the ideational plane: it is the upright body, with the head and both arms stretched upward, as though they were the three roots of a tree growing into the heavens, drawing life and light out of the heavenly ether. Theologians speak of this posture as the "orate position."[18] This prayer posture is so archetypal and universal that it easily developed into such basic symbols as the cross, the trident, the fleur-de-lis, and the old Nordic *man*-rune, also called the *elhaz-* or *algiz*-rune (ᛉ), symbolizing also the elk or Odin.

When Shankar is meditating on the inner glory of his being, the thrice-powerful weapon rests stuck in the snow with its blades pointing skyward. But then, when the measure is full and the time of doom and dissolution is at hand, he hurls the trident's prongs earthward. Again, we are confronted by universal symbolism: the sacred spear, resting and pointing upward, indicates dignity, rule, harmony, peace, and ritual purity. The spear turned upside down betokens bloodshed, war, hunt, disgrace, physical or sexual violence, and ritual pollution. It signals chaos, revolution and, at the same time, a new beginning, a new impulse.

The Plains Indians made sure that their lance tips never touched the earth. In the rare case that the unthinkable happened, only a long, complicated ritual, involving chanting and incensing with prairie sage, could restore purity. In European history, also, surrender and defeat were indicated by touching the standards and lances to the ground. (The sexual symbolism is evident—by touching the motherly earth, the weapon loses its purity and thus its magical potency. The lightning in it becomes grounded.)

It is significant as well that the man-rune (Υ), which Odin picked up as he hung upside down on the world-ash, is associated with thinking, making, measuring, and ordering—when turned upright. But when it is turned upside down ($\curlywedge$), it conjures destruction, dissolution, and madness.[19] It then becomes a "crow's foot," belonging to those black, carrion-eating birds that are at home on the battlefield and the execution grounds. It is contained in the anarchistic "peace symbol"( ). Though intended as a symbol of peace and disarmament, those who congregate under its auspices would like to undo the present establishment, which they consider aggressive, imperialistic, and warmongering.

People in archaic, animistic societies, our forebears included, felt that all tools and weapons have a spirit, which can be called by name. Shiva's trident is personified in a similar manner. Its name is Vijaya, "Victory." In the Puranas, the seers describe it as a young hero who carries in his hands a sharp ax, the sun, and also a noose. He is said to glow threateningly, like a smokeless fire, and shine out like the rising sun. His brows are knitted somberly, like those of a warrior scanning the horizon.

An unusual cornucopia of symbolic associations clings to the three tips of the trident. Swamis, vying with each other for the most spiritual interpretation, liken them to the three primal qualities (gunas), the three hills of Benares, or the Trimurti (Brahma, Vishnu, Shiva—the three reflections of the One, the Sada-Shiva.) Swami Swahananda interprets the three prongs as the three weapons of victory over the ego-demon's three apparently invincible castles (the physical, ethereal, and emotional armor of the human being). The three blades are: *vairagya* (nonattachment), *jnana* (gnosis, true knowledge), and *samadhi* (spiritual concentration).

For the simple Hindu, however, the trident is just what it appears to be, namely, a weapon with which God jabs and kills nasty demons. One such demon who felt the power of the trident was Andhaka. Blinded by lustful desire, he thought he would be a better mate for lovely Parvati and tried to carry her off. Shiva scooped him up with his fork and made the demon dance until he became so hot that his sins burned off. While dancing, however, he became ecstatic and

The symbol of the Sikh faith

began to praise the lord with a loud voice. Shiva, who is easy to please, was so delighted that he adopted Andhaka as his son.

The Sikhs, an old warrior caste from the Punjab, have also taken the trident, though in modified form, as their symbol. For them, the three prongs are composed of two crossed scimitars with a double-edged blade in the middle. Like Shiva sadhus, they let no scissors touch their head hair or beards and have sworn by this sign to be ever ready to defend dharma, if need be at the cost of their lives.

6

THE GODDESS

———— ᏭᎤᏚ ————

*Why does the God-lover find such pleasure in addressing
the Deity as Mother? Because the child is more free
with the mother, and consequently she is
dearer to the child than anyone else.*

RAMAKRISHNA, NINETEENTH CENTURY

In the sacred lore of the Aryan herdspeople who colonized the Indus
Valley, female divinities play nearly as insignificant a role as in the
sacred writings of the Hebrews. Pastoralists, the anthropologists have
found, live in a patriarchal universe.* In the course of time, however,
all the Vedic gods find themselves married to illustrious goddesses and,
finally, with the rise of the Bengali Mother cult and Shakti cult, the
Goddess becomes equated with the entire universe. She becomes the
personification of maya, the illusion of an infinite multitude of separate
existences, forms, and names, and of *kala,* the illusion of the coming

---

*The relative "weight" of male or female function in society is more or less determined
by ecological and economic factors. Pastoralists moving over wide, often hostile terrain
with their herds tend toward a more patriarchal organization of their daily life, whereas
planters and simple horticulturists tend more to a matriarchal organization. With the latter, the land was "owned" by the matrilineages (female line of descent). This made sense,
not only in that the fertile earth itself was seen as a "mother of life," but also, because
groups of related women did the work of planting and tending the crops. This was also
the case in pre-Aryan, pre-Muslim India. The cult of the Divine Mother is very ancient
in India and preceeds pastoralist invaders. In the course of time, Indian culture has
arrived at a synthesis of both traditions. Indeed, the cult of the Great Goddess is, within
popular Hinduism, still increasing in importance.

*Shiva appearing in
his female form
as Maheshvari*

and going of time. She is worshipped as the energy (shakti) that sets everything in motion, sustains it, and lets it dissolve.* In all this, Shiva is only consciousness. He is the Self, while she is his Being, which he contemplates in his meditation. He is the resting pole around which she dances her seductive dances. Her infinite number of masks and veils that simultaneously reveal and conceal, totally fascinate and spellbind the observer, plunging him into a kaleidoscope of sublime beauty, abysmal horror, unfathomable sadness, or peaceful gladness.

Since Shiva is only the silent, immobile witness, whereas she is the power herself, the devotees of Shakti and Devi have concluded that it might be best to direct one's attention and prayers exclusively to the Goddess. Not the distant Father, but she, the Mother of All, protects her children and fulfills their wishes. Periodically, Christians have followed a similar mode of thought, turning foremost to Mary the Virgin, who bore God and who is the Mother of the universe.

Indian monism demands that there be only one ultimate reality. Therefore, Shiva and the Goddess are not really two, but one: he is the center of being and she is the energy radiating from it. They cannot be separated, yet her (illusive) forms and expressions are without number. Consequently, the universe is filled with more gods and "realities" than there are grains of sand on the seashore. At the same time, the One (which is many) is threefold, expressing itself in the trinity of Brahma, Vishnu, and Shiva-Rudra. How Shakti arose from this triune Godhead is told in the *Varaha Purana*:

Once, the Creator, the Upholder, and the Destroyer met on Mount Kailash. They were heated with anger at the uppity demons that plagued them like lice in the hair. As their angry glances met, a column of smoke rose in the

---

*The relation of *maya* and *shakti* is like that of the clay to the potter's wheel. The one is the substance or matter of creation, the other is the formative force.

focal point and in its midst stood a most beautiful maiden, as fresh as a blue lotus bud opening to the gentle, warm caress of the morning sun. Shyly she bowed her comely head before them. When the perplexed gods asked who she might be and why her color was white, red, and black, the radiant woman replied, "Don't you know me, noble Lords? I am the concentration of your energies. I am your Shakti!"

All three wanted to possess her. Brahma, who overcame his confusion first, commanded her to divide into three parts, according to her colors. Thus, the three great goddesses came into being: snow white Sarasvati, whom Brahma took as his wife; Lakshmi, who is of auspicious red color and was taken by Vishnu; and Parvati, the black goddess, whom Shiva chose as his companion. The three goddesses who appear in this image are, of course, the three primal elements (gunas) that make up the creation: the light, sattva; the active, rajas; and the dark, dull, tamas. They are the primordial Mothers, the thrice-dynamic matter, out of which the world of appearance (existence) is woven. In principle, they are the same three ancient Mothers that spin out the fate of the world in Celtic, Germanic, and other Indo-European mythologies.*

Sarasvati, the white goddess who rides a swan, is a river goddess who inspires the flow of thoughts, words, and imaginings of poets, thinkers, and speakers. As the muse of artists and healers, she is shown holding a lute *(vina)*, a rosary, and a book. Her relationship to other Indo-European white goddesses and swan maidens, who can foretell the future and heal the ailing, is unmistakable. The Celts knew her as Brigit or Birgit, or simply as the White Goddess.

Sarasvati

---

*The three goddesses of fate of the Nordic legends—Urd, Wierd, and Skuld—or the three *moerae* of the Greeks, are expression of this archetypal female trinity. In most cultural traditions in the Old and the New World, the colors white, red, and black are recognized as primal, magical colors. White is the color of the beginning; it is milk and semen. Red is the color of life, of blood, and of living fire. Black is the color of death, of excretion, humus, and decay. The same colors (made from chalk, ochre, and soot) were used in the Paleolithic cave paintings. The color symbolism lived on in alchemy: the black raven is decay *(negrido)*, the white lily is resurrection, and the red lion is the symbol of life.

Shiva and Parvati

Lakshmi, the red-complexioned, faithful wife of Vishnu, who tenderly massages his feet as he awakens from his sleep on the world serpent, Sesha, is the personification of good fortune, or luck. She is the Fortuna, whose cornucopia pours out the riches for which every merchant and householder prays. As we have seen elsewhere, she appeared during the churning of the ocean and is, like the Greek Aphrodite, the foam-born goddess of beauty as well. Like the Greek Athena, her animal companion is the owl.

As happens with beautiful women all too often, the white and the red goddesses are jealous of each other and refuse to live under the same roof. Thus the artist or poet who loves the muse, Sarasvati, might draw the ire of Lakshmi and will often have to go without material wealth. On the other hand, the successful businessperson might swim in money but will have little time or attention from the muse. Rare is the blessed soul who has the favor of both goddesses.

But now we shall turn to the black goddess, who became Shiva's bride. Many more stories are told of her, for she is the Goddess!

❧ DEVI ❧

We have already gotten to know Devi, "the radiant one" or simply "the Goddess," as the self-immolated daughter of righteous Daksha. According to the *Kurma Purana*, she always was, and always is, the other half of Shiva.[1] The story tells of a grumpy grandfather Brahma, who was very upset when he discovered that his mind-born sons had no intention of being fruitful, multiplying, and thus populating the earth. As his angry thoughts concentrated, they took on the form of a hermaphroditic being, which he commanded to split into two. The masculine half he called "Rudra" and the feminine half, "Sati (Uma)." The Creator gave Sati to his foremost son Daksha to be born as his youngest daughter, whom Shiva was destined to wed.

After Sati had entered the flames and removed herself from existence, Rudra's power and glory waned until he was no better than a mangy dog. It is obvious that no god can be without his female half, his shakti. In the *Vaivarta Purana*, Shiva, maddened by the pain of separation, admits this when he cries of Uma's loss:

"Arise, arise, my beloved Sati! I am Shankara, your Lord! With you I am almighty, the foundation of all, the giver of all bliss! But without you, my animation, I am but a corpse, powerless and unable to act! Let your smiles and glances, let your words, sweet as ambrosia, rain upon my pain-scorched heart. Why, oh mistress of my soul, will you not speak to me?

Icon of Uma-Mahashvara

Mother of the Universe, do you not see me weeping? Why are you disobedient to me? Why have you forgotten your marriage vow?"

After having thus lamented, he lost his senses completely. He even forgot who he was. Exhausted by fatigue and anguish, he collapsed at the foot of a pipal (fig) tree. Vishnu, who found him in the forlorn state, started to cry bitter tears of compassion as he tried to console him, "Oh, Shiva, Shiva, come to! You will find your Sati again, for you and she are inseparable like fire and heat, like snow and cold, like sun and light!"

Shiva managed to open his tear-swollen eyes, "Who are you, you light of splendor? Are you God? Where am I? Who am I?" was all he managed to utter before sinking into darkness. (The tears that both shed filled a lake that is, to this day, a place of pilgrimage.)

As Shiva's despair reached the limit of what was bearable, Sati's voice was suddenly heard from the heavens, saying, "Be strong, oh Mahadeva, Lord of my soul! Wherever I may be, I am never really separated from you. Soon I shall be reborn as the daughter of the mountains and again I shall be your wife! Grieve no longer!"

Indeed, in due time, what the voice had foretold came to pass. The king of the mountains, Himalaya, and his wife, Mena (whom swamis take as a personification of the ether, or akasha,) had two daughters. The elder one they named Ganga, and the younger one, who had been Uma-Sati in her former life, they called Parvati. We shall soon see how she conquered the heart of the ascetic meditant, Shankar, and how she became the mother of the demon-killer, Skanda.

Shiva and Parvati often wander unrecognized, as beggars, throughout the world, testing the souls of people. Most of the time, however, they live in a simple abode on Mount Kailash, where Shiva loafs around while Paravati busies herself with household chores, like any good Hindu mother. But it is not just endless matrimonial bliss. Quarrels, fights, and then tearful making up are as common with them as with most married couples.

Many husbands like to read interesting excerpts from the Sunday newspapers to their wives. In the following Keralese folktale, Shiva is no exception. He loves to read and explain the Vedas to Parvati. Parvati enjoys this, but, as with most women, her mind sometimes drifts to more immediate concerns.

Once, having read the Vedas out loud for several hundred years, Shiva glanced up and happened to notice that Parvati was not listening. Being more than annoyed, he lashed out at her.

"I see that the Vedas are too difficult for you! You should have married a rude, illiterate fisherman! That would have been more your level of intelligence!"

At that very moment, Parvati disappeared from Mount Kailash and reappeared as a squalling infant under a tree, somewhere near the south Indian seashore. Just then, a group of simple fishermen happened to walk by and find her. The chief of the fishermen took the baby home and put it in his wife's arms. They decided to call her "Parvati" and raise her as their own daughter. Being cared for tenderly, she grew up as the prettiest child in the little thatch village.

In the meantime, Shiva was as miserable as a dog in the premonsoon heat. He was sorry to have scolded her and felt depressed and alone. His faithful bull, Nandi, not able to bear his master's decline of spirits, proposed, "Dear Lord, why don't you just go down there and fetch her again?"

"How would that be possible? She is about to be married off to one of these fishermen!" Shiva replied in a voice that betrayed immeasurable self-pity.

Suddenly Nandi had a flash! He jumped down into the sea, turning himself into a huge white shark, and started to terrorize the coast by attacking the boats and ripping up the fishing nets. The fishermen held an emergency council, trying to find a way to get rid of the menace. Finally, the chief of the tribe rose and spoke. "Any young man who manages to kill this shark shall have my daughter as his wife!"

Since Parvati's grace, beauty, and industry were unequaled, young fishermen from far and near were eager to risk life and limb in order to have her. But none of them were able to catch the white sea monster. At long last, with all their reserves exhausted, they decided to ask for God's help. They formed a large lingam out of wet sand, decorated it with flowers, and poured milk and coconut juice on it while they prayed to Mahadev. The chief's pretty daughter prayed as fervently as any of them.

Shiva heard their prayer. Slipping into the appearance of a black-skinned youth from a far away village, he walked in upon the scene. Overjoyed that his plan had worked, Nandi let himself be easily caught and killed by the youth. After the white killer shark was dead, the marriage feast was celebrated. During the sacred rites, the couple took on their radiant divine forms. They blessed the astonished, simple fishing folk, climbed on Nandi, who had changed back into his bovine form, and departed for the northern mountains.

Often the divine couple plays dice as a pleasant pastime. Shiva wagered his trident, Parvati wagered her jewels. One time he had a bad streak of luck. He lost not only his weapon, but his snake, his skull bowl, his drum, his smoking pipe, and finally even his loincloth. Peeved, he went alone into the pine forest. There he met Vishnu, who felt sorry for him. "Play another game," his friend advised him. "I will slip into the die."

Not only did he win all his belongings back, but he won Parvati's jewels, and even her shawl. As she stood there, shivering in the cold mountain air, she became suspicious and called him a cheat. Shiva was outraged by her accusation and demanded an apology. As they quarreled Vishnu appeared and revealed to Parvati the secret of Shiva's gambling luck. In order to pacify her, he explained: "The dice rolled not according to your wishes, but according to my wish, for my spirit had entered them. So neither one of you really won or lost. The game was an illusion and your quarrel a product of delusion." On hearing this, Parvati and Shiva realized that life was like their game of dice.[2]

That was not the first time they quarreled over a game of dice:

Once, as they were rolling the dice, they got into a heated argument, for they had forgotten to keep track of their scores. Shiva was sure that he had won, but Parvati insisted that she had the higher score. In order to cool his temper, Shiva left the house and took a walk in the forest. The sage Narada, who loves stirring up trouble among the gods, could not help but notice the bickering and decided to spice it up somewhat. In his honey-sweet voice, he told Parvati that he had just seen Shiva as a handsome young Bhil tribesman, roaming the forest and looking for one of those affectionate, seductive native women. At the very thought, Parvati's blood boiled, for she was as jealous as she was beautiful. Instantly, she herself took on the form of a sexy young Bhil maiden and went walking in the same forest. The heavy silver rings around her arms and legs shone like moonlight on her smooth, black skin. Colorful feathers of forest birds were woven into her full black hair, and her slender body swayed to her singing like a bamboo reed in the wind. Kama's flowery arrows hit the bull's eye of Shiva's heart when he saw her. Instantly he turned himself into a Bhil forester and stepped up to her. He became mere putty in the forest girl's hand.

"Oh, most beautiful maiden, marry me on the spot!" he said.

The almond-eyed native girl smiled teasingly. "But, sir, you already have two queens: Ganga, who lives in your hair, and faithful Parvati at home!"

"Don't let that bother you, my little forest flower. I shall send Parvati back to her parents and make Ganga your maid servant!"

"But," retorted the Bhil maiden, "you are so ugly with your matted, unkempt yellow hair, your horrid snakes and ashes. Anyway, your home is but a lean-to and you carry a beggar's staff!"

"Darling, I will get a haircut, shave, and shower. I'll chase the vipers off and throw the stick away. I will build you a palace of jewels, ivory, and gold!"

"Well, all right," she smiled, flashing her perfectly white teeth, "but it is the custom of our tribe that in order to woo a maiden, the suitor has to dance a dance to win her heart!"

Nothing was easier for Nataraja. On the spot, he started dancing like crazy. He was sure she would be impressed. But just as he went to grab her hand, he saw Parvati standing in front of him and froze in shame.

Another time, as Parvati tenderly wrapped her arms around Shiva's neck, he commented, in his way, "Sweetheart, your supple body is like a black snake wrapping itself around the white trunk of a sandalwood tree. I am pale white, but you are as black as the dark half of the moon. You are Kali, the black one, black as coal, black as a crow."

Parvati took these intended compliments in the wrong way and her feelings were very hurt. As tears rolled like pearls down her cheeks, she sobbed, "How can you insult me so meanly, calling me black! As if you have no faults of your own! But have I ever even hinted at them? The whole world knows your choleric temperament, how you knocked out poor Pushan's teeth . . . you monster! And your creepy companions, your snakes and skulls . . . how you run around shamelessly naked!"

She worked herself into a real rage. No "but, darling" could bring her out of it. Finally, Parvati convinced herself that she should leave him. She made up her mind to go into the wilderness and do penance until Brahma would be forced to grant her wish for a lighter skin color. As she turned her back on Mount Kailash, all the ghosts and goblins and everyone, including Nandi and Ganesha, ran after her, crying, "Mother, dear mother! Where are you going? Don't leave us! You know that when you are not here we can barely stand Shiva's moods."

"Don't worry, my little darlings. When your Mommy has finished her austerities and her skin has turned light, then she'll be back," she said to calm them, and then, turning to Nandi, she said, "You, my son, are the gatekeeper. Guard the door until I come back. Don't let any strange woman enter, so that this lecherous playboy of a husband does not diddle around while I am away!"

Lifting baby Ganesha into her arms, she said, "I'll take you with me, for I know he makes just as much fun of your elephant head as he does of my dark complexion!"

At that, she hurried on her way. Halfway down the mountain she came upon her aunt, the old mountain giantess Kasumamodini, and told her everything that had happened. They gossiped until the rocks started sweating and then, just before going on, she asked her aunt to throw an eye on Mount Kailash once in a while, to see if her husband was carrying on with another woman. Finally, after a journey of many days, Parvati found a hidden forest suited for meditation. She dressed in bark cloth and fasted. In the summer, she sat between four fires in the scorching sun and, in the winter, she stood in icy cold mountain streams.

In the meantime, Adi, a wicked demon, had found out that Parvati was out of the house. He saw it as a unique opportunity to avenge his father, Andhaka, whom Shiva had slain. Adi was not afraid of Shiva, for Brahma's boon had made him invincible, that is, as long as he stayed in his proper form. But already in order to sneak past Nandi the watchful gatekeeper, he'd had to turn himself into a snake. Then, again using the power of illusion, he took on the appearance of Parvati. Every hair, every pore, every curve, every smile, the tinkle in her voice and the twinkle in her eyes were exactly copied. The only difference was that this false Parvati had teeth hidden in her vagina.

*Icon of Uma-Shankar
as half-woman/half-man*

Smiling sweetly, she approached Shiva. "Darling, don't be upset that I went away angry. I have forgiven and forgotten your insult. Now I long for your kisses!"

Though she was Parvati's splitting image, Shiva became somewhat suspicious, for he knew that once Parvati's mind was made up on a plan, she was bound and determined to carry it out. Again he scrutinized her carefully, investigating every detail. No doubt, this was Parvati. But suddenly he noticed a tiny hair out of place and, seeing through the illusion, recognized the dangerous demon in front of him.

"Might as well turn the demon's destruction into sport," he thought, as he strapped a thunderbolt onto his penis. Then he jumped on the false Parvati and bore into her so that the monster died, screaming.

Unfortunately, just at that moment, Parvati's old, gossipy aunt passed by Mount Kailash. Thinking she had caught Shiva carrying on with a strange woman, she turned herself into a breeze of air and flew straight to the grove where her niece was doing penance. Parvati was as hurt as any woman can be when a husband is unfaithful. She cursed Nandi who had failed to guard the door as he should have. "May he turn into a heartless, cold stone for not obeying me!"

Her fierce anger, energized by the rigorous ascetic exercises she had done, sprang out of her in the form of a fiery lion. She was just about to plunge herself into its roaring jaws in order to commit suicide as she had done when she was Uma-Sati, but grandfather Brahma, her guru, stopped her. He told her not to be rash and act foolish. Knowing that it is a grave sin not to obey one's honored spiritual teacher, she just stood there, trembling. Now Lord Brahma granted her a boon: the darkness left her body and took on an independent form, that of Kali. And Parvati shone with the light, golden complexion of the rising full moon. Thus she received her new name, Gauri (the brilliantly shining, or golden, one). Before giving his student her final blessing, Brahma reassured her, "My child, you and your husband shall be so close that you will melt into each other, becoming one person, known as Ardhanarishvara, or Uma-Shankar." The mighty lion, born of her rage, became her mount, on which she would ride out against demons anywhere in the world.

All her wishes having been fulfilled, the Goddess, Gauri, hurried back to Mount Kailash. Just as she was about to enter the portals of her home, Nandi, who did not recognize the transformed Goddess, lowered his horns, blocking her path. "Be gone, strange woman," he bellowed. "No one may enter, but Parvati, our dear Mother! A wicked demon, taking on her appearance, stealthily wormed his way past me. After my Lord killed the intruder, he ordered me to let absolutely no woman pass this threshold!"

At these words, Parvati's heart melted, and she realized that her aunt had not observed correctly. Now she was sorry to have cursed Nandi to become a silent stone. But the white bull, who finally recognized her, said, "Dear Mother, even your curse is a blessing! I won't mind becoming a stone!" Ever since, one sees a stone Nandi in front of every Shiva temple. Some say that Nandi was actually born the son of a woman named Stone and spent a lifetime serving Shiva in human form.

ᘍ DURGA ᘖ

Like Shiva himself, his Shaktis have light and dark sides. They can take on gentle or fierce appearances. In her manifestation as Durga, "the inaccessible," the Goddess partakes of both. Noble Durga is neither the gentle mother and wife, like Parvati, nor is she the terrible, violent ogress like Kali; rather she is a sovereign, independent amazon. As is the Greek Athena, who sprung fully armed from the forehead of Zeus, and the valkyries, the shield maidens of Odin, she is a warrior. As Simhavahini, "the lion-rider," she is associated, like Kybele, Freya, and other ancient goddesses, with predatory cats. Like a cat, she hunts her prey: the demons of hate, vanity, and egoism. She is the nemesis of all those who violate dharma.

The warrior goddess received her name from one of her victims, an asura named Durga. Because of his pitiless self-torture, this asura had gained so much power that he could drive the gods from their thrones. The Puranas tell that:

The celestials were reduced to homeless beggars, dressed in rags, picking

Durga on her lion

through the garbage to survive. Demonic "Durga" forbade the worship of the gods, for only he was to be worshipped. Temples were set up in his honor. Soon chaos spread throughout society and throughout nature, for the Brahmins were afraid to recite the holy mantras from the Vedas. Not satisfied with how the world had been created, the mighty asura changed the weather patterns, drained swamps, leveled mountains, and rechanneled the rivers. The stars could no longer be seen as the sky was filled with dust and smoke. The seasons became irregular so that there were fruits and flowers in the winter. Nonetheless, Earth brought forth record harvests, mountains of grain and butter, but only because she was afraid of the mighty demon Durga.

The increasingly loud anguished cries of the maltreated animals, the overworked human beings, and the fearful gods finally rose to Mount Kailash and woke Shiva from his meditation. As he enjoyed resting in his bliss, he turned the task over to the Goddess. She mounted her lion and rode against the asura, who countered by sending tens of thousands of snorting giants to meet her. Their monster arms ripped out mountains and tall trees with which they wanted to bludgeon her. At that, she split the ogress Kalaratri "black night," from her being. Kalaratri's breath was so hot that it burned the monsters to ashes. New fiends appeared, as thick as hail, and pounded upon the goddess on the lion. Shakti destroyed them all and then went after the asura king, Durga, himself. Using his power of illusion, he constantly changed his appearance. He turned into a huge buffalo, then he became smaller than a fly, only to change into an elephant bigger than a mountain; but each time, she thwarted him. Finally she killed him, in his original form of a thousand-armed giant. In memory of this brilliant victory, Parvati takes on the name Durga whenever she goes to battle riding her lion.

The *Vamana Purana* tells of Durga's greatest battle. It tells how she freed the black buffalo-demon, the king of the asuras, Mahisha, from his evil karma by dispatching him:

No asura had ever been as powerful as Mahisha. Not only had he enslaved the three worlds, but no god, even among the great gods, could undo him. When the divinities met to deliberate, the terrible anger flashing out of their eyes met in midair, forming a fiery focal point, causing a giant conflagration in the midst of which arose a virgin shining brighter than all the heavens. She had three eyes, dark, flowing hair, and eighteen arms that whirled like the spokes of a rapidly revolving wheel. In each one of her hands she held a weapon, or a lordly insignia, of one of the anguished gods. She held Shiva's trident, Vishnu's discus, Brahma's beads and water pot, Varuna's noose, Agni's lance, the wind god Vayu's bow, the sun god Surya's quiver of arrows, and Indra's thunderbolt. Kubera, the god of the underworld, provided her with a heavy metal club. Yama, the god of the dead, gave her his sword and shield. Vishwakarman, the divine architect, handed her his battle-ax. On and on, the gods bestowed all their powers upon her. Armed in this way, she knocked the asura down and, standing on his back, cut off his head with her sword.

Durga's victory over the buffalo demon is a favorite icon for all those who need or seek strength and energy, such as truck drivers and soldiers. She is depicted as a radiant maiden sitting astride a lion whose fangs and claws are sunk into a bleeding buffalo bull. One hand grasps the severed head of her adversary by its scalp, while the other hands hold the weapons and insignias of the gods. All the while, her face is calm and gentle, as if nothing out of the ordinary were happening. She is the peaceful eye in the middle of the storm. The chaos and destruction surrounding her seem to be of no interest to her.

Once upon a time, somewhere toward the end of the last world age, the Dvapara Yuga, two asuras named Sumbha and Nisumbha, incarnations of extremely sophisticated egoism, gained power. The *Markandeya Purana* tells how they submitted to ten thousand years of the most horrid self-castigation—hanging upside down over fires, holding up their arms until they resembled withered bird's claws, lying on beds of nails or hot coals, and completing all the martyrdoms one still occasionally sees being performed by fakirs and ascetics on the banks of the Ganges or in the Himalayas.

The gods trembled at their implacable determination. In order to hinder these asuras, they sent the love god, Kama, and two of the most bewitching damsels of heaven to distract the penitents. Kama's flower arrows hit their mark. As Sumbha and Nisumbha looked up, the seductive

Apsara—a heavenly dancer

image of the voluptuous, dancing apsarasas burned itself into them. Momentarily, they forgot themselves and were filled with desire. After some five thousand years of carnal pleasure, however, they regained their senses, realizing that they were about to be cheated of the fruits of their suffering. Enraged, they drove the lovely apsarasas from their forest lodgings and continued their self-martyrdom more determinedly. Slowly, piece by piece, they cut strips of flesh from their bones and sacrificed it to Shiva. For a thousand years they did this, until they were but bleached skeletons. Everything they possessed, they sacrificed to Shiva—everything save their pride! With extreme devotion, they forced Mahadev to descend personally from his throne and listen to their pleas. They felt they had gained enough merits to warrant immortality. But Shiva explained to them that only if they could bring their last sacrifice, that is, letting go of their egotistic pride, could their wish be fulfilled. Then, they would merge with his Being and attain immortality. But being demons, they were not capable of abandoning themselves fully to the Lord, so they had to settle for lordship over the entire universe.

Their boon having been granted, they immediately cast the gods into the dust, for nothing was allowed to shine except they themselves. Their arrogance became so unbearable that even Brahma and Vishnu could stand it no longer. The Creator and the Upholder hastened to Mount Kailash to voice their concern. When Mahadev finally rose out of his trance and listened to them, he had to explain that nothing could be done, for the accumulated merits of Sumbha's and Nisumbha's sufferings permitted them to continue wielding power. He was not going to interfere! Before fading into bliss again, he told them they might try talking with Durga. Perhaps, if all the suffering creatures prayed to her, she would do something.

As one might expect, the Mother of the Universe had compassion with her offspring. Taking the form of a simple country girl, she walked through the mountain valleys, carrying a water jug on her head. No sooner had she appeared than the spies, who served as the eyes of the demon lords throughout the world, sighted her. As she was beautiful without measure and apparently innocent and unspoiled to boot, they quickly gave report to their masters, hoping to be rewarded for finding such a delightful morsel, which promised to satisfy the debauched lusts of their lords. The asuras sent messengers to the maiden, inviting her with flattering words to the palace, where the jewels and fineries of the world would be laid at her feet. The maiden merely laughed a cheerful laugh at this offer and told them, much like proud Brunhilde of the Nibelungen Saga, "Whoever wants to have me, must first defeat me in battle!"

The messengers became piqued at her haughty answer. "Don't you know, young lady, with whom you are dealing?"

She only continued laughing and went merrily on her way. Sumbha was infuriated when he heard what had happened. It was time to teach that wench some manners and respect! He ordered one of his captains to go and simply seize her. When the captain and his henchmen were about to lay hands on her, the tender maid roared like a lion so that their eardrums broke and their bones shattered. Only a handful of those who had not come so close managed to escape and tell their lords what had happened.

Now the asuras sent out a large troop to catch her and put her in chains. She met them sitting on a donkey, laughing. As they were about to bind her, she suddenly turned into a raging beast that pounced upon the warriors and devoured them, like a monkey devours ripe mangos. Gleefully, she sliced off the head of the commander and drank his blood, from which she became so drunk that her eyes started glowing madly.

Now a general alarm was sounded. Huge armies of rakshas, asuras, giants, and other allies were drummed up and set in motion. The titanic empire resembled a stirred up anthill. They surrounded the Goddess, who was now seated on her lion, and launched an attack from all sides simultaneously. She killed them all with ease until the only one that was left was the supreme commander, Raktavijas, a master of black magic. He challenged her to a duel. Immediately, he fell under the pranks of her lion and bled from a thousand wounds. He should have died instantly; but lo and behold, each drop of his blood turned into a new demon, as large and as strong as Raktavijas. The gods, watching from afar, shook like aspens in a storm, for they were sure that this would be Durga's end.

By now, the goddess was raging! Her anger leaped out of her in the form of a heinous black fury who is called Chandi (Kali).* She was made of the same poison that had discolored Shiva's neck. Lusting for blood, she pounced upon the wounded demons and sucked them dry. She lapped up every drop of blood that sprayed before it hit the ground and turned into another demon. Finally, after having dispatched the black magician, Durga killed the asura kings, Sumbha and Nisumbha, while another aspect of her, black Kali, ate the corpses that littered the battlefield, ripping them like a jackal. Radiant in victory, Durga rose back into the highest heaven while the universe sang her praises.

---

*The Great Goddess has many aspects. As a warrior woman, she is Durga riding a lion. Chandi is one of Durga's "personalities" or aspects. Popular Indian imagination identifies Chandi with Kali.

ᛥ KALI ᛤ

Black goddesses—mistresses of the night, the earth, and the dark of the moon—have been honored throughout history all over the world. In the Occident, they survived into Christianity as the Black Madonna, worshipped from Spain to Russia. The Black Madonna of Czenstochow, the patroness of the Polish people, is the best known. (In modern secular culture, her archetype seems to shimmer through the image of the matter-devouring "black holes" which astrophysicists have discovered in outer space, or, on a more mundane level, in the black-clad femmes fatales such as pop singers like Madonna.) However she appears, she is an expression of the dark, fertile, unknowable abyss of Being out of which all is born and into which all is again reabsorbed. None of the black goddesses, however, is as terror inspiring as Kali, Shiva's most awesome Shakti.

Kali Ma, "the black mother," is bloodthirsty and cruel like a man-eating tigress. She is time (kala) that mercilessly devours everything that dared manifest itself in the world of existence. She absorbs all, destroys all. For is it not true that every moment is immediately destroyed by time, every present becomes in an instant the past? Her ravishing hunger devours each second. Who can withstand her? Truly, she is sheerest evil for the ego, that sense of personal identity that longs to build itself a monument, give itself some hold, some sort of permanence.

How desperately humanity has tried to escape her clutches! Egyptians mummified their bodies, alchemists searched tirelessly for the "elixir of life," Hernando de Soto looked for the "fountain of eternal youth" in far-off Florida. And even now, laboratory chemists are trying to synthesize "the pill" that would extend life indefinitely, while gene-technologists place their hopes in the miracle of genetic engineering. In California, those who can afford it let themselves be quick-frozen in dry ice at the moment of death, in the hope that future scientists will be able to raise them from the dead. Others place their hope for personal continuance in sperm and ovum banks. In every case, it is the ego that wants to remain, that struggles heroically against all odds. Yet the strug-

Kali

gle is hopeless. Like a vampire, black Kali sucks life's blood and devours the corpses.

A common icon shows Kali drunk on blood and gore, dancing madly in the midst of a battle and doomsday fire over the bodies of the slain. There is no one to stop her! Even Shiva lies as a pale, bloodless corpse under her feet. With one of her four arms she is swinging the severed head of her opponent, and another hand is twirling a bloodstained scimitar. Except for a girdle of hacked-off arms, a necklace of fifty skulls, and earrings made from the corpses of children, she is stark naked. Wild, disheveled hair swirls around her head, while her three bulging, bloodshot eyes roll about in lunatic frenzy. A long, lolling red tongue, eager to lap up blood, hangs down her chin.

For the ethnocentric Westerner, Kali and her cult (including the sacrificing of buffalo bulls and billy goats) remain an abomination. British imperialists found in the colorful excesses of Kali worship welcome proof of their own moral and spiritual superiority. (That focus provided a ready pretext for ignoring their own dubious role in the exploitation of an entire subcontinent, under the guise of the civilizing mission of the white man.) But the swamis raise an admonishing finger, not to be too hasty in judgment. Is the image of a maltreated dead man, nailed upon a cross, not equally gruesome, and yet, the signpost of one of the most sublime spiritual mysteries?

It is the nature of such symbolism to transcend common reason and sense. Kali stands for the dark mystery out of which all arises and into which it disappears again. The ego, bound and limited by reason and the five senses, is in no position to be the judge. In a deeper sense, Kali is the loving Mother, who, through the power of time, graciously destroys the monstrous ego-illusion. "Fear not!" she gestures with her right hand as she blesses her devotees with the abhaya mudra, while her other hand, extended in the varada mudra, indicates the fulfillment of one's true wishes.

According to Swami Harshananda of the Sri Ramakrishna Ashram in Bangalore, the fifty skulls of Kali's necklace are the

Chamunda—one of Kali's many forms

fifty sounds of language, which cause the ether to vibrate and through which the entire universe will remanifest.[3] Nothing is lost. The destruction is but making the way for constant re-creation. The severed arms dangling from her belt stand for the selfless, and, hence, karma-less, deeds we have dedicated to the goddess. The loose, wild hair is expression of her unfettered freedom. Shiva, the core of Being, is clothed in his Shakti, which emanates from him, but there is nothing that can cover Shakti; therefore, she is shown completely naked *(digambara)* and black.

Naturally, not everybody interprets the icon of Kali in such a sublimated manner. Bengalese and Nepalese peasants celebrate the Black Mother in a much more concrete way. They satisfy her blood lust by sacrificing black billy goats or water buffalo bulls in front of her idol. The devotion shown during such ceremonies stands in stark contrast to the efficient butchery at our Western meat factories. As the earth drinks the blood, she will bring forth rich harvests. (The association of blood sacrifice and soil fertility is anthropologically common enough that it needs no further comment.)

Since there is no resisting the power of such a goddess, one can but submit to her will and soothe her with sacrifices.* In the *Kalika Purana,* Shiva tells his sons, the bhairavas, that Mother Kali can be pleased for five hundred years with the blood of a gazelle or of a rhinoceros, but the blood of a human being satisfies her for a thousand years.

Calcutta, the city of Kali, in the heart of Bengal, appears to the Western visitor as strange as the goddess herself. No one remains neutral about it: one loves it or one is appalled by it. In the midst of a slum, crowded with homeless Hindu refugees from Muslim persecution in Bangladesh, Kali has her main temple. There, sensation-seeking tourists who dare run the gauntlet of cripples, beggars, and thieves, may witness one of these animal sacrifices. This is the neighborhood where the white-robed nuns of Mother Theresa swarm out like vultures, collecting the dying and destitute. For many Bengalis, there was little doubt that the old nun, dressed in a white sari (white, as the color of death in

---

*The sacrifice to Kali can also be an expression of atonement. For example, in *Autobiography of an Unknown Indian,* the Bengali writer Nirad C. Chaudhuri tells readers that when he returned from England as a young man, after having finished his studies, his uncle sacrificed a bull in front of the idol and bathed him from head to toe in the warm blood, in order to purify him of the moral and spiritual filth he had picked up in the land of the *mlechhas,* the unclean foreigners.

Asia), was none other than the goddess herself, for who else would care so much for the dead?

With Sri Ramakrishna (1834–1886), the Bengali saint who started as a temple servant at Kali's temple in Calcutta, the cult of the Black Mother reached new ethical heights. He honored every woman as Kali. In contrast, there are occultists for whom Kali worship has degenerated into pure black magic. As they slash the sacrificial animal, they call out the enemy's name, assuming that he'll die in the same manner. Murderers and criminals, like the thugs, often dedicate their atrocities to the wild goddess.

The thugs (also *phansigars* = stranglers) were ordinary peasants who belonged to a secret endogamous society that worshipped Bhowani-Kali by periodically going on expeditions during which they joined pilgrims and travelers, whom they strangled and robbed, when Kali provided them with favorable omens. Strict ritual and taboo regulated the undertakings of these were-tigers of Kali.

The thugs trace their origin back to Kali's battle with the demon Raktavijas, whose every drop of blood turned into a new monster. When Kali got tired of licking up so much blood, she made two men out of the sweat of her arms. She gave them knotted handkerchiefs and told them to continue killing the demons she pointed out to them, by strangling them and not shedding any blood.

The cult of the stranglers seems to be old indeed. Already the carvings in the Ellora Caves show thugs doing their work; and Old Persian legends tell of them. Villagers tolerated them, while some maharajas even taxed their loot. They carried on undisturbed until a clever British officer, William Sleeman, uncovered their activities and brought many hundreds to the gallows. The thugs themselves believed that Kali was punishing them for having abandoned their dharma by wantonly killing holy men, women, and a certain class of merchants that the goddess had tabooed. Sleeman was quite surprised to find out that most of the thugs were formally Muslims. When asked how they could worship a Hindu goddess, they told him that Kali was none other than Fatima, Muhammad's daughter—another example of Indian syncretism. Ever since the partition of India in 1947, there have been isolated rumors of a revival of the thuggees.[4]

The dacoits—armed gangs of peasants who plunder trains and the villas of the rich and ambush the police—operate also under the auspices of Kali. The female dacoit leader, Phoolan Devi, who terrorized

*Kali dancing on
Shiva's corpse*

the wild hinterlands of Uttar Pradesh during the late 1970s and early '80s, was worshipped by the local peasantry as an expression of the goddess. For several years, they hid the "dacoit queen," and fed her and her gang, making it impossible for the four-thousand-man security force to apprehend her.

The most common iconographical representation of the uncanny goddess shows her in frenzied dance on Shiva's lifeless, bleached body. The interpretation generally forwarded by Hindus is that Kali, inebriated from the blood she drank, was dancing her victory dance. Her gyrations were so wild that the earth threatened to come unhinged. In order to bring her back to her senses, Shiva laid himself under her feet. Being a normal Hindu woman, she was thunderstruck with shame when she saw her husband at her feet, for a woman's place is at the feet of her husband, not vice versa. Feeling ashamed, she stuck out her tongue. Historians of culture venture another interpretation. The icon represents the final victory of the indigenous black Mother Goddess of the originally matriarchal Dravidian cultures, over the male pantheon of the white, Aryan invaders. But there is another interpretation possible. Though he looks lifeless, Shiva, the archetypal shaman, is in a state of deep trance (samadhi). His anima has left its physical body in the form of Kali in order to accomplish wonderful, world-saving deeds in the supersensible world of gods, demons, and spirits. At the same time, the icon makes some of the basic tenets of Hinduism visible. It shows Shiva as the unmoved ground of being, upon which the ever changing, shimmering, endlessly varied play of divine energy (shakti) unfolds. Shiva is the resting pole around which Kali dances the dance of illusive existence.

❧ ANNAPURNA ❧

Like many of his devotees, Shiva lives as a beggar on earth. His daily round of begging keeps his poor family alive. Often, however, he cannot even get that together, for he is given to smoking hemp or eating bhang, which helps him forget his earthly misery. Whatever meager crumbs or few grains of rice that might be left from the day before are usually eaten by Ganesha's rat or Karttikeya's peacock. Often Parvati and the children must go hungry as in the following common folkloric story, which was related to me by a sadhu.

One day, Narada, the roguish messenger of the gods, came by the hovel they called home. Shaking his head in feigned indignation, he teased the poor woman. "Yes, indeed, your old man is a *bhola* (fool). He smokes dope while his wife and children are starving!"

That was more than Parvati's pride could bear. Taking Ganesha on her arm and leading little Karttikeya by the hand, she decided to go and do the begging herself. After a few hours, having sobered up a bit, Shiva finally started his rounds, only to find his pleas unheeded and the doors slammed in his face. How could he have known that his wife had been everywhere before him? Utterly disappointed and close to tears, he came home with an empty begging bowl. Parvati, however, met him on the doorstep with a full bowl of rice and started to feed him with a spoon. Ever since, this manifestation of the goddess became known as Annapurna, "she who is rich in food." Shiva was so overjoyed at her kindness that he hugged her, pressing her so

Annapurna feeding Shiva (Nineteenth century)

hard to his side that they melded together to form one being. In this half-male, half-female form, they are known as Ardhanarishvara.

There is another version of the story:[5]

One day Shiva lectured his wife: " The world is an illusion. Nature is an illusion. Even food is just maya."

That was too much for Parvati to bear; after all, she is the mother of all material things, including food.

"All right," she shouted as she walked out the door, "If you think I am just an illusion, let's see how you and the rest of the world get along without me."

Her departure caused havoc in the universe. Time stood still. The seasons did not change, the earth became barren. There was no food to be found in all the three worlds. Gods, demons, animals, humans hungered and cried like children who had lost their mother. Even the sages cried, "Salvation makes no sense to an empty stomach."

News reached Shiva that Parvati had reappeared in Benares and set up a kitchen for hungry pilgrims. He ran there as fast as he could, and joined the endless line of hungry creatures waiting for alms. As he held up his begging bowl in front of her, he said, "Now I realize that the material world, like the spirit, cannot be dismissed as an illusion."

Parvati smiled and fed him with her own hands.

Annapurna—
the goddess of food

In Varanasi, the city of beggars and saints, Annapurna has a famous temple. The kind goddess is shown as a light-skinned matron holding a bowl of rice and a serving spoon. Anyone who worships her, as Shiva did, will never have to go hungry. It is said that because of her constant presence in the holy city, no one has ever starved in Varanasi. She herself will not eat unless everybody else has been fed.

Annapurna seems to be an ancient Indo-European goddess. The Romans worshipped an Anna Perenna, whose feast they celebrated in springtime with wine-drinking excursions into the countryside. Legend tells of the time when the plebeians battled with the patricians and the Romans had to flee to the surrounding hills. They were about to die of hunger when suddenly the goddess appeared and fed them cakes she had baked.[6]

⁓ GANGA ⁓

The Indo-Europeans of the days of yore experienced all rivers as female divinities. In India this is still so. For the Hindus, Mother Ganges, or Ganga Ma, as they lovingly call her, is the purest and most heavenly of all river goddesses. Like Parvati, her younger sister, she is the daughter of the king of the mountains.

Stories tell that after Sati had immolated herself in the fire and was about to be reborn to the mountain lord and his wife, she split herself into two persons, Ganga and Parvati, both of whom were married to

Shiva. In some Bengali accounts, Ganga is even made out to be the first wife of Shiva. He has to sneak out of the house at night to meet with his dark lover, Parvati, in the garden. In any case, both goddesses play the role of a mother for Shiva's son, Karttikeya. In many popular folktales, the beautiful river goddess appears as Parvati's rival. Parvati is so jealous that she heaps abuses upon her, calling her a harlot and cursing her to be born as a *chandali*, an untouchable prostitute, a status equal to that of a dog or a pig. But Ganga pays her back often enough. She washes away the sand lingams Parvati builds or even tries to sweep her sister away in her floods.

Once, in the beginning of time, Ganga, a proud, independent maiden, frolicked in the wide, flowering fields of heaven. She had no desire to go down to earth. Indeed, she was vehemently opposed to the idea. How the meditation of a saint brought her down will be told in the following story, which is related in the *Ramayana* and frequently told as part of the oral tradition:

Sagara was an ancient king who had two queens. One queen bore him a son and the other queen bore him a gourd, which contained sixty thousand seeds—which, after they had been placed in milk, also turned into sons. One day, in order to thank the gods for all the boons he had received and also to increase his realm even further, the king decided to stage a great horse sacrifice.

Such an *ashwamedha* was by no means a simple affair. The stallion chosen was allowed to roam where it pleased for a span of one year. Armed nobles and princes had to follow it to make sure it was not lost or, even worse, abducted by another king. In the latter case, it meant war. The loss of a consecrated horse was an omen of the greatest misfortune.

Sagara's sixty thousand sons took it upon themselves to follow the sacred horse. However, despite their vigilance, the unthinkable happened: the horse disappeared without a trace. Indra, fearing the impeccable king might become too powerful, had abducted the animal and hid it in the deepest region of the underworld (Patala). The thunder god knew that a monarch who succeeds in completing one hundred such sacrifices would automatically become the next Indra, the next king of the heavens.

The sixty thousand princes had no choice but to search all worlds to find the stallion. They combed all lands, searched the wide seas, and climbed all mountains. It was of no avail. Finally, they started digging deep into the earth, down to the mighty elephants that hold it up. Disturbed, the elephants shifted weight, causing the earth to tremble and quake. This, in turn, bothered the rishis and the gods, making them very angry. At long last, the searchers reached Patala, deep, deep under the earth, and saw their horse grazing peacefully next to a meditating sage. Wasting no thought, they took him for the culprit who had abducted their animal and rudely roused him from his contemplations, threatening him with their weapons.

"Hand over our horse, you thief!"

They should have known better! One simply does not get away with disturbing a meditant! His anger took the form of a ball of fire that shot like lightning from his forehead and burned all sixty thousand to ashes on the spot.

King Sagara waited for many years, but his sons did not return. Nobody knew what had happened to them. However, the ritual, once begun, had to be completed, for it amounted to a promise made to the gods and, if word is not kept, the consequences are unspeakable. Thus, the king sent out his last son to find both the horse and his brothers.

For many years he searched and searched. In the meantime, old king Sagara died. Finally, the son died also, and the grandson continued the nearly hopeless search. But being keen of senses, he picked up the trail of his sixty thousand uncles into the underworld. At long last he reached Patala, where he came upon the old, meditating rishi and the consecrated horse peacefully grazing next to him. Being more polite than his predecessors, he waited and did not speak until the holy man addressed him first and revealed to him the fate of his uncles: "They were rude and deserved their fate! Now, they are bound in hell!"

"Great rishi," the young man asked carefully, "Is there no way to save them? For how shall the ancestors gain peace if there are no grandsons to sacrifice and pray for them?"

"There is only one way. If heavenly Ganga can be made to flow from heaven into hell and wet the ashes and bones, then only will they be cleansed from their sin and may go to heaven!" Then, gruffly, as is the manner of rishis, he told him, "Now, take the horse, and be gone!"

To bring the river of heaven down to the lower world would not be easy. It would take more years of strict penance than were left in the young king's life. Only his noble son Bhagiratha, Sagara's great-grandson, had the ability, purity, and will to undertake this difficult task. He traded the palace for the wilderness, his silks for bark cloth, and he meditated for ten thousand years without losing concentration until Brahma appeared, asking him which boon he desired. When Lord Brahma heard his wish, he sadly shook his head and told him, "What you desire is impossible! The earth could not bear the impact of that mighty stream cascading down upon her. Only if Shiva were willing to brake her fall by letting her flow through his hair, might it be possible."

Bhagiratha's filial piety and devotion to dharma left him no choice. For another ten thousand years he centered his mind on the god with the matted hair, while performing the most difficult ascetic exercises. Finally Shiva appeared to him and promised to help.

*Shiva catching Ganga
in his dreadlocks*

Ganga, the proud maiden, was in no way pleased to trade the pleasures of heaven for a journey to the underworld. But the power of the sage's austerities left her no choice. Sullenly, she looked down upon Shiva, who was ready to catch her in his mountain of matted, tangled curls.

"I shall wash him away!" she thought to herself gleefully. But Shiva read her thoughts. He caught her in his felted hair, like a fish in a net, and held the struggling maiden there for another ten thousand years, in order to dampen her pride. Bhagiratha nearly despaired. Finally, Shiva loosened but a single hair and she came rushing down his head and down the mountainsides as the seven main rivers of Earth. Since that day, Shiva became also known as Gangadhara, "carrier of Ganga," and the river is lauded as Harasekhara, "Shiva's crown."

The young river flooded the once dry plains. Wherever she passed, the land greened and blossomed. Happiness spread among humankind and the beasts. Rippling, splashing, gurgling, clapping her wave-hands, she followed the sage Bhagiratha, who was guiding her way to the underworld, where the bones of his fallen ancestors awaited her reviving touch.

Then, an incident occurred that almost doomed Bhagiratha's effort. In her careless passing, Ganga's singing and splashing disturbed the meditations of the powerful rishi, Jahnu. Using his unspent ascetic power, he

*Ganga and dreadlocks—
attributes of Shiva*

simply drank her up, swallowing the entire river, and returned to his contemplations. All creatures, great and small, but, above all, Bhagiratha, pleaded that he release her again. Finally, moved out of respect for Bhagiratha's penance, he let her spurt out of his ear. Her sojourn through the rishi made her even purer than she had been before. Finally, her waters reached the enormous pit that Sagara's sixty thousand sons had dug and filled it with her flood. It became the ocean. On and on she flowed until, at long last, she reached the underworld where her mere touch brought the dead back to life.

Ganga is an ancient Indo-European name related to such words as *going* and *gang*, indicating constant movement. The sacred river is an external picture of the stream of life's energies, the flow of wisdom, and the constant flowing of Shiva's shakti energy. Indeed, to the natives, the river does not flow with mere water, but with liquid shakti. The patient, selfless sacrifice of a saint and the divine grace of God, in combination, brought this virginal stream from heaven in order to heal and purify a sorrowful world. Whoever bathe in her stream not only wash the dust from their body, but also the sins from their soul. Descending into the deepest depths, she reconnects that which is dead with the stream of life and carries it upward again into heaven. The Milky Way shows her path across the sky. And, way up there, in the northern sky, we can still see the seven great rishis, the seven stars of the Big Dipper *(Arctos major)*, meditating on her "riverbank." The eternal cycle completes itself when she descends again to the earth as fertilizing rain and bubbling mountain streams.

Kashi on the Ganges

Ganga's water is the soma offering poured on the ever hot Shiva lingam, to cool it down. In this way, Ganga belongs as much to the lingam as the more earthen yoni of dark Parvati. Together, Ganga and Parvati are Shiva's companions. For a lingam puja (worship of the lingam), nothing is better suited than libations of water from the river Ganges.

The Ganges also stands for the ever flowing stream of consciousness, in whose passing, master meditants— fishermen in the spirit—watch the eternal archetypes glide past their third eye. It is the original "television," which wiser souls once watched to find out the ways of the gods. On Earth, there is no better place to watch this television than in the holy city the Indians

A Brahmin teaching on the banks of the holy river

call Kashi, "the shiny one." It is Shiva's favorite place on earth. Anyone who still has an inkling of spiritual vision will notice it immediately when sitting on the banks of the Ganges in Benares. Effortlessly, like schools of golden and silver fish, the archetypal images that live in the soul, will pass in front of one's inner eye. It is no puzzle that every year hundreds of thousands, even millions, of pilgrims visit this *thirtha* (ford) to the higher worlds. It is a life-changing experience to join the multitudes bathing in the early morning hours when the rising sun turns the water into liquid gold.

Countless old people come to Benares to await death on the banks of the holy river, for it is said that all who die here, with the name of God on their lips, will achieve salvation. For thousands of years the funeral pyres have burned here and constantly the chant of the pall-bearers is heard: *"Rama nam satje heh!"* (God's name is truth.) Gently, Mother Ganga takes the dead into her bosom. Innocent souls, those of cows, children, and saints, as well as those, like lepers, whose suffering during life has purified them, are put directly into the water. All others, because of their sins, must pass through the portal of the fire of the pyre. Their ashes are then put into the waters of the river.

Ashrams and thousands of temples flank the shore of the glistening river. River dolphins surface and submerge again, gracefully and rhythmically, giving the impression of the passing of

Yogi on a platform in the middle of the Ganges

gigantic river serpents. Wooden boats pass. Little boys drive herds of water buffalo to their daily, refreshing bath. Pilgrims bathe and build little lingams of mud along the shore, decorating them with marigolds and sweet-smelling incense. Black-skinned fishermen cast their nets. Washers, standing in the water up to their knees, wash the city's clothes and lay them to dry on the shore. Jackals hurry along the bank, hoping to find an edible morsel, while eagles and vultures turn majestic circles high up in the sky. Barbers squat in the shade of pipal trees, waiting to shave the crania of mourners or pilgrims. Brahmins, having taken their purifying bath, read loud and ostentatiously out of some holy scriptures. At the same time, boatloads of pious pilgrims, singing "OM Shiva Mahesvara Mahadev," pass on their way to have darshana with a 226-year old yogi who has installed himself on a platform in the middle of the wide stream.

No harsh motor noises desecrate the atmosphere. Because of the drifting, submerged sandbanks, no steam or motor ship can safely pass. The British had tried to introduce regular steamship travel between Benares and Allahabad, but, it is said, a yogi, disturbed by the smoke and noise, merely pointed his finger at the monstrosity, at which it instantly rammed into a hidden sandbank. It is, indeed, a special place, a good place for finding one's Self. A common saying is that only a fool would ever leave Shiva's wonderful city on the Ganges once he has found it. But again, it is also said, "You can leave Kashi, but Kashi will not leave you!"

At Varanasi, Ganga turns for a short while northward, toward her origin, much like a newly wed bride who turns back to take one last look at her native village before going off to her husband's home. In this gesture, the river curves like a crescent moon. This, too, it is claimed, is the moon that sparkles as a diadem from Shiva's locks.

7

THE DANCER IN
THE FLAMES

————— ∾ —————

This is my greatest desire: without fail,
one day you'll show yourself to us,
My father with locks twisted like the
flames of a lighted fire
the place where you dance, in full night,
over the high flames . . .

ARPUTA TIRUVANTATI,
TAMIL POETESS, FOURTEENTH CENTURY

Let us visit once again the hidden pine forest, where honorable hermits and their chaste wives are meditating and practicing asceticism, and see how Shiva makes fools of them. In this version of the story, there are not just seven rishis but tens of thousands. They have shaven their heads in penance; they despise all mundane joys and passions. Unremittingly, they preach to the common people that the universe is infinite having no beginning and no end and that there is no God who saves souls, but that each must work diligently on one's own salvation. (The suspicion rises that this story tells of the struggle of emerging Hinduism with the dogmas of the Buddhists and Jains.)

Gracious Shiva, seeing the damage these fanatics were doing, decided to free them of their delusions. Using the power of his magical illusion, he stepped into their world as a most handsome young yogi. Vishnu was with

135

*Nataraja, the
cosmic dancer*

him in the form of a beguiling Mohini, a heavenly nymph. At the sight of the young Adonis, the rishis' wives were dazzled. Forgetting their duties, like silly girls, they daydreamed of being caressed by his strong, white arms and kissed by his full lips. They let the water jugs slide from their hands and break; they let the food scorch in the pans.

Their husbands made fools of themselves likewise. Unthinkingly, they threw away the fruits of thousands of years of hardest penance in order to feast their longing eyes on the voluptuous curves of the heavenly maiden. But then, they suddenly regained their senses and were terrified to realize that their resolves had so weakened. Their shock quickly turned into hateful anger, which consumed the rest of the fruits of their asceticism. They meanly rebuked their wives and began to hurl the vilest curses at the handsome yogi and his seductive female companion. Combining their magic powers, they ignited a fire into which they chanted mantras of death and destruction. On and on they chanted, fanning the flame into the form of a monstrous, murderous tiger. This they directed to tear the strange, naked interloper to pieces. But the yogi skinned it with the nail of his little finger. Next, the hermits let a gigantic poisonous viper rise from the magic fire; but Shiva wrapped it around his neck as though it were a silk shawl. Seeing their efforts fail, the furious ascetics combined all their remaining strength to conjure the most terrible weapon of which they could conceive. It was a wicked, black, misshapen dwarf with an invincible club. But as soon as he leaped out of the flames, Shiva bowled him over and began to dance light-footedly on the squat torso, taking on his divine emanation as Nataraja, the king of dancers, revealing himself as the lord of the universe and of eternity.

At this, the poor rishis fell to the ground, trembling with fear, while all the gods of the universe appeared to behold the wonder of the dancing god. The world serpent Anant-Shesha, on whose back Vishnu sleeps in the intervals between creations, was so enthralled by the splendor of the spectacle, that he asked Vishnu for leave. His reptilian heart was filled with only one wish, and that was to be allowed to go on a pilgrimage to Mount Kailash. There, he wanted to engage in severe penance so that he might find out the meaning of this overawing cosmic dance.

Ganesha worshipping Shiva

The holy family:
Shiva, Parvati,
and Ganesha

Nandi, Shiva's Bull
(Godowlia, Varanasi)

Stone nagas in a temple park
(Tirumakudal Narsipur, near Mysore)

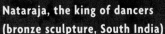

Ardhanarishvara,
the half-man/half-woman god
(Kumbakonam, Tamil Nadu)

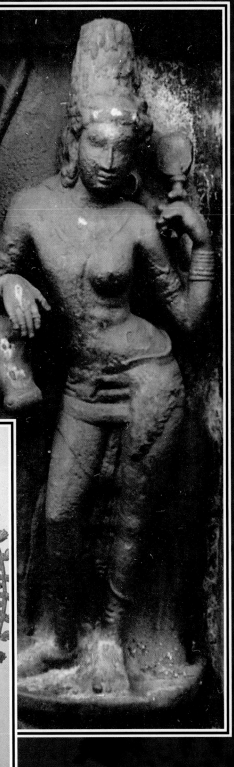

Nataraja, the king of dancers
(bronze sculpture, South India)

Swami Ganapathi Sachchidananda worshipping the Shiva lingam (Mysore)

Sadhus on the banks of the Ganges (Varanasi)

Worship of Bhairava
(Batuk Bhairav Temple, Varanasi)

An unusual Shiva sadhu

Bhairava (Kathmandu, Nepal)

Kali in a small shrine at a Durga
Temple (Durga Kund, Varanasi)

Durga killing the buffalo
demon (popular statue)

Durga in a festive garment
(Durga Kund, Varanasi)

Lingam worship (Assi Ghat, Varanasi)

101 Lingams in a small shrine (Talakad, near Mysore)

Thus it happened that the thousand-headed, jewel-crowned primordial serpent spent eons in single-minded devotion. Nothing distracted him, until one day, Shiva, appearing as Brahma riding on the gander, told him, "Your devotion is perfect! I shall reward you with eternal paradise!"

But the snake refused paradise. Instead, it wanted to be allowed to continue watching Shiva's dance forever. At this, Shiva took on his own radiant form and taught Ananta the essence of wisdom, which are the Vedas, and promised him, "You will shed your serpentine form and you will be born of a human couple. When you are old enough to leave your parent's home, your footsteps will lead you to Chidambaram. There, in the shade of a hallowed grove, you shall find my lingam, which is cared for by an old meditant. You may help him in his duties, for here, at the Chidambaram Lingam, I reveal my eternal cosmic dance to all who have eyes to see."

Ever since, Chidambaram, a town on the coast south of Pondicherry, is a much-visited place of pilgrimage. It was here that the now world-famous bronze casting of Shiva-Nataraja, dancing in a ring of fire, originated.

Let us now look at this dancing god. Like Shankar, his face is calm and collected, and cobras and rudraksha beads decorate his limbs. But otherwise, he is in total motion, his hair swirling wildly around his head. Ganga is no longer visible as a jet of water, but as a tiny, hard-to-see female figure, riding the waves of his hair. The hand drum (damaru) no longer hangs silent on the trident, but vibrates energetically in his upper right hand. Every one of his four hands is flashing a special gesture, or mudra, expressing esoteric meaning. The upper left hand, held cupped like a half moon *(ardhachandra mudra),* contains a blazing fire. A third arm, bent like the trunk of an elephant *(gajahasta mudra),* reminds the worshipper of Ganesha, the clever bull elephant who overcomes all resistance. It points down toward the uplifted left foot, indicating cosmic lightness and nonattachment. The fourth hand stretches its open palm toward the beholder in the abhaya gesture, signaling, "Fear not! May peace be with you!"

Shiva's right foot presses upon the demon-dwarf Muyalaka, "the relentless one," trodding him to the ground. The brutal dwarf is the symbol of the smallness of egoism, caught in samsara, the illusion of life and death. He is also called Apasmara,

The damaru,
Shiva's hand drum

"the epileptic," for our egoism and spiritual blindness cause us to continually stumble and fall. Gravity, graveness, and heaviness of soul have pulled him down, for he has forgotten the cosmic joy and lightness of divine laughter and light. But when the divine feet touch him, the dwarf begins to sing ecstatically, much as the Tamil Shaivite poet, Pampitti Chittar:[1]

> *The Good Foot*
> *which is lifted up*
> *I've seen.*
> *I've seen the Light too:*
> *I've seen the dancer inside*
> *the Pure Space:*
> *the feet imprinted on*
> *the attacking head*
> *are the True Guru's Feet,*
> *so*
> *dance snake!*
> *Dance!*

Of course, the downtrodden pygmy can also be interpreted as the mortal body of a shaman, lying entranced, witnessing the glory of his immortal, higher Self. Indeed, the dwarfish ego, which continuously seems to trouble those trying to follow a spiritual path, is a necessary precondition, in order that the Divine might manifest itself. The problem of most mortals is that they identify themselves with this ego, instead of realizing their divine Self.

❧ SHIVA'S DANCES ❧

In Shankar, resting motionless in meditation, the three primal principles, the red, white, and black gunas, are in harmonious, undisturbed balance. But when Shiva becomes Nataraja, these elements are swirled into motion, churned and infinitely mixed and remixed. When he starts the drumbeat, the Oneness of Shankar's silence is shattered. The countless trillions upon zillions of rhythms and pulses of Creation start their beat, for all of Nature is dance: the dance of wind and waves, the rounds of seasons and tides, the swirl of planets and galaxies, the reveling of elves, elemental beings, and angels, the frolic of the animals, the coming and going of thoughts and feelings, going on endlessly. At long last, even the scientists cannot ignore the metaphor and begin to talk meaningfully of the dance of subatomic particles swirling through the cosmos as ever transforming fields of matter and energy.[2]

What is dance, but the continual loss and instantaneous regaining of balance? Shiva's dance is the fine edge of the universe tumbling into chaos and destruction and the simultaneous recreation of poise, in a continuous, ecstatic, spontaneous whirl of creation-destruction-creation-destruction.

Holy men drunk on God, and lovers caught in the contagion of Shiva's bliss, start dancing through life in a similar way, moving lightly on the razor's edge between life and death, petrifaction and conflagration, dissolution and new creation; they dance ecstatically along, in the here and now, between the past and the future. Only those persons, apparently mad, who have discovered their own "Shiva-nature" can dance so freely, gracefully, and fearlessly; otherwise they would fall into panic and stumble in terror like Muyalaka the dwarf. Shiva's liberated souls are berserkers, high on the sword dance of existence, dervishes twirling out of the fetters of ego and high-wire artists stepping across the yawning chasm of the void. They are surfers on the crest of the steadily rushing, rolling, cascading wave of their life. Any instant, they could be dropped into the abyss of death. Even to think about it constitutes a "wipe-out." But they do not think, like the encapsulated ego-pygmy thinks. For them, there is no subject, no "other" to think about, for they are one with the wave, here and now, one with the entire ocean! They have understood the meaning of the abhaya gesture of Shiva's open hand. Thus, they dance the dance of liberated souls. Like Nataraja, they are surrounded by a mantel of blazing flames: it is their aura of light, their shimmering rainbow cloak, and it is the glow that accompanies all saints.

As Nataraja shakes his drum, the first sound *(shabda)* arises. Like the proverbial Buddhist's sound of one hand clapping, it is the sound originating from the One, not from the interplay of two opposites. It is the *Ur*-sound, the primordial vibration upon which all other vibrations follow. It is the OM, the first syllable, which, if it fell silent, would mark the end of the universe. It is the all-moving Logos, which generates all phonetics, all languages, starting with the first of all languages, Sanskrit, developing into the Babylonian babble of the multitude of tongues and finally into the growling, grunting, snorting, and chirping of the animals.

The sound of the drum moves the ether (akasha), which in turn sets the elements into motion—the air, then the fire, then water and the solid matter. Now Brahma begins to breathe. Out of his forehead the "creators of the world," the demiurges or *prajapatis*, are born, and from them arise all the creatures and things that fill existence. With the sound of the drumbeat begins the cosmic game, the *lila* of the One and his Shakti. Shakti, God's feminine energy nature, comes alive as a tiny point (bindu) or as a golden egg *(hiranyagarbha)* and begins to expand into infinity, populating the universe with countless ever changing forms and names, which multiply, thrive, wither, and die, only to reappear metamorphosed.

Like all icons, the one of Nataraja's dance has a multitude of interpretations. For the Hindu believer, it is a symbol of the totality of being: the drum represents the continuous process of creation *(srishti)*, the open hand stands for the preservation *(sthiti)* and the hand pointing downward, for the destruction *(samhara)* of the universe. The foot that grinds the dwarf into the dust represents the veiling *(tirobhava)* of the universe in darkness, while the uplifted foot shows God's grace *(anugraha)*.

Another way of interpreting the icon is as a visual expression of the most holy Shaivite mantra: *OM NAMAH SHIVAYA.* The hand holding the fire is the *NA*, the resting foot is the *MA*, the hand with the drum is the *SHI*, the hand pointing downward is the *VA*, and the open palm is the *YA*.[3]

The Ananda Tandava (Sanskrit *ananda* = joyful, *tandava* = vigorous, dynamic dance), shown in the Chidambaram representation, is the best known of Shiva's dances. But, as the god of dancers (Nateshvara), he dances many different dances—one hundred and eight, say the swamis. On the burning ghat of Manikarnika, on the banks of the Ganges, he dances a wild, crazed dance with his drunken imps and ghouls, devouring the mortal remains of the deceased, freeing them of their material husks. In Benares also, he dances the dance of victory over the elephant demon who took pleasure in vexing the saints and mocking the holy Vishvanath Lingam. Before skinning the elephant monster and freeing him from his demonic incarnation, Shiva danced, eight-armed, on his head, drumming wildly, swinging his trident, twirling the sling in which sinners ensnare themselves, and wielding a sword and a skull. Other dances show him holding the restless deer or the double-bladed ax, indicating steadiness and keenness of spirit. Hissing vipers entwine his limbs even as he dances. These reptiles can be interpreted as the fascinating *tremendum* his being radiates, or as the five external senses that can poison the soul, or even as aspects of Shesha, the cosmic serpent to whom it was granted to watch the dance forever.

In the Urdhva Tandava, Shiva dances in a contest with naked Kali to see who is the better dancer. Since Kali represents the blind, unfettered, black, absolute energy (shakti) of the universe, she is sure that she is the very best dancer. As they dance, she is able to imitate Shiva's each and every movement perfectly. But, then, one of Shiva's earrings falls, which he effortlessly catches with his foot and replaces on his ear in a single swoop without her even noticing it. That establishes him as the king of dancers once and for all.

His dance steps mark the creation and the destruction of the universes. In the Kodu Kotti dance he rocks destructively in heavy-metal style, bringing about the fall of civilizations. In the Pandam, he levels the three fortresses of the demonic ego forces. In the Kodu Kapalan, a demented Shiva swings the severed head of the Creator (Brahma) in his hands. In the Samhara Tandava, he dances, as the dreadful Bhairava, the total destruction of the universe and its disappearance into the void *(pralaya)* that separates the cycles of creation. All these themes find expression in the beautiful classical dances of India (the Kathak, Manipuri, Bharata, Natyam, Kathakali, Kuchipudi). Though often not understanding the complex symbolism, the tourist can nonetheless appreciate the aesthetic beauty of the movements.

Above all and foremost, however, Shiva dances in the fiery ring of our hearts. Here, in the center of our being, he, who is our own true Self, dances the joy of being, as well as the dance of doom that turns ego, greed, hate, false pride, and jealousy into pure ash. This, our flaming heart chakra, is his true burning ghat and funeral pyre.

ᰦ THE DRUM ᰧ

Indian cosmogony abounds with creation myths and creators. They create the world out of their sweat, out of their semen, out of their mind. They bring it forth by budding like plants or by chopping up the original sacrifice into many separate parts. The most common story of creation is one that tells of Vishnu. He is sleeping on the world serpent, drifting in the ocean of chaos. As he awakens, a delicate stalk starts to grow from his navel, forming a lotus bud. When the tender, fresh pink petals of the lotus blossom open, one sees therein the four- or five-headed, bearded grandfather of all creatures sitting in deep contemplation. In his meditation, the

Shamans "creating" the universe
with dance and drum

new universe is born. The gods spring from his brow while the demons escape his colon as farts.

The complex of creation myths surrounding Nataraja provides a very different picture. After Shiva has finished his meditations, he rises and begins to drum and dance. As the beat shatters the fathomless silence, the scintillating, illusory "reality" (maya) starts to manifest itself, twirling like a dancing girl dressed in veils of colorful silk, bewitching the senses and enthralling the mind. Only a shaman goes about manifesting his inner visions in this way. Using the power of song, dance, and drum, he conjures an entire universe for his spellbound audience. He lets the gods, ghosts, ancestors, demons, magic plants, and animals appear, and then he releases them into the stream of existence, into Time/Space on this side of Being. The worlds thus drummed into substantiality are not mere entertainment gigs, which catch the attention until "real" reality asserts its dominance once again. No, the shaman conjures the very matter of fact of existence itself, as far as the tribe is concerned! He is not a mere entertainer but a creator, a "thinger," lifting all things that be out of the abyss of the dark unconscious, the void, the "unthought of." Whatever his voice, drumbeat, and mime pushes into existence, remains. It remains for generations, as a basis for future thought, dreams, decisions, hopes, and expectations.

Every human being knows the mesmerizing power of the drumbeat. Already as a fetus in the womb, every individual has her mother's heartbeat as a steady accompaniment, long before a conscious sense of ego has developed. (In the same way, all string and wind instruments are reminiscent of the rushing of the blood through the mother's veins and of the mother's breathing.) Every drumbeat is a transmutation, permutation, or metamorphosis of the mother's oceanic heartbeat, which resonates at the basis of our soul for our entire life. Because of this, the clever shaman can use the drum as a bridge to the deeper layers of our psyche. With it, he can sound out the depths, penetrating to archaic layers of the soul, where there is not yet thought or reflection, where fine, pristine ethereal/astral vibrations have not yet jelled into solidity, where an ego consciousness has not yet hardened the flow of these vibrations into final, rigid forms. The drum can produce what psychologists call "hypnotic regression" and touch the deeper, archetypal self that is still one with the cosmos, open to all other forms of being and connected with the most distant stars. It can take one on the magic journey to Shiva himself, ferrying the initiate through wonder worlds and fairy tale realms, past the elemental beings, the gods and archetypes. A real shaman knows the paths that lead through these dimensions to the Source, for he is fearless, knowledgeable, and respectful. As he is not just a lunatic, he also knows the way safely back and brings with him the treasure of new creations.

His drum guides his steps. It is his "mount." Does the prattle of the drum not echo like the hoof beat of horses or reindeer? Because it is his riding animal, the shaman's drum is usually made from the hides of just such fleet-footed herd animals. In northern Eurasia, reindeer hide is stretched over the drum ring. Thus, it is said that he rides a reindeer through the air on his magic flights. The symbolism is still alive in the Nordic Santa Claus, who rides from the North Pole on a reindeer sled at the holy tide of winter solstice, to climb down the chimney into the hearth (heart!) where he leaves magical gifts and the nuts and seeds of new fertility.

In the right setting, at dusk, by the flickering campfire or in the light of the full moon, the gifted drummer can drive her companions into complete abandon or frenzy. These states, often amplified by psychedelic herbal drugs, lift the soul out of the restrictions of the mundane, ego-centered personality, allowing for "reprogramming" to occur. Such techniques, developed way back by the early Stone Age hunting societies, are not really completely foreign to us. Rock concerts and Holy Roller (Pentecostal) revivals exhibit many of these traits. The rhythm possesses body and soul, pushing the critical, rational, recently evolved cerebral function aside, while making room for the old reptilian brain to connect the person with the instincts and the collective consciousness that is the basis of the group spirit. All too often, such an altered state of consciousness seems to the cool, objective observer to be primitive, bizarre, and because of its sexual undertones, perhaps even obscene.

Drumming takes on new importance when the established cultural patterns wear thin and lose their adaptive function, when traditional modes of acting and cognizing lose their meaning, as happened when native, preliterate societies clashed with world colonialism. Creative energy and fresh courage is drummed out of the depths of the collective (or racial) unconscious. When this occurs, colonial administrators, traders, and missionaries become ill at ease. The natives are restless! It is time for a punitive expedition of the colonial military force, which in its turn also churns its drums to muster courage. In any time of war or crisis, the drum rules the movement of the people. The marching of troops is also a form of dance, a virile tandava, preparing the people for self-sacrifice in the name of values (God, Fatherland, Democracy) that transcend the individual concern for safety. In this way, societies master life-threatening crises.

The master drummer not only can excite and rouse to action, but she can slow the rhythm to the point that it puts the listener to sleep, hypnotizing him. Instead of exploding into ecstasy and rage, the participant is driven into himself in a form of "enstasy," or trance. In this manner, inner landscapes open up before the mind's eye and lift beyond mundane reality. This phenomenon has been researched thoroughly enough by now to be used commercially: there are soothing tapes for stressed business managers, gentle beats that help soothe the pain and anxiety at the dentist or put critical faculties to sleep while spending money at the supermarket. Then there is the slow, somber beat of the death-tolling drum, accompanying the coffin to the grave and putting the mourners in a contemplative mood.

A further inheritance from our Stone Age ancestors is the knowledge of arhythmic drumming, with a beat that counters the heart rhythm. Sorcerers used this arhythmic beat as a part of death-magic. For a long time, scientists, those curious priests of the Enlightenment, considered such death-magic impossible, pitching it, together with flying witches, voodoo dolls, and zombies, into the garbage heap of superstition. But a modern medical science has revised itself. It knows all too well how chaotic rhythms can induce subliminal anxiety, which might intensify to the point of panic. This occurs when the signals of the sympathetic and the parasympathetic nervous system (those "switch-on" and "switch-off" systems responsible for heartbeat, breathing, and endocrine glandular activity) are driven to chaos as a response to such asynchronic drumming. If the victim is subjected to this long enough, the organs are tremendously stressed. This, accompanied by frightful mental imagery, may actually lead to death. It is the rhythm of Nataraja's Samhara Tandava dance!

The slow, steady thumping of the drum skin can create hypnotic half-trance. A common event in any town on the Subcontinent can serve as an illustration: An emaciated man, covered with ashes, his matted, bleached hair piled up on his head like a turban, is wending his way through the crowded market. A small, silver Shiva-trident pierces each cheek and another fixes his outstretched tongue, like a butterfly in a collector's case. His hands hold a garlanded picture of Shankar, along with a mirror. As though he were saying, "Look at your Self," he invites to a Shiva darshana. All the while, his wife, one child at her breast and another child clutching the seams of her beggar's dress, is sounding a drum in a slow, steady, haunting beat, maintaining her husband's half-trance.

Another illustration from Nepal: An elderly *jhankrie* (Nepalese shaman) calls upon Lord Shiva as he steadily rattles the damaru. The little boy next to him starts rolling his eyes as he fades away into trance. When he is fully entranced, the shaman pushes the blade of a hunting knife through his neck. The youngster does not seem to notice; only his fingers and toes twitch uncontrollably and a small rivulet of blood trickles to the ground. Now he is ready to soothsay for the assembled peasants, answering his "yes" and "no" in a strange creaking voice that seems to come from far away. All the while, the damaru's rattle serves to maintain the trance.

The drum—the shaman's horse—is so vital that nothing regarding it is left to coincidence. When, for example, a Siberian magician proceeds to make himself a drum, he searches out a special tree, one that has been struck by lightning.[4] Out of its wood he will carve the frame of the drum. Often he sets up camp underneath this tree, or he might fell it and set it up in his lodge as the supporting pillar. It becomes his ladder upon which to climb into the upper and lower worlds, during his spirit séances. Upon this pole, symbolizing the middle of the universe, he ties his spirit horse, that is, he hangs his conjuring drum. In a similar way, Shiva hangs his damaru on the trident next to his seat. The Shankar icon shows the drum hanging just below the prongs, at what would be the level of the heart. This makes good sense, for the drum is but an externalized heart. The symbolic complex involving the trident, the tree, the bolt of lightning, and the heart must, indeed, be ancient.

Some representations show a buffalo horn also hanging from the trident. The horn, a lunar symbol, is, like the drum, a spirit caller. At the same time, it is the original drinking vessel, the holder of mead or soma. Today's sadhus identify the horn next to Shankar's drum as the chilam, the pipe for smoking ganja.

But now it is time to leave this shaman god, who dresses in the pelts of wild beasts and dances with ghosts and goblins, to his visions and his ecstasy. Reverently, we bow before this archetype of all shamans and the lord of the animals, sitting alone in the snow or dancing in a ring of fire. Turning to more recent times in the history of humankind, we shall meet Shiva again, this time as a happily married family father, as the companion of the Great Mother of the Universe!

8

THE IDEAL FAMILY

———— ⚬〰⚬ ————

When the little children ask
to sit on their father's knee,
then even the dirt on their bodies,
seems a blessing to him.

KALIDASA,
INDIAN POET, FOURTH/FIFTH CENTURIES

A poster or wall painting that frequently smiles at passers by from the gaudy blue walls of stores, *chai* shops, and the stands of betel nut sellers, shows the "Holy Family." Arranged in the manner of a classical family portrait, one beholds a friendly Shiva sharing his throne with his wife Parvati and their two children. Mount Kailash is no longer a barren, frozen waste, but a green, sunny mountain meadow in springtime's bloom, as pretty as anything shown in a prospect advertising holidays in the Alps! Even though snakes still dangle in his hair, ash covers his forehead, and rudraksha beads garland him, he is no longer the homeless drifter, the harsh penitent, or the wild shaman. With a golden, jeweled crown and leggings of saffron silk, he presents himself as the *pater familias*. The trident in his right hand is now the scepter of a king. His left hand, if not holding a shell or the drum, lies gently around Parvati's shoulder. A third hand is extended in the teaching pose *(varada mudra)*, while a fourth hand holds an unfolded lotus at heart level. No longer grayish white like that of an ash-besmirched sadhu, or dark like the Tamilian Nataraja, Shiva's skin glows in an auspicious blue, like the color of a clear summer sky. His eyes are gentle and mild, no longer

147

*"The holy family" from
an Indian comic*

shut in inner contemplation or bulging out angrily like Bhairava's.

Parvati, sitting to his left, as is becoming of a Hindu wife, ogles him tenderly with soft, doe-like brown eyes. She too shines regally in her colorful silk sari, golden crown, and jewelry gracing her ears, nose, arms, ankles, fingers, and toes. Like her lord, she has flexed one leg, pressing its heel to cover her private parts, while the other foot is firmly planted on the ground.

She is holding her pudgy, four-armed, elephant-headed son on her lap. It is baby Ganesha. His beady eyes twinkle merrily and confidently, as though he knows that he is the most popular of all the gods for the common Indian masses. In his upper right hand he carries a trident or an elephant goad *(ankusha)*, in his upper left, he holds a noose *(pasa)*. The open palm of his lower right hand communicates the gesture of blessing *(abhaya mudra)*, while his lower left hand clutches a large bowl of caramel candies *(modaka, burfi)*. It must be noted that he owes his bulk to his hopeless addiction to such sugary delights. Beneath his gargantuan feet hunches a little mouse or rat, his riding animal *(vahana)!*

In some renderings of the family portrait, the other son, the six-headed Karttikeya, is shown standing next to his father. He is a stout little fellow decked out with a helmet and shield, while holding a sword and a bow and arrow. A bright peacock parades at his feet, ready to carry the warrior child—who is none other than the god of war—to any battlefield wherever he may be needed.

A milk-white bull lies at Shiva's feet and a lion brushes against the legs of the Mother Goddess. Thus, all the gods have their riding animals, which are, at the same time, expressions of their lower (animal) nature. In the same manner, Brahma rides the swan (or gander) Hamsa, the personification of life's breath. Vishnu flies on the sun-eagle Garuda, when he is not sleeping on the world serpent; Yama, the god of death, rides a black water buffalo, whereas Kama, the love-inducer, rides a parrot; Agni, the fire god, rides a ram; and Saturn rides on a vulture. (Our heathen Western ancestors were equally at home with such symbolism for we find Zeus, like Vishnu, flying on an eagle, Odin riding an eight-legged steed, while Thor's chariot is drawn by goats, Freya's by cats, Nerthus's wagon is pulled by cows, and that of the spring goddess Oestra (Easter) by bunnies.)

❧ KARTTIKEYA ❧

Karttikeya, also known as Skanda or in southern India as Subrahmanya or Murugan, had a most difficult time being engendered and born, as we have already seen. The story tells us that the egocentric demon, the asura Taraka, undertook everything he could to become master of the universe. In merciless self-torture, he stood on one leg for years, balancing on one toe, while staring in the sun and refusing all food. For years he sat on red-hot coals or on nails, stood on his head, balanced on one hand, let himself be hung upside down from a tree and, finally, be buried alive by his disciples—all without losing concentration. Brahma, the boon giver, had no choice but to grant him his mad wish. Since there has to be a loophole in every boon, he wished that, if he were to fall, then, only by a son of Shiva. Ha, did he think himself clever! He felt safe and strong, for how could Shiva, the otherworldly meditant, engender a son? Besides, Taraka had read in the great epos, the *Ramayana,* that Shiva was not even capable of having children. It was recorded there that at the beginning of time, the gods had done everything possible to prevent Shiva and Parvati from reproducing, for they feared that any child of that mighty pair would be too much for the universe to bear. It had been easy for the gods to find Shiva in a good mood and to extract the promise from him, that he would remain childless. They knew that it is difficult for Shiva to say no. Parvati, however, became extremely angry with them for taking advantage of his goodness and cursed their wives to be barren, also. And that is how it is to this day that the immortals cannot have natural issue, born in labor from a maternal womb, but only illusionary, magically wrought offspring, born of their minds or formed from various bodily excretions.

Karttikeya

*Kubera, the lord of
the elemental beings*

So Taraka, cocksure of himself, commenced to maltreat the gods, stealing Indra's eight-headed horse, robbing the thousand sea horses of Kubera, the hunchbacked king of the elemental spirits and guardian of the earth's treasures, stealing the heat from the sun, turning the summers cold, changing the courses of rivers, and disrupting the normal succession of the seasons. In short, the asura's whims became unbearable. Now the gods bitterly regretted the promise they had elicited from Shiva and tried everything to bring about a fruitful union of the divine ascetic and the young daughter of the mountain, anyway. But, as we have already heard, the unequaled charm of youth did not move the naked meditant with the bleached yellow hair. Even Kama, whose arrows of passion no one can resist, was burned to ashes by Shiva's angry eye.

*Young Parvati doing penance
to gain Shiva's love*

Tender Parvati, who loved Shiva from the moment of her birth and since all eternity from the bottom of her heart, had to realize that beauty, youth, and charm were not enough. Perhaps, though, if she joined him in deep meditation, he would finally reward her with a glance. With that resolve, the maiden left the gilded palace of her parents and wandered into the wilderness, where she exchanged her silks and satins for rude bark cloth. Refusing to eat even a morsel, she meditated day and night on the image of her beloved, which she had always carried in her soul.

Then one day, a handsome young Brahmin saw her and demanded of her why she, a young, noble maiden of unequaled beauty, would torture herself so cruelly.

"You are the flower of youth," he reminded her. "You could have everything your heart desires!"

Her ladies in waiting, who, because of their devotion, had accompanied Parvati into the forest, let the stranger know that the princess was doing it in order to gain the favor of Shiva. At that, he burst into roaring laughter. "How is that possible? How can this beautiful child want anything to do with that dirty, monkey-eyed fool whose family and background are unknown, who smears his body with ashes, who plays with poisonous vipers, and wraps himself in bloody hides?"

Gone was Parvati's tranquillity of mind! Her face flushed as she turned away. "It is a great sin to say such horrid words, but an even greater sin to listen to them!"

A young Brahmin taunts
Parvati by mocking Shiva

But barely had she spoken than the rash Brahmin changed his appearance: There stood Shiva! He had only been testing her resolve. And thus, the great love came about after all.

A lot of arrangements had to be made. Shiva sent Narada, the honey-tongued messenger of the gods, to the palace of the mountain king Himalaya and his queen, Mena, to ask for the hand of their daughter in his behalf. The mother was hesitant, for not all she had heard about Shiva had been positive. But finally, at the urging of the gods, and because she knew her child's inner-most desire, she gave her assent. The parents hired the architect of the gods, Vishvakarman, to build the marriage platform. Stores of pastries, sweets, wine, curds, and barley cakes were stacked up and invitations to the gala festival were sent to all the guests. All the rivers and mountains, all the gods, heavenly musicians, and dancers were invited.

Finally, on the day that astrologers had determined to be most auspicious, the festival began. The gleaming chariots of the lords and princes of the universe, accompanied by troops of dancers, jugglers, elephants, and soldiers, started pouring into the city. Mena, mother of the bride, held watch from her tower, eager to see her son-in-law arrive. Once, she saw a hero, shining brighter than the sun, riding a white elephant bull, leading a drum-ming and trumpeting host of most noble companions, dancing maidens, and heavenly musicians.

"How beautiful," Mena sighed. "That must be Shiva, my future son-in-law!" But, alas, she was told that it was merely Indra, lord of the heavens, one of Shiva's servants. As one procession followed another, each more

Shiva with his entourage on the way to the wedding

grandiose than the one before, Mena had to be told again and again that its leader was not Shiva, but just another of his vassals.

All of a sudden, toward evening, a train of wildly drunken goblins, trolls, evil spirits, and bhutas (fiendish creatures) appeared. Howling or singing discordantly, fighting among themselves, grunting, huffing, slobbering and pissing on other guests, and carrying on in a most indecent manner, they rushed down the street. A dirty, unkempt beggar covered with snakes and powdered with ashes rode in their midst, bearing a skull in one hand and a trident in the other. Mena was about to call the guards—but then fainted when told that this was Shiva. When she came to, she was inconsolable. She would rather poison or drown her daughter than bear the disgrace of giving her to such a misfit!

Her husband agreed. "Lock the gates! The marriage is called off! He may be a great god, but he will not marry my daughter!"

Parvati started to cry.

At that, her father tried to console her. "Don't worry, child, we will find a better groom for you!"

She sobbed, saying, "No, I want only Shiva!"

Her mother could not believe her ears. "Oh, how terrible. I think that terrible yogi must be a sorcerer. He has cast a spell on our child!"

The gods had to work hard to calm her mind and to make Shiva promise to show himself in a more favorable light. Parvati herself prayed to Shiva: "Do it for me, my lord. Show them what they want to see!"

Shiva heard her prayer and appeared as the personification of all that a mother could wish for in a son-in law. Mena was astounded. "Is that the same one who rode the bull, who was dressed in a strip of elephant hide?"

"The same one," assured Vishnu.

"And who are those handsome boys and girls standing behind him?"

"Those are the ganas, the heavenly hosts, the groom's party."

Before she could ask more questions, Vishnu, Shiva's best man, admonished her that they must proceed, for the astrologically auspicious hour for the ceremony might soon pass.

Thus, at long last, the elaborate marriage ceremony began. The drums and horns were sounded. The Brahmins began their chants. Difficulty arose again when the groom was asked to attest to his genealogy, his caste, and his Vedic ancestors, and tell of his guru and his education. Full of shame, Shiva turned his head aside. But he was saved by honey-tongued Narada, who told them that, as the Primal Being, Shiva has neither ancestors, nor caste, neither guru, nor education, for he is the origin of all.

During the ceremony, old Brahma, functioning as the main priest, kept his glance fixed to the ground, for he dared not look into the radiant beauty of Parvati's face. But even Parvati's toes were so beautiful that he lost his self-control. Though he tried to squeeze his genitals between his legs to hide his shame, drops of sperm fell to the ground. This impropriety enraged Shiva and, again, the gods had to restore peace. (Out of Brahma's spilled seed, pygmy sages no bigger than a thumb were born. To this day, they are devoted to Shiva.)

Apart from such minor near-disasters, the festival was loud and gay, not much different from any normal Indian wedding. There was also plenty of bawdy joking. Vishnu, knowing how frightened snakes are of birds of prey, sent his eagle, Garuda, into the women's chambers at the very moment Shiva was being presented to his mother-in-law there. As soon as the vipers saw their enemy, they fled hissing into the darkest corners of the room, while the tiger-skin loincloth that they held in place slid from Shiva's body. The groom found himself standing exposed amid screeching women. Vishnu burst out in boisterous laughter, while Shiva grinned embarrassedly. Parvati could not keep a smile from her lips. Mena quickly extinguished the light. Later on, the women, who had fled the room like a flock of excited chickens, began to needle each other: "Well, I dare say, it certainly took you a long time to take your eyes off of him!"[1]

When they were finally alone, the innocent bride turned out to be extremely shy. India's greatest poet, Kalidasa, describes the honeymoon in his poem "Kumara Sambhava." Even though they ate betel and camphor together, her face turned scarlet red and she lowered her eyes when her husband was near. When he tried to touch her, she frightened like a bird. Only when she believed that he was sleeping did she dare throw a glance his way. Of course, he was a bit disappointed, for he would have loved to close her in his arms, caress her skin, bite her lips and breasts tenderly, and let his passions run free. But he loved her, so he was patient.

However, it did not take the blushing bride all too long to throw off her innocence and learn the art of lovemaking. Once, after she had taken a little too much wine, so that her eyes turned glassy and she could no longer pronounce her words clearly, with her sari disheveled and her rouge smeared, she lost the last of her girlish inhibitions. Soon she was better at it than the best courtesan. Soon the two did not leave their love nest day or night. They loved each other as mare and stallion, as bull and cow, as boar and sow, as wolves, as flies, as bees in the flower, as lecherous demons, as tender angels. They tried ever new, exciting positions that no other creatures had ever managed. Shiva's drive was that of a continuously erupting volcano underneath the sea. And thus they melded for a near eternity.

In the estimation of the gods, this near eternity of lovemaking endured a little too long. After all, they were suffering at the hands of Taraka and were yearning for a savior. They agreed to send the fire god, Agni, to spy on the divine lovers. In order not to be detected, Agni took the form of a turtledove and approached the love nest cooing and chortling, imitating Parvati's pleasure. Shiva, noticing the intruder immediately, lifted off from Parvati just at the moment of orgasm. We have already heard what happened then. Poor Agni, receiving the full load of hot sperm in his beak, was nearly burned to a crisp and staggered off to the river Ganga. The river, in turn, deposited the seed in a bed of reeds. There the six-headed infant was born, just in time for the Krittikas (Pleiades)* to find the baby and suckle it. Not long after, Shiva and Parvati came walking along the shore. Mahadev recognized his son

---

Krittikas, the Pleiades, a cluster of seven (in Indian tradition, six) stars near the constellation Taurus.

and placed him in Parvati's arms. Because the Krittikas nursed him, he is called Karttikeya. As Parvati's child, he is known as Skanda; some swamis insist that Scandinavia is named in his honor. As a son of Ganga, he is known as Gangeya; as the son of Agni, he is called Agnibhu; and as the offspring of the reed grass thicket, he is Sarabhu. A mere seven days after his miraculous birth, he ended the demonic reign of Taraka by killing him.

Scholars surmise that, originally, Skanda might have been an ancient Aryan war god whose cult merged with that of a Dravidian forest deity. Today, he is worshipped mainly in south India under the name Subrahmanya, "dear one of the wisdom seekers." His temples are found on forested mountaintops and he is wed to the forest goddess, Valliamma. As supreme commander of the heavenly warriors, he has long replaced the old Vedic god Indra. Subrahmanya's troops are accompanied by a host of dancing girls and prostitutes, as any great army of old, going off on its campaigns. Even now, the temple girls of south India, the *devadasis*, belong to him. They are his brides, much as the Catholic nuns are the brides of Christ.

As always in Indian mythology, there are a number of versions to the story of Karttikeya's birth. According to one legend, he came about when a shower of fiery sparks sprayed out of Shiva's eyes and fell into a lake. Six boys were born out of the sparks. Again, the heavenly sisters, the Pleiades, found them and nursed each one of them. But when Parvati saw these darling children, she hugged them hard, pressing them so strongly to her heart that their bodies melted together, leaving one infant with six heads and twelve arms.

Another story is told in the *Mahabharata*.[2] Since Shiva and Parvati are incapable of reproducing normally, they engendered a child by proxy, namely by fire and water, personified as Agni and Ganga. Shiva, taking on a Rudra-aspect, slipped into Agni and filled him with ardent desire, so that his seed might bring forth the longed-for hero. At the same time, Parvati took possession of the virginal Swaha, whose name means "the offering, or oblation," one of the many lovely daughters of Daksha, the chief sacrificial priest. The following version of the story was told to me by my good Indian friend Virendra Singh:

All this happened once upon a time, when the rishis were celebrating a great soma offering. All the gods had been invited to participate for the welfare of the world. Naturally, Agni was there, for his countless flaming mouths had to receive the soma libations poured for the gods. As Agni was flickering and dancing on the altar, he happened to notice the immaculate beauty of the rishis' smooth-limbed wives. He could not withstand such beauty and his passion flared up as high as his flames. In order to be closer to the women, he slipped unnoticed into their cooking fires. This way he could observe them in the privacy of their homes and occasionally lick the soft skin of their arms with his fiery tongues. Agni was so taken in by them that he did not notice beautiful young Swaha, who loved him dearly and longed to be with him.

As Agni's passion was not returned by the rishis' wives, he became restless and, at times, took on human form to work off his frustration by roaming in the forest. Swaha noticed this and thought of a way to trick him. By means of her magic power of illusion, she took on the appearance of one of the rishis' wives and let herself be surprised while collecting wood. Giving her womanly charms free play, she did not miss the mark. Agni ravished her with flaming passion. The next day, disguised as another one of the wives, she let herself be waylaid while hauling water from a forest spring. In this manner, she mimicked each and every one of the women he so fervently desired. After each rendezvous, Agni turned himself into an eagle and swooped out of the forest, so as not to be discovered by the cuckolded husbands.

Clever Swaha carefully collected all the semen her ardent lover had spilled during the trysts and placed it into the fecund waters of the Ganges. Soon thereafter, a six-headed baby was born out of Ganga's watery womb. The rishis, sensing a disturbance in the astral atmosphere, suspected that their wives had betrayed them and cast them out. Skanda, however, took pity on his six mothers and permitted them to enter heaven, where they shine as a cluster of stars to this day. He also fulfilled Swaha's one and only wish: to be forever united with her lover, Agni. Ever since, when the Brahmins carry on an offering ceremony or the housewives cook the daily food, they call out the auspicious name "Swaha" (or "Svadha") as they feed Agni's flames with oblations of butter or rice meal.

Esoterically, Karttikeya can be seen as the heroic principle of the soul that overcomes the outrages of egoism, anger, and illusion. The swamis interpret his six heads as our five senses plus a discriminating spirit working harmoniously together in mastering ego illusions. Swami Sivananda speaks of six rays emanating from the god and penetrating the world with spears of wisdom, dispassion, strength, fame, wealth, and divine powers.[3] The peacock, strutting vainly and puffing out his gaudy plumage, is as fitting a symbol of the blustering ego, as of the pretentious, proud warrior. Karttikeya shows that he has mastered these qualities and put them as servants at his feet.

An entire month, from the waning October moon to the November full moon, when the moon passes the Pleiades, is dedicated to this heroic son of Shiva, as are Fridays and the sixth day of each waxing moon. When times are especially hard, as in war or famine, or when an impending disaster has to be averted, some brave souls may take it upon themselves to swear the *kavadi* vow. Like the sun dancers of the Plains Indians, who attach themselves with thongs to the sun pole, or like medieval flagellants who, during plague or famine, martyred themselves with whips and carried heavy crosses to stay God's wrath, the Kavadis try to move Subrahmanya to mercy by self-imposed martyrdom. Like Shaivite beggars, they dress in red, do not shave or cut their hair, wear rudraksha-malas and pointed hats like magicians. They fast or take only a little fruit and milk once a day and pierce tongue, cheeks and other parts of their body with replicas of Subramanya's spear. They walk hundreds of miles barefoot, carrying two baskets *(kavadi)* suspended from a pole, decorated with peacock feathers. Into these, they receive the rice and other offerings people give them and bring the load to the Lord's temple on some distant mountaintop. Under their burden, some of the kavadi bearers become ecstatic and start to sing and dance, praising the lord. Those who vow the Agni-kavadi even walk over pits of red hot coals with their load, indicating that the Lord has taken total possession of them—at that moment, they are Karttikeya.

❧ GANESHA ☙

Skanda's baby brother, Ganesha, is surely the most popular of Hindu deities. Skanda is worshipped mainly in southern India and Ceylon, but the corpulent elephant god is known far beyond India's borders, being honored from Afghanistan all the way to Indonesia. The image of an elephant deity most likely has its roots in the Stone Age, when big game hunters confronted and were awed by the power of the mighty mammoth bull. At least there are plenty of Paleolithic cave paintings of such Ice Age elephants.

Like Skanda, who is basically a clone of Shiva, Ganesha is not a naturally born child; rather he was created parthenogenetically by Parvati. Of the stories of his origin, this one (likely to remind the

Stone age engraving of a prehistoric elephant (grotto "Les Comberelles," France)

American reader of the comic figure Baby Huey) is perhaps the most common. It can be found in both the *Matsya Purana* and the *Shiva Purana:*

Parvati feels lonely and neglected, as Shiva is always gone into his meditation and Skanda, as usual, is off demolishing some fiend or other. Thus, the Great Goddess decides to pass her time with a bath, washing herself in her own luminous glory. However, a constant stream of uninvited visitors keeps interrupting and annoying her, so that she finally decides to do something about it. Scraping some scum and dirt off her skin with her fingernails and mixing it with sandalwood and clay, she kneads a pretty little figure. Happy at the prospect of not being so alone, she breathes life into it and tells it, "My dear little son, you shall be the guardian of my threshold. You shall be mightier than all. Let no one enter these portals whom I have not personally invited!"

"Yes, Mother," quacks the little fellow, as Parvati departs to indulge in her bath.

In the evening, Shiva, having meditated long enough, comes home and is dumbfounded to find some little pipsqueak of a stranger barring his way. Neither friendly words nor threats can budge him from the threshold. At first Shiva thinks it is rather funny, but at last he loses his temper.

"Don't you know who I am!" shouts Shiva, the Lord of the Universe.

"Even if you were Brahma, I would not care. You can't come in."

Flushed with anger, Shiva turns into Rudra and orders his horde of goblins and ghouls to remove this stubborn little ass. But the tiny guardian knows no fear, for that had not been put into him during his creation. He resolutely grabs an iron rod and bashes his opponents mercilessly, smashing their skulls and breaking their bones until they flee in panic.

Shiva is increasingly embarrassed, for how will he be able to save face when the other gods and goddesses realize that his wife is not letting him enter his own house and home? Finally, he asks his best friend, Vishnu, what to do. Vishnu agrees that it is indeed a difficult matter, "Only if we trick this rogue will we be able to beat him, for he is clever and filled with dark, tamasic power!"

With that, Vishnu charged the mysterious gatekeeper but was received

with such a heavy blow that he faltered.
But, at the same moment, Shiva jumped
him from behind and lopped his head off
with his trident. The severed head rolled
down the slope and disappeared; perhaps
it was even eaten by one of Shiva's ghouls.
All the gods and ganas (heavenly hosts)
started cheering the victory of their lord
over the tamasic stranger.

Ganesha

When the Goddess emerged from
her bath and realized what the clamor
was about, she became inconsolable.
"My darling child! My darling child!" she
screamed, tearing her hair and beating her breast. Shaken by pain and
anger, she emitted bursts of destructive energy, which took the form of hundreds of thousands of raging furies. Wherever one looked, these female
demons of vengeance, with names like Gape-Jaw, Cripple, Hunchback, and
Droop-Head, raced about the world, blindly attacking the gods and the
demons, the rishis and the nature spirits. Shiva felt as though he had stepped
into a hornet's nest!

Soon, all the battered beings—the gods and rakshas, the rishis, gandharvas, apsarasas, humans, and beasts—joined in beseeching the Goddess to
show mercy. Piously folding their hands, they fell down before her and sang
her soothing songs. Finally she relented, telling them, "Only if you bring my son
back to life will I be satisfied; otherwise, my grief will destroy the world."

At once, all the gods, prajapatis (creators), and Brahmin priests assembled in order to revive the corpse by means of ancient magical ritual. The
effort seemed doomed to fail, for the head of the body was missing. But
Shiva knew how this could be remedied.

"Go north," he told them, "and bring the head of the very first creature
that crosses your path!"

It happened to be an elephant bull whose head was taken. Combining
all their radiant energy (tejas), the gods and seers concentrated on the body,
putting the heavy cranium in place while singing powerful Vedic spells and
sprinkling the corpse with holy water. Then, suddenly, the little red-skinned
boy started to quiver. He stretched and yawned as if nothing had happened.
Parvati's sorrow passed like a dark cloud from the sun's face. She folded the
child in her arms and once again let her maternal love beam out through the
universe.

Yakshini—a nature spirit serving the Goddess

The story just recounted is not likely one that the drumming shamans of the old Paleolithic hunters acted out around the campfires. It belongs, rather, to the great cycles of myth of the Neolithic agricultural civilizations. The livelihood of these matrifocal planters had sensitized them to the Earth Mother, whose offspring, the crops, are removed from her, thrashed, chopped up or ground up, partially to be eaten and partially to be replanted, to grow whole once again. It is the mystery of the flora, which appears as the Mother's child, son, or lover, who is maltreated, killed, buried, cried over, and magically resurrected. It is the Goddess as Creatrix and *Mater Dolorosa,* "the Mother of Sorrows." It is the archetype appearing in the "Pieta," Mary with Christ's corpse. It is Isis, who cries for her dismembered husband/son/lover Osiris. Osiris too is raised from the dead by priests who fit his body parts together and enliven him with powerful magic spells.

Demeter, the Mother of Sorrows of classical antiquity, is a figure similar to Parvati. Her beloved child, Persephone, was abducted by Pluto, the black lord of the dead and of the underworld, while she picked flowers on a sunny meadow. Inconsolable, Demeter searches all the worlds for her. When the Sun tells her that the child had been robbed with the consent of her husband Zeus, her bitterness knows no end. Overwhelmed by her maternal sorrow, she withdraws from creation. In her absence, the earth is dry and barren, famine breaks out, and the fertility of humans, plants, and animals vanishes. The gods and priests do all they can to soothe her anger, but she has sworn that not a blade of grass shall grow unless her child is resurrected from the dead. The northern goddess, Frigga, experiences a similar sorrow when Loki kills her son, Baldur, the sun god.

A story that always elicits chuckles, when it makes the rounds at eventide by the flicker of the fire, is that of the race between soft, pudgy Ganesha and his athletically inclined brother, Skanda:

The boys, in a bout of sibling rivalry, agreed to race around the earth. Whoever got to Mount Kailash first would be the winner and would get the prize of the two beautiful shaktis,* Riddhi (prosperity) and Siddhi (success,) as wives. The spartanic hero, Skanda, immediately jumped on his peacock and disappeared in a cloud of dust on the western horizon. Fat Ganesha, on the other hand, struggled to get on his poor, squeaking mouse, nearly crushing it. The moon, peeking out from behind a cloud, burst out laughing at this charade, vexing Ganesha even more. "May you, too, get fat and then skinny, then fat, then skinny for all eternity!" cursed the elephant-headed boy.

Ganesha, being stubborn, did not give up; and being clever, he stopped to think, reasoning, "My mother and father are the universe. So, if I walk around their throne, I will have walked around the universe!"

The argument was acceptable; thus he easily won his two wives. When Skanda returned, huffing and puffing, a few months later, to find out that he had lost, he denounced his jumbo brother as "the lord of cheaters!" (Gamblers have picked up the epithet, for they devote their vice to the elephant god.) Peeved, Skanda refused to speak to his parents or brother, and left for the south, to live in the mountain wilderness of Krauncha. Like many a macho warrior, he never married.†

The story of a race between gods (such as this one) or animals (such as Aesop's fable of the turtle and the hare), where the smarter one overcomes the faster one, is common folklore in many cultures.

Another popular story is that of Ganesha's birthday (Ganesh Chaturthi), which falls on the fourth day of the waning moon in August (Bhadrapada):

On the morning of that day, Ganesha merrily saddled his mouse in order to ride to town. There, his devotees—who are many—had prepared large bowls of sweet rice balls, pudding, and other goodies for him to eat. After a while, having eaten like a gluttonous pig, his guts became so heavy that his mouse started groaning and moaning under the load. Suddenly, a snake crawling

---

*Shakti = dynamic energy, personified as the female consorts of the gods

†According to the south Indian version, Indra, the king of the *devas*, gave Skanda his daughter Sena, a veritable warrior-maiden, as his wife. He married her according to the Vedic rituals. Later, while wandering the dense jungles he came across Valli, a beautiful tribal girl, who stood in the middle of a millet field shooing away the birds. The two got married by "natural rites," with the trees and animals as witnesses. Thus, Skanda too was blessed by two shaktis.

across the path frightened the mouse so that it stumbled, spilling the rider. As Ganesha crashed to the ground, his bloated belly burst open, spilling all the rice balls and candies. Quickly, he stuffed it all back in and grabbed the snake to use as a belt to hold his stomach together. Seeing this, the moon burst into laughter and, again, Ganesha was disgruntled. He swore that whoever looks at the moon on his birthday, even for a second, would be hounded by bad luck. Since that day, no sensible Hindu will look at the moon on Ganesh Chaturthi.

The stubborn elephant is, like the double-faced Roman Janus, a guardian of the threshold and god of beginnings. His bright vermilion red figure decorates the main entrance of every orthodox Hindu home. Since elephants are said to have an excellent memory, as well as being clever, this lovable pachyderm becomes the patron of all thick-skulled scholars and writers. Every book written by a scholar (this one not excepted) begins with the mantra honoring the first of all pundits, *Om Shri Ganeshaya Namah*. The sacred white thread *(yajnopavita)* draped over his shoulder indicates that he is a Brahmin. Of our physical body, he guards the lower entrance, the anus. (The dangling penis is taken as his trunk.) For this reason, he is also associated with "dirty," left-handed *(vamacara)*, and esoteric magic. (The left hand is used to wash the anus after defecating.)

Having only one tusk, he is called Ekadanta, "one tooth." He lost his second tooth in an argument with Parasurama, "Rama with the ax." Parasurama—who is none other than Lord Vishnu in his sixth incarnation—was a devoted follower of Shiva. His battle-ax and bow were

Ganesha using his tusk to write the epic Mahabharata

Shiva's personal gifts to him. One day, Rama took a pilgrimage to Mount Kailash to touch his lord's feet and to pray to him. But there at the gate the stodgy thick-skulled one stood and refused to let him enter, whereupon Parasurama struck him with the ax, splitting his tusk off. Later on, the severed ivory tusk served as a style for writing down the epic *Mahabharata*, which the sage Vyasa dictated to Ganesha.

Ganesha and his two wives, Riddhi and Siddhi

Otherwise, the cozy elephant god is recognized as the cause of all hindrances, as well as the remover of them. As the lord of obstacles, he is known as Vighnaraja. No one whose soul is not purified will get past him and his two Shaktis, Success and Prosperity. Many souls who have started their pilgrimage to Shiva and Parvati to obtain salvation have been held up by the temptations of wealth and fame, for it is Ganesha who sends these dubious blessings. In that sense, the corpulent lover of sweet goodies is a dangerous tempter and seducer. It is not by mere coincidence that he was formed from the scurf and dirt of the goddess's skin. Only those souls who have washed away the dirt from themselves and have become one with Shiva, realizing Shivoham (I am Shiva), can pass this formidable gatekeeper.

One story illustrating this point tells of a time at the beginning of this age, when barbarians, savages, unclean women, and others who knew nothing of offerings, penance, charity, or the study of the Vedas, were able to gain easy access into heaven. They had learned that all they had to do was to visit the Shiva temple at Somnathpur, for all their sins to be forgiven. After all, Shiva is easy to please! Soon, the heavens were filled with teeming rogues and rascals, while the seven hells were becoming depopulated. The gods, Yama first and foremost, were quite irritated and begged Shiva and Parvati to do something about it. The Mother took heed of their complaints. She scratched black, oily scurf from her arms and molded it into the four-armed, elephant-faced god. When he had dried sufficiently and his senses were awakened, she gave him this order: "When people make their way to the Shiva temple of Somnathpur, put the following obstacles in their

Ganesha's tusk symbolizes insight as does the horn of the unicorn in Western myth

path: money and property, wealth, fame, success, power, sex, and progeny. But all those who see through your tricks and worship you, let them enter!"

The sling, which Ganesha-Vighnaraja holds in his right hand, symbolizes all the temptations of wealth and success in which people are apt to get ensnared and miss their true purpose of living. The prod in his other hand is the sign of the compulsions and constraints that dominate our lives, but also of the goading necessary to lead us toward God realization. His huge elephant ears are but winnowing fans for separating the grain from the chaff or our wordy prayers. The curvature of his trunk reminds us of the sacred OM.

His singular tusk is, like the horn of the unicorn, the symbol of single-minded concentration, of penetrating insight, and of esoteric mastery. The double-bladed battle-ax he sometimes carries was a common emblem of Bronze Age agricultural societies (it shows up in the hands of the Cretan goddess) and is associated with the waxing and waning halves of the moon, perhaps being also an intuitive visualization of the left and right halves of the brain.[4]

Contrary to all expectations, considering his body size, Ganesha loves to dance, being almost as light-footed as his father. Just as surprising is that he rides a tiny mouse. The little, gnawing rodent, Musaka (from Sanskrit *mus* = to steal) is a fitting symbol for that diminished aspect of the mind that scurries here and there, gathering its data, facts, and information. It is a picture of the restless, nervous intellect, which cannot find the quiet depth of true insight. It is important to put this "Mickey Mouse" in its right place: under foot, as Ganesha has done.

Ganesha is Gajamukti, the elephant face. Swamis read mystical significance in the very name gaja (elephant), for its component syllables, *ga* and *ja,* mean "end" and "beginning," respectively. In this way, Ganesha is the alpha and omega of creation. Auspicious swastikas decorate his (and Vishnu's) temples, where he is served with incense, red flowers, and sweets.

❧ NANDI THE BULL ❧

A common icon shows the divine family of Shiva, Parvati, and the little rascal, Ganesha, riding on a massive white bull. This gentle beast is Nandi, "the fortunate one," Shiva's faithful servant and chamberlain, leader of his hosts (ganas), guardian of the Shiva lingam and gatekeeper to all of Mahadev's sacred sites. In perfect devotion and love (bhakti), he honors his master, for he is the expression of dharma (the right path, duty). In his anthropomorphic form as Nandikeshvara, he appears as a youth with a bull's head, much like the ancient Cretan Minotaur. Like Shiva, he has three eyes. Two of his four hands are placed together in a devout *Namaste* (I greet God in you), the third hand holds a deer, and the fourth holds a double-bladed battle-ax.

That Nandi is indeed a very old being is obvious when one knows his parentage. His father is the archaic turtle, Kasyapa, one of the primal creators (prajapati), who created the celestial gods as well as the first man, the lawgiver, Manu. His mother is none other than Surabhi, the cow, which contains all the gods and fulfills all wishes. Both the cow and the turtle figure as primal beings in many old mythologies.

The hunters of the Old Stone Age were already impressed by the power of this bovine, as a number of cave paintings showing aurochs and bison bulls indicate. The Plains Indians saw in the white buffalo bull the incarnation of *wakan,* the power that sustains the universe. Anyone who has worked on a farm and had to deal with these veritable mountains of muscle will share that traditional respect. These mighty sires of the herds are concentrations of sheer power and sex drive, providing a most handy universal symbol of masculinity.

Nandi, Shiva's bull

The sacred bull

Literally "bull-headed," they are ready to gore their rivals, charging them blindly with horns lowered, in order to defend their territory and their herd of females. There is no reasoning with such snorting, stamping, drooling hulks, for their essence is the pure, unmediated will to rule and fecundate. Such absolute drive and will, unadulterated by thinking or even feeling, makes the bull, Nandi, a fitting symbol for the unwavering, unerring desire to follow dharma, to realize one's true nature.

For the Indo-European tribes, whose livelihood depended upon their livestock, the concept of wealth coincided with the number of cattle owned. To this day, a capitalist is a rich person, owning lots of heads (Latin *capita*) of symbolic cattle. Words like fee (Old English *feoh* = cattle, property) and pecuniary (Latin *pecus* = cattle) confirm this connection. The bull, as multiplier of the herds, was held in highest esteem and was mentioned in one breath with the sun, the cosmic law, and the king. The bull fertilized the herds, just as the sun fertilized the earth and the king—the grand sire—fructified his realm. The bull actualizes the Law (dharma) on the pastures just as the king actualizes it in the commonwealth and the sun does so in the sky. They are each in their own realm the upholders of divine law and are, thus, incarnations of the same essence.

It is meaningful that according to tradition, Gotama Buddha, a son of an Aryan king, was born in the astrological sign of Taurus (Vrishabha). In the Vedas, the greatest of the seers are addressed as "bulls among men" and the most powerful gods are called "bulls among the gods." Even today, older and respected males are addressed as "Sir" (from Middle English *sire* = procreator, sire bull). In order to see whom the gods had chosen to be the next king and upholder of the law, the Indo-European Celts sacrificed a white bull, cooked him in a cauldron, and let a druid bathe in the broth in order to obtain clairvoyant confirmation.

The ancient Persians, also an Indo-European people, associated the white bull with the sun, the eternal law of right and wrong, and Mithras (Sanskrit Mitra), the "friend of humankind." This god of the light and companion of the heaven god, Varuna, was the embodiment of law and order and the guardian of oaths and contracts. His cult grew, over time, far beyond the borders of Iran. Everywhere in the Middle East and in Asia Minor, we come across his name. Roman legionnaires brought the cult of Mithra and his white bull back to Rome, where it fell on fertile ground, especially among the soldiers. The old Romans were no strangers to the cult of the bull, for already in their earliest days they had sacrificed white bulls on Capitol Hill. The cult of Mithras (who sacrifices the bull in order to renew the world)—with its baptismal and communion rites and its festival of the invincible sun *(sol invictus)* on the 25th of December—became a formidable rival to early Christianity.

Among the Zoroastrian Parsees of Bombay, the archaic cult of the white bull continues to this day.[5] Priests consecrate albino bulls in special temples. Their hairs are considered to be accumulators of a mysterious divine force, and so, after a week-long prayer, they are clipped, wrapped around spools (thought of as energy condensers), and sent to the outlying parishes. The pure white animal is taken to be an expression of the archangel Behman, guardian of the animal kingdom. He represents also the world soul, tormented by Satan. When God on high perceived its anguished cries, he took pity and sent Zoroaster to reestablish Truth and Peace.

It comes as no surprise that Hindus also see a connection between the white bull and the eternal cosmic law. Nandi is none other than Dharmadevata, lord of dharma.

Once upon a time, as the sage Dharmadevata sat meditating, he was overwhelmed with awe and fear at the realization of the never-ending cycles of creation and dissolution. What seems so permanent to the mind, he realized—the mountains, the oceans, and the heavens of the gods—were all but bubbles on the stream of eternity, as ephemeral and doomed to destruction as everything else. Is there nothing that endures? Surely, one day of the Creator Brahma lasts 12,000 heavenly years, or 4,320,000 human years (as one heavenly year equals 360 human years). When Brahma sleeps, the world dissolves; when he awakens in the morning, it is created anew. One hundred years Brahma lives—for us human beings, an inconceivable span of time! Then he dies. But, the entire life of Brahma is but one day for Vishnu, and every day as Vishnu awakens from sleep on his serpent bed, he brings forth a brand new Brahma. Finally, however, when the Great Night of Being absorbs everything, even Vishnu must pass, only to reappear and set the unfathomable cycle in motion once again, and so on infinitely.

Dharmadevata shuddered at this realization. The cruel prospect of endless repetition of suffering existence made him a restless wanderer. At long last, his feet took him to Kailash, Shiva's throne. Using his yogic power, he took on the form of a white bull and threw himself at Mahadev's feet, pleading, "Lord, take me as thy vehicle! For only in thy constant presence can I bear it!"

Shiva was pleased. "Gladly, my dear Dharma," he said. "This is how you shall pass through the ages: in the first age, the Golden Age, you shall walk with ease on all four legs. In the second, the Silver Age, you will limp on three legs. In the third, the Copper Age, you shall hobble on a mere two legs and finally, in the dark Iron Age, the Kali Yuga, you shall stand insecurely on one leg only!"

The mighty cosmic bull rules the imagination of not only the nomadic, patriarchal, pastoral peoples but equally that of the rather matrilineal, sedentary societies of planters and peasants. In the earliest agricultural civilizations, the white bull accompanies the Great Goddess of the earth, the heavens, and the moon as her fecundator, her impregnator. Late Stone Age hunters in the Zagros Mountains, flanking the Fertile Crescent, must have first captured and penned wild oxen *(Bos primigenius)* for ritual and sacrificial purposes. By Neolithic times, a full-fledged Bull-Mother-Goddess cult flourished in the region. In the early Neolithic settlement of Catal Hüyük (Anatolia, 6000 B.C.), archaeologists have discovered plastered walls with paintings of bulls and women

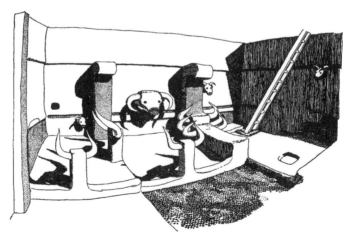

Shelves with the skulls of holy bulls (Neolithic, Catal Hüyuk, Asia Minor)

giving birth, as well as shrines with sculpted ox heads and horns.

Mother goddesses, youths dancing on the backs of bulls, and the half-human, half-bull Minotaur (born of Poseidon's white bull and a king's wife) confront us in the pre-Hellenic Mediterranean cultures. In Memphis, on the edge of the Egyptian Sahara, one can still marvel at huge underground chambers in which embalmed, mummified bulls were entombed. They were the Osiris-Apis bulls, representative of the ever dying and resurrecting god who

Shiva and Parvati on Nandi

was worshipped along with the Great Mother Isis. Into late antiquity, the baptism in the blood of a sacrificial bull was part of the initiation into the cult of the lion-riding mother goddess Cybele, whose lover is the dying/resurrecting phallic youth, Attis. Even the thunderbolt-hurling Godfather Zeus of the Indo-European Greeks took the form of a white bull to rape Europa, while the oriental god of inebriation and wine, Dionysos, entered the Mediterranean world riding a white bull, surrounded by clamoring women, satyrs, nymphs, and sprites. His followers, the maenads and bacchanalians, ran wild in intoxicated frenzy, carrying cymbals, snakes, swords, leaving their hair wild and uncombed and occasionally tearing living bulls apart and devouring their flesh raw.

The cult of the Great Mother and the fertilizing bull that is sacrificed to her covered nearly the entire ancient, civilized world. India is no exception. The motives carved upon the soapstone seals and the statuettes of the pre-Aryan Harappa Empire along the Indus River indicate this. To this day, there are remnants of this ancient cult of fertility: in the Occident, the Spanish bullfights, under the auspices of the Virgin Mary; in the Orient, the sacrifice of buffalo bulls to the Black Goddess in Bengal. Given all this, we can appreciate that the icon of Shiva and Parvati riding a white bull represents a successful synthesis of age-old Indo-European and pre-Aryan cultural elements.

In the rural villages of the Subcontinent, stories and fables make their rounds. The most popular of all are those telling of Shiva and Parvati traveling incognito through the world, either on foot or riding their bull:

Once Shiva and Parvati were riding through a town on Nandi, when they heard people whispering behind their backs, "Will you look at that! My, that's cruelty to animals, those two fat people sitting on that little bull!"

Shiva, not wanting to offend anyone, got off and walked next to Nandi. Again, nasty comments could be heard. "Look at that henpecked husband. He has to walk, while she plays the big lady and rides!"

That was a little too much for Shiva's pride, so he changed places with Parvati. However, that did not stop the slander; another barrage of vicious tongues assaulted their ears. "That male chauvinist pig! He rides comfortably while his poor wife has to walk in the dust!"

At that, they both agreed to walk. Perhaps then, the people would be a bit kinder to them. But now the townspeople laughed and pointed their fingers at them. "Look at these fools! They have a strong animal, but they are too stupid to ride it!"

Shiva and Parvati were baffled.

"Now what?" they thought, as they stood there. Nandi smirked and winked. "How about this? I'll ride on you. Maybe that will please these people!"

At that Shiva and Parvati realized that in society, no matter what one does, one cannot please everybody. So, why not do what one thinks is right in the first place? With that realization, they both climbed on Nandi's back and rode on undisturbed.

Lord Shiva not only rides a bull, but sometimes he turns himself into one. It is well known that he likes to meditate up north in the Himalayas, at a scenic spot called Kedara, or "the field" (where salvation grows). One day, as he quietly sat there, he heard the five Pandava brothers, the heroes of the *Mahabharata,* clamoring up the path to see him. They came to worship him in order to atone for sins they had heaped upon their souls by slaying blood kin in battle. But Shiva had no desire to see them. He changed into a bull and ploughed into the earth. However, his hindquarters got stuck and were promptly adored by the five penitent warriors. These haunches and hooves can still be seen there, but in this dark Kali Yuga age, they have turned into mere crumbling rock, their true essence being visible only to a clairvoyant. Shiva's bovine head came out in Kathmandu Valley in Nepal, where one can still worship his horns at Pashupathinath, the temple of the lord of the animals.

Other storytellers claim it was Brahma from whom Shiva fled at Kedara in the form of a bull. Brahma knew that if he took a pilgrimage to Kedara and achieved a vision (darshana) of Shiva's lingam, he would find instant liberation. But Shiva, who never got along very well with the Creator, took on a bull's form and charged into the ground. Brahma managed to catch him by his hind hooves and hold him there. The bull's penis, however, surfaced at Kashi (Benares) as a great lingam. When its

Temple in Kedara

power became known, Brahma hurried to Benares, sacrificed ten horses (at Dashashwamedha Ghat) and then was allowed to worship the lingam.[6]

The mounts (vahanas) of the gods are commonly interpreted as the negative side of the deities' personalities, as their lower nature, which must be put into the proper place and dominated in order that universal harmony can be maintained. Ganesha's mouse, as we have seen, is the personification of the nervous, covetous intellect; the lion or tiger of the goddess is wanton cruelty; and Skanda's peacock is the vanity of the victorious warrior. Nandi, too, can be seen in this perspective. One legend has it that he once was a powerful demon, against which Shiva had to struggle hard to bring him under foot. Nandi stands for aggressive male sexuality. The very words *bull* and *phallus* can be traced etymologically to the same Indo-European root word, *bhel* = to swell. Related is the English use of the word *balls*, referring to testicles, as well as to having courage (to "have balls"). Related also is the bel, the tropical wood apple tree, whose round, swollen fruits look like a bull's scrotum and are dedicated to Shiva and used in his worship. Shiva, as the king among ascetics and as the master of yoga, has perfect control over the powerful sex drive. To him, this bull is not a problem, but a faithful servant.

For the Hindu, even to this day, any white bull is a manifestation of Nandi. Some ashrams keep a herd of purebred white Zebu cattle, which have not been mongrelized by crossbreeding with Jerseys, Holsteins, or Swiss Simmentals (from the sperm banks of international

*Free-ranging sacred bulls
in Benares (Varanasi)*

development and foreign aid organizations). Such holy Zebu bulls are kept immaculately clean, and their majestic horns are painted red and tipped with gold.

At the funeral of an important person, a "bull among men," it is the custom in India and Nepal to release a bull calf, dedicated to Shiva, and allow it to roam as it pleases. This practice of bull-freeing *(vrisosarga)* is said to please the ancestors *(pitri)*. Places such as Benares that are auspicious for cremation abound with such cud-chewing beasts. Standing like meditants, motionless in the streets, they help slow the traffic to a tolerable, relaxed speed. Leading an unfettered existence, they browse on what they find—garbage, paper, weeds, and an occasional gift from a devotee. If they are still hungry, they might steal fruits or vegetables from the stands of street merchants. Unlike Spanish fighting bulls, they are unbelievably gentle, moving calmly through the bazaars as if each and every person is just another cow of the herd. They are not even upset by street urchins teasing them or throwing rocks at them, but tolerate them like feisty calves. Only at the sight of a rival bull or of a nervous, camera-laden tourist, who smells and acts different, might they lose their calm. The owners of the sacred cows let their animals also wander the streets to look for fodder and are happy when such a bull regularly bestows them with a calf.

When one of these colossi dies, his last rites are performed in style: He is adorned with flowers, smoked with incense, and given a drink of Ganges water before boatmen tug him to the middle of the current where fish, river dolphins, ravens, and vultures feast on him. His soul will be reborn as a human being.

Because he rides a bull, one of Shiva's thousand and eight names is Vrisavahana, "the bull rider."

9

THE DESTRUCTION OF
THE SACRIFICE

*The sacrificial lamb brought for the festival
ate up the green leaf brought for the decoration.
Not knowing a thing about the kill,
it only wants to fill its belly:
born that day, to die that day.
But tell me:
Did the killers survive,
O Lord of the Meeting Rivers?*

BASAVANNA,
SOUTH INDIAN SHAIVITE POET, TENTH CENTURY

Almost imperceptibly, yet steadily, the stars shift their relative position. In a little over two thousand years, the sun's spring position, the vernal equinox, will have moved into another sign of the zodiac, giving its radiations a qualitatively new impact. The changes one observes in nature are connected with the beat of these great cosmic rhythms, as are the major transformations of human culture. The scholars call this evolution. Thus, with the passing of the great herds of mammoths, woolly rhinoceroses, wild horses, and bison, the roving bands of Paleolithic hunters and their "Atlantean" magic began disappearing also. Animals were tamed and peasants started to grub the earth to raise corn and tubers. A growing population organized itself into castes and classes, and built cities and temples, while philosophers contemplated the succession of ages: the Golden Age became the Silver Age, the Silver Age turned into the Bronze Age, and now we find ourselves in the grip of an Iron Age.

Just like the external world, the inner world of the soul also changed. The immediate vision available to all, the "seeing God eye to eye," gave way ever more to priestly authority and ritual, which in turn was replaced by ever more rational, ego-oriented thinking. The dancing, drumming, immanent, androgynous, shamanistic trickster-god was replaced by regal, celestial deities who control the seasons and the waxing and waning of vegetation and by a life-giving, yet bloodthirsty, Earth and Mother Goddess. The animal god of the hunters faded or metamorphosed into a number of persons, such as the phallic lover of the goddess, the fire god, the god of the herds, or the devil. But in recent times, even these images faded, being replaced more and more by a transcendent, virgin-born Logos, whose brilliant light ever more vaporizes into thin air, leaving in its void an apparently absurd universe of matter/energy.

But let us see what happens to the old shaman god of the hunters in India. He metamorphoses into Rudra, the Aryan storm god, who, in turn, absorbs the indigenous, Dravidian lord of the animals. In this combination, he gains ever more power in the minds of the common folk, so much so, in fact, that it becomes uncanny for the Aryan sacrificial priests and Brahmins. Like a sponge he soaks up all the other gods, until they are merely his masks, which he can change at will. He expands into the infinite, becomes identical with Purusha, the fatherly primordial spirit, while the goddesses are but the rays of his fiery aura of energy. They become his active power (shakti) and his magical force of illusion (maya). He becomes all encompassing, so that the Aryan gods of sky, light, and cattle are but mere dwarves next to him. Finally, the Brahmins, who at one time possessed godlike powers and whose minds brought forth the worlds, are forced to bow to him, who was once the howling god of storms and of the dead, and to appeal to his mercy, calling him Shiva, "the gracious," Shambhu, "the kind" or Shankar, "the peaceful."

The old folktales, the Puranas, witness his rise to sovereignty and his conflict with the Aryan seers and sacrificial priests. In this section we shall see how they tried to block his rise to power and how, step-by-step, Shiva reveals himself as Mahadev, the God of Gods. On the dizzying heights of Shaivite metaphysics, he becomes absolute Being/Consciousness/Bliss (Satchidananda), which is the sum total of all and everything. All oppositions of day/night, good/evil, I/Thou, being/non-

being, male/female, and life/death are but
the ethereal, spontaneous game (Sanskrit
lila = play of the gods) of his Shakti, his
feminine power, his dancing mistress,
whose gestures bring forth universes and
absorb them again.

Vishnu, Shiva's best friend

Since Mahadev is all, he is not jealous
of a God—like Jehovah or Allah—who tol-
erates no other gods. Shiva is pleased by all
cults and all religious devotion. The multitude of religions, churches, and sects reflect
only the various stages toward realization
of his being. Souls enmeshed in the pangs of
illusion need loud, colorful, bloody rituals
and gaudy idols. Others need sackcloth and
ashes, sermons and soda water, while still others need anemic philosophical speculation. Shiva is gracious to all, no matter under what
name or in what tongue they call upon him. They are all right, for they
are all Shiva. They are but Shiva himself praying to Shiva.

With this kind of thinking, it is no wonder that in Hinduism every religious expression is tolerated, from the primitive cults of local deities to the
archaic Vedic rites at meal preparation, weddings, and funerals. There is
no real conflict even with the Vaishnavas, who honor Vishnu as the God
of Gods. He, too, is Shiva. As Hari-Hara or Shankaranarayana, Vishnu
and Shiva have melted into one person of whom the right, masculine side
is more Shiva and the left, feminine side is more Vishnu. The Sanskrit
Puranas tell the following anecdote about Hari-Hara:[1]

Once upon a time, the gods approached Lord Vishnu because they were
upset and at a loss to explain why the world was in such a mess. They
wanted to know why everywhere war, hatred, unhappiness, and vice
seemed to hold sway. When the delegation, led by Indra, arrived at Vishnu's
palace, the Preserver told them, "Let us go to Shankar, for he is wise!"

They climbed the icy slopes of Kailash but saw no one. Amid the glaciers
and rocks, there was no sign of either Shiva or Parvati, nor of Nandi the
white bull. Vishnu told them, "Beloved, your selfishness has made you blind,
for Hara is here! You must purify yourselves, bathe in milk, sing the
Satarudriya hymn, take only hot milk, hot butter, or hot water as food and
then, after three days, your eyes shall be opened."

Vishnu and Shiva as one person (Hari-Hara)

The dumbfounded gods followed the instructions, but still their vision was as though they were snow-blinded. "Oh, Jaganatha, Lord of the World," they cried out, "Where can we find the trident bearer, that we might honor him?"

At that, Vishnu pointed at his chest, "He is in me, as I am in him; can't you see?"

As he spoke, he revealed his lotus heart. As its petals opened, the sacred lingam was revealed. The gods hastened to worship it by pouring milk over it, covering it with vermilion, fragrant sandalwood paste, trifoliate bilva leaves, flowers, herbs, and lotus blossoms while chanting the 1008 names of Shiva. But at the same time, their minds were disturbed—for how could Hari (Vishnu) and Hara (Shiva) be one and the same? Did not Vishnu have light, *sattvic* qualities, while Shiva had dark, *tamasic* qualities? Reading their thoughts, Vishnu took on Ishvara's (Shiva's) form. They could no longer tell the difference between the three-eyed god with the matted hair and cobra necklace and the other one with the disk (chakra) and seashell. Capitulating before the mystery, they prostrated themselves and worshipped.

ॐ THE ARYAN BACKGROUND ॐ

The Aryan (Iranian) tribes of Persia and their Vedic cousins in India honored the same nature deities, as did other Indo-Europeans of the Eurasian steppes. Above all, they worshipped the bright, radiant Devas, "the shiny ones" (Persian *daeva*; Latin *deus* = god, *dies* = daylight; Sanskrit *dyaus* = day, sky; Greek Zeus; Anglo-Saxon Tius) and the soma-quaffing Suras. At their head stood the god of high heaven, Varuna (Persian Uruwna; Greek Ouranos; Latin Uranos; German Urahne) the ancestor of all and kingly guardian of the eternal law, the Rita (Old Persian *arta*; Latin *ritus*; English *right*), to which all creatures, even the gods, have to submit. Equally sacred was Varuna's companion, or son, Mitra, the god of light and guardian of fidelity and all oaths and contracts.

All personifications of light were worshipped. Among the first and foremost was the sun, Surya. He was the leader of the soma-inspired

Suras. In his honor the Hindus of the "twice-born" castes still recite the Gayatri Mantra mornings and evenings. Sacred was Ushas (related to Greek Eos; Latin Aurora; Anglo-Saxon Eastre, or Easter, the spring goddess), the virginal light of dawn. Sacred were the heavenly twins, the Ashvins, the physicians of the gods, whose swift, shiny horses pull the sun on its course.*

Sacred were a number of atmospheric gods, such as Indra, the thunderer, and the prototype of the hard-drinking, hard-fighting Aryan warrior whose thunderbolt gashes the gut of the cloud demon and releases the fertile water for the fields and pastures. Not to be forgotten was the Mother Earth, Prithiva Mater (the Gaia Mater of the Greeks), the wife of Dyaus Pitar, or Father Sky.

What unfolds in front of our eyes is the picture of an unspoiled nature religion, which perceived the Sacred in word, water, blood, and above all, in light and fire; and which had no need of temples or idols, but worshipped out of doors. In everything, the Indo-Europeans felt an all-pervasive, cosmic, magical, numinous force, the Brahman, which was personified as 33 or 3339 gods. (In modern India, the number has inflated to 300,000,000.) By means of the sacred word, in the form of the mantric chants, and by the ritual of sacrifice, this numinous force could be manipulated.

The sacrificial rite (Sanskrit *yajna*) was the bridge leading to the gods. It was a great cosmic sacrifice that had created the world in the first place and each new sacrifice was a continuation of the creation, bringing new boons. Under the open sky, on a platform strewn with fresh grass, between three fires, the Aryans offered their most sacred possessions—horses, bulls, rams (in that order)—as the "graceful tongued" hymn singers *(hotar)* sang out, as the fire priests puffed and churned the fire, as the "gentle handed" magicians *(atharvan)* prepared the offerings, as the soma priests pressed the magic plant and poured libations, and as the Brahmins, the presiding priests, cast their spells. Agni (related to Latin *ignis* and Lithuanian *ugnis* = fire), the ever famished, flaming "mouth of the gods" received the gifts and transported them to the celestials.

The sacrificial rites of the Indo-Aryans, like those of the related Celtic druids, generated a magic force that was meant not merely to please or

---

*The Ashvins, the Vedic twin gods of healing, are related to the Greek Dioskouroi, the Gemini of the zodiac. They live on in Christian mythology as the twin saints Cosmas and Damian, the patrons of doctors and pharmacists.

placate the gods but to control them, to force them to fulfill wishes and demands. Such a priesthood that could be compulsory upon the gods was indeed very powerful. The blessing or curse of such a Brahmin, who, besides having mastered esoteric knowledge, also led a virtuous life in line with the cosmic law, was feared by man, god, and demon alike. To this day, a large number of Indians fear and respect the mantra-knowledgeable, ascetic and Brahmin and are careful not to rouse his ire.

The Aryan dead went to the realm of Yama (Persian Yima, related to the Nordic Ymir), the primordial human, who was the first mortal to die and, thus, the king of the realm of the dead. For that purpose, the common dead were buried. Nobles and priests, however, were cremated, like an offering received by Agni and carried into the world of the heavenly light, to become godlike. Valued possessions like horses, weapons, and servants were often sent along. The wife who entered the blazing funeral pyre of her husband of her own free will was giving proof of the nobility of her character. Such a woman was revered as a Sati, a "virtuous one."*[2] This old Indo-European custom of voluntary widow-immolation was practiced in heathen Scandinavia up to the tenth century A.D. The Arab traveler Ahmed Ibn Fadlan gives a detailed description of the practice among the Vikings (Rus) who had anchored their dragon ships on the banks of the Volga in the tenth century.

Pieces of meteoric iron, falling from the sky as "thunderstones" with blazing tails, were magic fetishes since the Early Stone Age; and wild horses were among the favorite game of all early hunters. However, it was not until the second millennium B.C. that a new epoch of history unfolded—when some unknown Indo-European tribe of the Asian steppes tamed the horse and harnessed it to light war-chariots; and the Indo-European Hittites (who worshipped Vedic gods) smelted and smithed iron, somewhere south of the Black Sea. Soon Indo-European tribes, inspired by the terrible god of horses, war, and iron (who the Greeks called "Ares" and the Romans "Mars") spread in successive waves throughout central Asia, Europe, and Asia Minor, and spilled over into the Indus River valley. Wherever they went, they took their gods, cults, spells, rites, and language. Confronted by subjugated tribes and civilizations everywhere, they tried every means possible to retain

---

*The practice of the voluntary self-immolation of widows is occasionally still practiced in northern India, even though it is illegal.

the purity of their culture. The Aryan priests of India did their utmost to keep non-Aryan *(anarya)* elements from polluting their culture and their blood. The conquered Dravidian natives were enslaved and excluded from all rites, including those of marriage, meal taking, and funerals.

History records similar attempts of the early Indo-European Greeks and Romans to maintain the purity of cult and blood. (Ancient Greek democracy was meant only for the aristocrats.) These ideas are the direct historical antecedents of apartheid, racial segregation, Indian reservations, caste arrogance, and, equally, the atavistic concepts that a half-educated Hitler tried to superimpose on a modern, twentieth century industrial society in Central Europe.

Sooner or later, the Aryan priesthood had to acknowledge that despite their efforts, slowly but surely, the non-Aryan elements were being absorbed and integrated. Stealthily, changes crept into the pronunciation and intonation of the all-important Brahmanic spells, while the complexion of the dominant population darkened. At the same time, indigenous gods and spirits that the Brahmins had banned into the underground rose and gained power in the popular imagination, demanding their own cults and mingling with their Aryan counterparts. It was the uncanny fear that the ancient Sanskrit mantras might lose their effectiveness by being mispronounced that led the sage Patanjali (in the sixth century B.C.) to write his famous treatise on phonetics and grammar, which, in its thoroughness, satisfies even modern scientific criteria. It was the fear of losing racial purity, of "thinning out the blood," which they believed carries the spirit, that led the Brahmins to transform the rather loosely structured Indo-European three-class system (priests, nobles, commoners) into the absolutely rigid, endogamous caste system. Though even now the upper castes are lighter in skin color than the lower castes, the segregation must not have functioned too well, for there is no break, only a sliding continuum. Even now the wish for partners with a "wheatish complexion" is frequently voiced in the want ads for marriage candidates in the Sunday papers of India.

At the same time that they were imposing racial and social segregation, the Brahmins fixed the, up until then, verbally transmitted sacred lore into writing to guard against heretical changes. In this way, the books of wisdom, the holy Vedas, came about. But even at that, it took numerous Upanishads to explain to later generations what was meant by the Vedas. Later on, in the folktales, or Puranas, the amalgamation of native Dravidian traditions and Aryan lore is nearly complete. In them, old Indo-European gods frequently shrink to insignificance or sink altogether into oblivion. Indigenous deities take on Aryan symbols and attributes, declaring themselves to be the guardians of the Vedas.

The story that is about to be told is an echo of the mighty struggle between the Brahmanic priests of the Vedic sacrificial religion and the newly emerging, synchretistic image of the God of emerging Hinduism. This is a central tale in Hindu folk mythology, found in the *Taittiriya Upanishad*, the *Mahabharata*, and the *Ramayana*. The story is told with various embellishments by village storytellers, who were my main source.

ꣷ Daksha's Great Sacrifice ꣶ

Daksha is the son of the creator god, Brahma. He was born of Brahma's mind, or, in another version, of his right thumb, for Daksha means "the right" (related to Latin *dexter*). For some ten thousand years this noble son of Brahma heated himself in strenuous ascetic exercises and, as a result, was made the chief of the prajapatis, who are the minor creators (demiurges) and patriarchs.

Since Brahma's mind-born creatures could not multiply, he ordered his son Daksha to invent sexual intercourse so that creation might multiply as it should. Thereupon Daksha, as chief priest, sacrificed the androgynous cosmic unity, creating males and females among the gods, titans, nagas (serpent deities), cattle, birds, heavenly singers and dancers, and all other creatures.

But when Daksha's sons heard of the mysterious, three-eyed god, they lost their sexual desires and refused to multiply. Instead, they followed Shiva's footsteps as wandering monks, losing themselves in the infinity of the universe. At that, the chief priest and cocreator became very annoyed with the ascetic god. But he went on creating many other creatures, including sixty very beautiful daughters, of whom ten are married to Dharma, twenty-seven to Soma (the moon), and the rest to various gods.

The youngest and most lovely daughter is shiny Uma (light). Already as a child, she had fallen in love with the mysterious three-eyed god. When the maiden mentioned her heart's desire to her father Daksha, he

Brahma, the Creator, the father of Daksha

would not even hear of it. Had he not already had enough trouble with this madman? In no way could he approve of a dirty beggar, an uncombed long-hair with snakes dangling from his ash-covered body, and a dope fiend, to boot, as his future son-in-law!

When Uma became of marriageable age, her marriage was not arranged, as is the custom with common people. Being a princess, she had the right of *swayamvara*, that is, the privilege of choosing her own husband. All the princes and outstanding bachelors of the three worlds were invited to the swayamvara festival, in order that she might pick one as her proper and fitting mate. Naturally, Shiva, the social outsider, was not invited.

Uma looked about the great hall where thousands of young, eligible nobles, one more handsome than the next, vied for her attention. But as she looked, she became ever sadder. Her tear-filled eyes could not discover her one and only true love among them all, so that she might place the flower garland around his neck to indicate her preference. With a gesture of desperation, she finally flung the wreath into the air, as she was unable to choose another. Miraculously, Shiva appeared all of a sudden and caught the wreath. Daksha was aghast. Grandfather Brahma, however, told the irate father that it was destined and that he should bless the marriage. When the elaborate wedding ceremony was completed, he presented his new son-in-law with a milk-white bull, as Aryan custom demands. Then, mounted on the back of the animal, which they named Nandi, the divine pair rode north.

As they approached Kailash Mountain, Shiva's wilderness home, the wolves began to howl and the ghosts to wail. Forest devils and rock gnomes rolled down the slopes, laughing insanely and merrily. With wild dancing, drinking, and buffoonery, they celebrated the honeymoon couple. Finally, the god and goddess retired to the mountaintop where they lived without a roof over their heads (today we would probably say without running water, electricity, television, or central heating) and spent their days in blissful lovemaking.

One day much later, Daksha, the chief priest, staged a gigantic sacrificial celebration, a yajna, to which all the celestials, the rishis, and the seers were invited. As the proud prajapati, Daksha, entered the sacred, grass-covered arena, all the gods and goddesses, even great Vishnu, rose from their seats. Only Shiva did not stand up. That apparent slight grievously upset Daksha. Never again would he invite this shameless son-in-law to a sacred ceremony! Neither this mischief-maker, nor that ruined wench who was once his daughter but now was seen dancing in the company of ghouls in graveyards, should ever again receive a portion of the sacrifices reserved for the gods. This Daksha swore by all that was holy.

Sometime thereafter, Daksha organized one of the greatest of Aryan sacrifices, the *ashwamedha* (horse sacrifice). Shiva and Uma did not find out about it until they saw all the brilliant chariots of the gods whizzing by on their way to the sacrificial fields and a relative stopped to tell them what was going on. Uma was quite upset. "How dare my father refuse Thee, who art the Universe itself, thy proper share of the offering! How canst Thou sit there so calmly as though it concerneth Thee not?"

Shiva tried to calm her gushing anger. "What difference does it make, my beloved! These bloody sacrifices mean little to me. Those who sing to me in their hearts and offer their souls to me in devotion are dearer to me than these arrogant Brahmins with their burnt meat and monotone chanting!"

But these wise words did not appease Uma. She insisted on her right as a goddess to be part of the horse sacrifice. Uninvited, she went to the ceremonial ground with a small retinue. Her reception was frosty. Though she humbly touched her parent's feet, her greeting was not even acknowledged. She, nonetheless, demanded to know, in the assembled presence of the gods, why she and her husband had not been invited. The impudence of his daughter caused Daksha to explode angrily, "That horrible man of ashes! That chief of all that is ugly and contemptible! Not Shiva, the gracious one, but Ashiva, the wicked one, should he be called! Let it be known once and for all, this devil is banned from all the rituals of the righteous!"

This curse was too much for lovely Uma to bear. Some say that her anger heated her so much that she burst into flame. Others say that she jumped into the ritual fire and burned like a sacrifice. In this way, she became the first suttee *(sati)*. Ever since, it has been the custom of honorable Hindu widows to cremate themselves voluntarily on the funeral pyre of the husbands (at least until British colonial law put a stop to it). After this dreadful event, the priests drove Uma's retinue off, hurling curses, and then continued the ceremony.

When Nandi and the sadhus told Shiva what had happened, it was his turn to become angry. His wrath exploded volcanically. In a burst of rage, he tore a bunch of hair from his scalp and thrashed the ground so hard with it that it split and turned into the two most terrible creatures the world had ever seen. Towering infernally, there stood a thousand-headed, thousand-legged, pitch black monster, dripping with blood and armed with invincible weapons, including huge fangs. It was Virabhadra: outrage made visible! Next to him loomed black Bhadrakali, hunching on a mur-

Shiva's hordes attacking the sacrifice of the priests (from an Indian comic)

derous tiger, naked except for a necklace of severed heads and a skirt of ripped-off arms, terrible and bloodthirsty: the picture of destructive revenge! They silently awaited Shiva's orders. "Go! Destroy the sacrifice of the Brahmins!" was his command.

In the meantime, at the sacrificial ground, ill omens indicated that things were going awry. Jackals were heard howling between the uttering of the sacred spells. Daksha felt a stinging pain in the left side of his body. Black thunderclouds, out of which three-pronged lightning bolts flashed, darkened the blue sky.

Suddenly, with a roaring din, the wild storm broke out over the field and, with it, the terrible horde of howling storm spirits (rudras and maruts), with Virabhadra and Bhadrakali at their head, descended upon the celebration. Reaching for their weapons, the gods swung themselves on their mounts, only to be battered and scattered by the attacking horde. Meanwhile, the mighty rishi Bhrigu, pouring libations into the sacred flames while uttering powerful spells, raised a magical army of demons to fend off the attacking rudras. But it was all in vain. Finally, after Indra had fallen wounded from his elephant and Vishnu was knocked unconscious, the gods fled to Mount Kailash to beg Shiva to restrain his anger and show mercy.

All the while, Shiva's unsavory hordes lay waste to the ceremonial site. They set the tents aflame and threw the priests and singers, as well as the sacrificial posts, to which the horses were still tied, into the river. They knocked the eyes out of the head of the old Aryan guardian of private property, Bhaga. (For this reason, one of Shiva's thousand and eight names is Bhaganetraghna, "destroyer of Bhaga's eyes.") Virabhadra rammed his foot into the mouth of the Aryan god of cattle, Pushan, breaking all of his teeth out so that, henceforth, he could only eat mush and bananas. They urinated into the holy fire, thus defiling it. And finally, Virabhadra sliced off Daksha's head.

There is another version of the story, which tells how an enraged Shiva takes personal part in the battle. Stepping out of the southern sky from the region of the constellation of Orion, he appeared as Sharva, the archer. The frightened sacrificial altar, taking the shape of a deer,

Shiva placing a goat's head on Daksha's body (from an Indian comic)

fled into the sky. Finally, it fell back to earth and took refuge in Sati's (Uma's) corpse. As Sharva chased his quarry, a drop of sweat fell from his brow in the form of a fireball. As it descended, it transformed into an ugly, cramped, swarthy man with the bristling hair and the bloodshot eyes of a rabid dog. He has horrendous jaws and wears the red garb of someone condemned to death. His name is Jvara, "fever."

Long after the battle was over, fever raged over the land. Brahma appealed to Lord Shiva to do something about this dreadful, sweat-born creature, for it was depopulating the earth. When something is created, it is impossible to make it disappear again, so Shiva decided to dilute it by splitting this Jvara into many less-potent portions. It turned into the headaches of elephants, the lava flow of volcanoes, the green slime on the surface of waters, the laziness of snakes, the infertile, alkaline spots on fields, the blindness among cows, the constipation of horses, the eye ailments of cuckoos, the hiccups among parakeets, the liver diseases among sheep and, of course, the hot and cold flashes that humans call fever. In this way, evenly distributed, fever became tolerable.

The gods acknowledged their defeat and lay prostrate at Shiva's feet. Their hands folded, they accorded him first rank, praising him as Mahadev, "God of Gods." At that, he was very pleased. He threw off his manifestation of wild Rudra and turned into friendly, peaceful Shankar. Now the gods begged him to bring their fallen comrade, Daksha, back to life. Being in a happy mood, Shiva fulfilled their request. But, since the cocreator's head was missing, having been either burned in the fire or devoured by one of the ghouls, Shiva took the head of a billy goat and, with superb surgical skill, fastened it to Daksha's body. From then on, this prajapati is always shown with the head of a goat. Having been raised from the dead, he prays to Shiva without cessation, bleating "bom, bom, bom," as (Indian) goats are known to do.

Now that Daksha's illusions of grandeur had been destroyed and his spirit, formerly clouded by false pride, had cleared up, his father, Brahma, could initiate him into the truth. He told his goat-headed son, "Surely, the Gracious One, whose banner is the white bull, has freed you from your illusion. It is he, Shiva, who dwells in all hearts! It is to him that the singers of the Vedas, who are one with Brahman, have sung their verses. He is the Self, the Seed, and the Goal. To him all mantras are directed. Truly, those who think that Vishnu, Womb of the Universe, is somcone other than Shiva, are mistaken and do not understand the Vedas!"

Some of the priests and rishis, who were scorched by the conflagration of the battlefield, or who had swum to safety, still cling to the mistaken notion that Shiva is unclean and of little worth. They continue to believe, to this day, that only Vishnu is worthy of worship. Though they are reborn as Brahmins again and again, as a result of their asceticism and impeccable lives, they remain in error. Only at the very end of this Kali Yuga will they achieve insight.

☙ SHIVA THE SINNER ❧

As we already know, after the battle the berserker god sank into gloom and depression over having lost his beloved Uma-Sati. Forgetting his true nature, he wandered and erred through desert and wilderness. Ever deeper did he glide into mental darkness (tamas), so that, by the time he reached the Himalayan pine forest where the hermits and their wives meditated, he was but a madman. At least, that is how the pious anchorites saw him. To the holy men who were so proud of their brahmacharya (ritual sex abstention), he was but a naked, filthy devil with a constantly erect virile member. Their wives, on the other hand, with the exception of only one, saw in him a temptation, a magnet of lust.

The rishis and their wives really stand for the human spirit and the human soul. Both are caught up in illusion and cannot recognize God when they see God. The thinking (the masculine side of the psyche) projects its own weaknesses and fears upon him, while the feeling (the feminine side) falls into unwholesome fascination. But Shiva is really void of characteristics. He is but a mirror of their state of being. He is the symbol for the Self, which really cannot be made into an object, either of thinking or feeling. The Self is always beyond these. In the same way, no magic, no theurgy, no rite, and no offering can compel the Self.

The stories of Daksha's sacrifice and of the hermit's austerities in the pine forest express the tension between the Vedic Brahmins, eager to compel the powers of the universe, and Shiva, who cannot be compelled and who seems dangerous and terrible because of it.

This tension is also mirrored in the following story, in which Shiva kills Brahma, the foremost of the Brahmins. The murder of a Brahmin was one of the most heinous sins of which the mind of a true-blooded Aryan could conceive. The murder of a noble (kshatriya) could be atoned for with a wergild of a thousand cows, the killing of a commoner (vaishya) with a hundred cows, the killing of a slave (shudra) with ten cows, but that of a Brahmin could not be atoned at all![3] How the sacrilege of Brahma's slaying came about is told in the Sanskrit Puranas:

Lord Vishnu rested in the infinite void between creations, in dreamless sleep, floating on the dark sea of chaos. At the dawn of a new cycle, he stirred. Keeping the pure, light nature (sattva) for himself, he let his active, creative nature (rajas) take the form of the lotus-born, five-headed Brahma; while his dark, sluggish nature (tamas) took the form of a three-eyed being with matted hair and a bead rosary in his hand. Simultaneously, Ahamkara, that terrible force of egoism, arose from the world soul and took possession of the latter two figures. That is why tamasic Rudra, blinded by egoism, assaulted grandfather Brahma with abrasive words: "You senile old gray gander, where do you come from?"

The Creator, his dignity having been slighted, replied in an equally harsh, provocative tone. His fifth face distorted in a horrible grimace, he sneered at Rudra, saying, "I'll tell you who you are and where you come from! You are pollution and darkness! You are nothing but a destroyer!" (Today, old Brahma would surely have used such an expression as "terrorist, punk, and anarchist.")

Rudra responded accordingly. He fixed him with his third eye and then, using the nail of his little finger, he sliced off the Creator's fifth head. The skull of the murdered primordial Brahmin stayed stuck to his hand. He could not shake it off.

That is how great Shiva exteriorized the luckless personage of Kalabhairava, the murderer of Brahmins, who is also known as Kapalika, "the one who carries a skull." Upon this unfortunate being, who was really a part of himself, Shiva lay the following curse: "Misshapen, stinking, and limping, you are condemned to restlessly wander and beg. People will spit at your shadow and, wherever you go, you will be pursued by an ugly fury of vengeance, a flaming ogress with gaping jaws and crocodile teeth, Brahmahatya (murderer of Brahma). She will always pursue you until you reach my holy city, Benares. There, where all sins are turned to ashes, the skull, the symbol of your shame, shall drop from your hand."

Having been thus cursed, the malefactor roamed the three worlds without respite. Whoever was able to see God in him was blessed. But, for the most part, nothing but hate, fear, and loathing greeted him, and people avoided him like the plague. One day, he and the unsavory company of ghouls, goblins, and other creatures of hell that had joined him stood before the portals of Vishnu's jeweled palace. He held out the skull, which served as a begging bowl, and asked for a handful of rice. But the gatekeeper, Vishvaksena, would not even tolerate him near the gate and was about to unleash the hounds on him. Again the murderer committed a murder. With his iron trident, he decapitated Vishvaksena. When Vishnu rushed to see what the ruckus was about, he immediately saw through the filthy, misshapen beggar's exterior and recognized Mahadev. Using his disk, the great god whose mount is the eagle split open his very own head so that the blood streamed forth like a mighty river.

"Mahadev, great Lord," he said to the beggar with the trident, "Let this blood be my alms to fill your bowl!"

For a full thousand divine years, the blood gushed into the skull but could not fill it. Next, Vishnu commanded the horrible fury, which had pursued Kalabhairava wherever he went, to be gone. But the spirit of vengeance would not let go, for it was her dharma to pursue the sinner. It was not until later, when they reached the sacred city where, at the beginning of time, the column of light had manifested, that the demoness plunged back into hell, departing with a blood-curdling scream. At that, the skull dropped from Kalabhairava's hand.

Having freed the great sinner from his burden, Mahadev burst into spontaneous dance at the place where the skull fell. All the gods watched in awe and went into ecstasy. Since that time, any sin, no matter how grave, can be cleansed in Varanasi. Kapalamochana, "the pool or place where the skull fell," is to this day a place of pilgrimage. It is a place of power, where one can wash away the most heinous sins.

Before Shiva repaired to his home on Mount Kailash, he installed Kalabhairava as the city magistrate and chief of police. The Baranasi, that is, the citizens of Benares, refer to him respectfully as the "devourer of sin" and believe that he, like Yama, writes all their transgressions into a book. In order to please him, they celebrate a festival in his honor during the cold nights of the waning moon of Margashirsha (November/December).

All murderers, robbers, thieves, and other criminals adore Shiva-Kalabhairava—or his black female counterpart, Kali—for no other deity would be able to understand or have as much compassion for their own suffering, hardship, and fear as the god who was himself guilty of murder and hated by society as an outcast. Which god would grant them forgiveness, if not this one who himself had to wait so long to atone for his guilt?

As the god of sinners, Shiva is easily moved to grant mercy at the slightest sign of penance. There is, for example, the story of a certain culprit named Durdhara:

This Durdhara was about as low and nasty of character as can be imagined. He did not even respect the holy cow but ate beef without batting an eye. The money he gained through theft and extortion, he squandered on wine and women. He did not refrain even from raping his mother-in-law or from planning to murder a Brahmin. One day, a gardener surprised him as he was about to steal flowers, which he was going to use to seduce the wife of another man. As he jumped over the garden fence, he flung the bouquet to the ground, hissing, "These are for Shiva!" These mere words earned the culprit enough merit that he was allowed to throw a glance into heaven for a mere second. During that moment, he glimpsed a heavenly maiden looking back down at him. Her compassionate glance struck him to the core. In that instant, he regretted all the misdeeds he had ever done. But, despite his rue, he was hellbound, for the consequences of one's deeds follow inexorably. Nonetheless, the heavenly maiden pleaded on the sinner's behalf that he might be able to take a pilgrimage to Benares before the jaws of hell were to snap shut on him. As Durdhara approached the city gate, the gatekeeper stopped him, telling him that because of his vile nature, he stunk so much that he would not be allowed to enter the holy city. Once again the angel helped him. She let holy water rain from the sky to wash away the odor. As he set foot on the sacred grounds, his sins caught fire and enveloped him in flame. His misdeeds burned off his soul and rose into the sky, coloring it blue.

Since Shiva is proverbially easy to please, miscreants believe to this day that they can circumvent punishment and avoid harvesting the bitter fruits of karma by dedicating their crimes to Shiva or to Kali. Even today, goons and professional terrorists *(gundas)*, pocket thieves, robbers, and even the *dacoits* (armed peasant bandits) are devotees of Shiva. Weatherbeaten hippies, the flotsam and jetsam of the psychedelic sixties who still hang around the tourist spots in Goa, Bombay, or Kathmandu and survive dealing drugs, like to tattoo themselves with Shaivite motives: tridents, cobras with flared hoods, or Shankar's visage. Indian petty criminals like to slip into the red gowns of Shaivite sadhus and, pretending to be holy men, engage with the careless, nosy Western tourists and take them for all they are worth.

The swamis and gurus, however, warn against facile interpretations. Shiva's grace cannot be taken as license to commit crime. Stories like that of Durdhara are only allegorical, much like the story of Krishna's secret love affairs with the herdsmen's wives: they tell of God's love for each individual soul. When the Puranas call Shiva the "lord of thieves," it refers to the act of grace that steals our hearts at an unexpected hour, much as a thief in the night. It does not mean that he will protect burglars from the law. In the same way, Shiva's wanton cruelty is not a license for brutality, nor is it directed at human souls, but at the demons that plague the souls of his devotees.

Swamis, probably worried about the moral implications of Shiva as a Brahmin killer, have tried to move the story into a better light.[4] The fifth head of Brahma, they explain, was a god-devouring Moloch. The frightened gods begged Vishnu to free them from this terrible ogre. But Vishnu, who is the Preserver, was unable to do it. Shiva, who had already drunk up the poison that would have destroyed the world, declared himself willing to take on the portentous deed. In the form of Kalabhairava, he severed the monstrous head and agreed to carry it wherever he went for it was too heavy for the earth to bear and its heat would have dried out the ocean. He suffered it all out of his love for the earth and its creatures until, finally, he deposited it at Kapalamochana, the place of the skull. (It is interesting to note that Golgotha, the place where Jesus died as a "sinner" and redeemed the world, also means "the place of the skull.")

10
SHIVA AS
THE DEVIL

───── ⌒\ᴑ ─────

You can make them talk
if the serpent has stung them.
You can make them talk
if they're struck by an evil planet.
But you can't make them talk
if they're struck dumb
by riches.
Yet when Poverty the magician enters,
they'll speak at once,
O lord of the meeting rivers.

BASAVANNA,
SOUTH INDIAN SHAIVITE POET, TENTH CENTURY

By the first millennium B.C., in Persia as well as in India, the Aryan sacrificial cult had petrified into formal ritualism, no longer capable of satisfying the spiritual needs of the populace. It could deal with neither the tensions of a society in transition from pastoralism to sedentary agriculture, nor with the external threat of marauding tribes (Turanians) from central Asia. The inevitable revitalization of the social order took a totally different turn on the Iranian plateau, than it did among the Vedic cousins settled in the Indus and Ganges river basins.

☙ ZARATHUSTRA ❧

Sometime nearly three thousand years ago (scholars are still squibbing about the exact date), Zarathustra (Greek Zoroaster), "the man rich with camels," herded his beasts in the sparse desert of eastern Iran. In that wasteland he experienced a vision, an overawing new revelation of God, so powerful that, in its wake, the world has not to this day come to rest. There, in the loneliness of the wild mountains an angel of white light, a messenger of the "Wise Lord," Ahura Mazda, appeared before the trembling herdsman, revealing to him "Truth." This Truth concerns all of us, for it is the primogenitor of all the great mono-theistic religions of the West. The inheritors of Zarathustra's vision are not only the Persian fire wor-shippers and their priests, the *magi*

Ahura Mazda—the great God of Zarathustra

(magicians), along with their descendents in India, the Parsees; but also among its children are Judaism, Christianity, Islam, and numerous eso-teric cults. It is by no means mere coincidence that the three Zarathustrian astrologer priests, the so-called "Wise Men of the East," were present at the birth of Jesus at Bethlehem.

The east Asian religions do not treat good and evil as totally distinct ontological realities, for they are nothing but illusion (maya) or the play (lila) of God. Therefore it poses no great theological dilemma that Shiva can appear as God or as Devil. The form in which God appears is but a reflection of the soul of the beholder.* Zarathustra, however, saw the nature of reality differently. In his awesome vision, the universe becomes fundamentally divided into truth/falsehood, good/evil, white/black, and God/Satan. An unbridgeable chasm splits the two halves of the universe, and the individual human being, caught in the middle, is called upon to

---

*The spiritual traditions of indigenous peoples do not generally split the world into absolute dichotomies. In their "cultural construction of reality," tribal peoples such as the American Indians attribute to each being, be it a stone, a plant, an animal, or any other phenomenon, its own unique power. Depending on the situation or in what man-ner one approaches it, this power can be helpful or harmful. Good and evil are thus not absolute, but situation bound.

make her own ethical, moral choice between them—a choice of either/or. Threatening God's (Ahura Mazda's) perfect creation is the spirit of Evil, Angra Mainyu (Ahriman). While Ahura Mazda guards the *asha* (the eternal Law and Order, Truth, Justice), which the Hindus call *dharma*, Ahriman spreads lies and illusion *(druj)*. The uncompromising battle between the two principles rages throughout the universe, ripping apart macrocosmic Nature as well as the microcosm of each soul.

Ahura Mazda is Lord and Master. He has no need of a wife, like the Hindu idols. Nor is his image of pure light sullied by a miasmic jungle of colorful and lewd tales and legends or graven images. He is the Creator, who brought forth all that is good: the starry sky, the primordial white bull, the human beings, cows, dogs, the earth, the elements, the angels, and all the virtues.

His satanic opponent, however, tries to spoil the Creation wherever he can. He perverted some of the stars, turning them into malefic planets; he ruined many of the animals, turning them into snakes, rats, reptiles, amphibians, flies, and other unclean, creepy crawly things. He brought all impurities and sicknesses, all things mean and ugly, all lies and illusions into the world. At the beginning of time—that is, at the beginning of the Four Ages, some twelve thousand years ago—Ahriman entered Creation. His first evil act was to kill both the primordial bull and Gayomard, the androgynous primordial human being, with the result that physical matter, sexuality, and all the painful passions came into existence. These he stirred into the perfect Creation, mixing it up so that good and evil, light and dark were hopelessly intertwined. Like a sorcerer stirring his cauldron, adding the vile to the pure, he planned to ruin the Creation completely; but God and his heavenly hosts, the *amesha spentas*, the angels and archangels, thwarted his efforts.

Zarathustra's followers believe that the situation became ever more desperate as time wore on. Then the merciful God heard the sighing and moaning of his maltreated creation and sent a prophet—Zarathustra—to bring the right teaching. He was born of a virgin who, upon bathing in a holy lake, received the unspoiled sperm that had been kept hidden in its waters since the beginning of time. Despite the devil's efforts to destroy the infant, he managed to grow up to be a simple herdsman and then to spread the right teaching.

Zarathustra was a champion of sobriety, condemning self-torture and asceticism as much as inebriated ecstasy. The best way for human beings to escape the clutches of the devil and to separate the good particles of light from the hold of darkness is to live the simple, natural country life, working at tilling the soil, raising grain, growing fruits, rooting out weeds, draining marshes, irrigating deserts, treating one's animals well, especially the cows and dogs, and always speaking the truth. (Because of the high rank accorded agricultural husbandry, the theosophists, anthroposophists, and other occultists see Zarathustra as "the great initiate of the second post-Atlantean period," whose divine inspiration inaugurated the culture of sedentary farming communities.) Zarathustra condemned all the magic and idolatry that had, in his eyes, polluted Aryan worship. He preached against blood sacrifices, established cow protection and the maintaining of the purity of the elements. Ever since, in order not to pollute the elements, the dead may neither be buried in the earth, nor dumped into water, nor burned in fire. The Parsees have built "Towers of Silence," where the dead are laid out, to be eaten by vultures.

For the end of time, Zarathustra prophesied a final battle between the forces of good and evil, in which Ahriman and the damned hosts will be defeated and banished forever into the pits of fiery hell. Another deliverer (Saoshyant), a savior like himself, will appear just before this apocalypse. Then the dead shall rise for their final judgment. As they cross a razor-sharp bridge over into paradise, their own conscience will appear to them as an angel if they are good, or as a demon, terrifying them and causing them to plunge into a lake of fire below, if they have been wicked. Another image is that of a molten stream of metal that will torment the evil but will feel like soothing, warm milk to the just. Finally, the earth will disappear in a great conflagration.

What is especially interesting in Zarathustra's vision is his redefinition of the old Vedic gods, the *daevas* (Sanskrit *devas*). They are turned into devils, companions of evil Ahriman. Ancient Indo-European deities, such as Indra, the wielder of thunder, the Ashvins (the heavenly twins), and Sharva, who is none other than Shiva-Rudra, are expressly mentioned as evil spirits. Daeva worshippers are threatened with eternal hellfire.[1] The *ahuras,* led by Ahura Mazda (who is really a metamorphosis of the old Aryan lord of high heaven and guardian of the moral and cosmic order, the god Varuna), become the heavenly hosts opposing the evil daevas.

The ahuras appear in the oldest Indian writings as the *asuras* (from Sanskrit *asu* = breath, air, hence divine; related to Nordic *asir*). In the Vedas they are divine lords, neither especially good nor bad. Only later Indian writings (Brahmanas) speak of them as foes of the devas, or gods. The Upanishads confirm that, at first, the asuras and devas were equal in virtue and vice; but because the devas loved the truth, they became divine, while the asuras, who loved advantage above truth, became demonic. Popular folktales tell that the gods derived from Prajapati's breath but the asuras from his stinking intestinal winds. At one time, they had all cooperated. They had churned the ocean of milk together, dividing their work equally. But when it came to the prize to be won, the nectar of immortality, the antigods were cheated. They were deprived of the divine, inebriating soma, which is also called *sura*. Thus, say the tales, the antigods are *a-suras*, glum nondrinkers, while the gods are suras, drinkers, drunk on divine bliss and ecstasy.

We can see that Zarathustra turned the sociology of the supernatural worlds topsy-turvy. To him and his followers, the worshippers of the *daevas* (devas) became nonsober, idol devil worshippers. There was little doubt as far as they were concerned that the devotees of Shiva-Sharva were worshippers of the Evil One.

The image of Satan, which spooks through all Western religions, has its roots in Zarathustra's condemnation of the old gods, specifically of Shiva. Shiva is the arrogant Lucifer, who refused to stand up and bow at the presence of the Creator (Daksha) and is, therefore, cast out of the heavens to dwell as an outcast in the wilderness with demons, ghosts, and goblins. Shiva, the ash-covered ascetic who loves to dance on burning funeral pyres (the symbol of the passing worlds of illusion), was turned into the filthy devil, dancing in the sulfurous fumes of hellfire, in which the souls of the damned are roasting. His trident became the devil's pitchfork. The animal skins he wears became the devil's own hairy skin. His seemingly uncontrolled, volcanic sexuality, his phallus, his passionate indulgence in drugs, especially witches' drugs like hemp and thorn apple, his proverbial unwillingness to work, and his habit of begging were all thoroughly condemned. His shiny diadem, the crescent moon, was easily turned into horns, identifying him with other horned, shamanistic gods that savage heathens are apt to worship.

Mahadev's adders and vipers became, in Zarathustrian eyes, the very insignia of evil. In older cultures these long-lived reptiles, with their ability to shed their skins, were respected as the symbol of life renewing itself, as omens of fertility, of wisdom, and of healing (e.g., Aesculapian serpents of ancient Greece). The divine serpent belongs to the Mother Goddess, like the lingam to the yoni. Often the masculine divinity takes on an ophidian form to slip into the moist, dark caverns under the earth, to fertilize the Earth Mother.[2] Even Odin turned into a snake in order to enter the abode of an earth giant, seduce the giant's daughter, and make off with the mead of immortality. In India to this day, women worship nagas in order to be blessed with children. When the Bible speaks of the seduction of the Mother of Humanity by the clever serpent, Lucifer, at the tree of paradise, it is in line with ancient tradition. However, it is given a negative twist and order is

Worship of the nagas (snakes)

not restored until the immaculate, heavenly virgin, Mary, crushes the old serpent under her heel. A Persian folk story, reflecting the Zarathustrian bias, tells that women were cursed to menstruate because of Eve's illicit intercourse with the serpent.

The Zarathustrian imagination that discovered the devil and hellfire also brought forth the popular image we have of angels and archangels, as messengers of God and as personifications of the virtues. They were shown in long, white robes, fluttering through the air with dovelike, feathery wings, doing the bidding of Ahura Mazda, their heavenly Father. Even our common image of the good Lord as a strict but loving old man with a long, white beard, wearing a white robe, approximates Old Persian icons of Ahura Mazda.

To Westerners born and raised in a Judeo-Christian cultural setting, these images and ideas are quite familiar. There is a good reason for this—our Western worldview was nurtured by the Old and the New Testament, both of which are replete with Zarathustrian contents. In the year 587 B.C. Jerusalem was besieged, looted, and burned, its temple razed to the ground by the armies of the orgiastic, goddess-worshipping Babylonians. The Chosen People were scattered, many taken into captivity where, as the Psalm tells:

Western Devil with pitchfork

> *By the rivers of Babylon*
> *There we sat down and wept*
> *When we remembered Zion.*

Some fifty years later, the Persian warlord Cyrus the Great overran Babylon in the name of Ahura Mazda, freed the Jews, and let them rebuild their destroyed temple city, Jerusalem. During these years of crises, the cult of Yahwe, the tumultuous god of Mount Sinai, took on new dimensions. The synagogue and a calendar of festivals appeared and, equally important, many of Zarathustra's teachings entered the beliefs of the Hebrews: the belief in God as a universal, not merely tribal deity; the belief in a hierarchy of angels serving God; the doctrine of the existence of Satan (Shaitin) and his fallen hosts as the opponents of God, in an absolute dualism of Good and Evil; the belief in the inevitability of the final battle (Armageddon) and the longing for a coming messiah; the dogma of a day of judgment, of the resurrection of the dead and their final reward in everlasting heaven or their punishment in everlasting hellfire. Heaven and hell became clearly defined, in contrast to the previous belief in a *sheol*, a shadowy place for the dead.

During the hardship of the Roman occupation, the yearning for the arrival of the Messiah was especially strong. The Essenes, a group of monks dressed in plain white, like the magi, built agricultural communes in the desert near the Dead Sea. Given to serving God by performing purification rites, fasting, and working the soil while awaiting the "Teacher of Righteousness," they bear full evidence of Zarathustrian influence. John the Baptist seems most certainly to have been associated with them, and Jesus of Nazareth also.

The towering image of Zarathustra, the moral prophet and voice in the wilderness, possessed by righteousness, stands in sharp contrast to the image of the Shaivite sadhu, the ecstatic shaman, the Taoist mystic, or the Buddhist begging monk. He is the model for all the Biblical preachers and prophets to follow, and for the Christian and Muslim zealots that have been hammering their message into the brains of the western half of humanity ever since. We see him reappear as readily in Muhammad as in Jean Calvin, the father of the Puritans, in American revivalists (à la Jerry Falwell or Billy Graham) and hard-line conservative politicians; he is alive in the fanatic fundamentalism of Osama bin Laden as well as in the moralism of Karl Marx. In the person of Ayatollah Khomeini, who struggled to purify his people and refused to compromise with the Great Satan, the bearded prophet had appeared once again in his land of origin, Persia.

After the heathen warlord "Alexander the Damned" (as the Parsees still call the Macedonian conqueror) demolished the proud empire of the Zarathustrian Persians and burned all their sacred writings, the brilliant star of this religion started to set. Covertly, though, the great river of vision lives on, not only in Judaism and Christianity, but also in other streams, such as Manichaeanism, with its ample influence on occultist and esoteric movements (e.g., Rudolf Steiner's anthroposophy).* Islam, too, which has declared total war on Satan and all idols, proves itself a grandchild of Zarathustra with its concern for ritual purity, its obsession with body fluids and excretions, and its mandatory five daily prayers.

In each case, the message remains the same, created by the same dramaturge but enacted differently on different stages. The cosmic drama is a linear, historical one. It starts with a creation and concludes with a happy end. Sandwiched in between is the treachery of the villain, the battle between the good creator and the evil destroyer, the arrival of the messenger of the good (a prophet or savior) and the moral injunction to all and everyone to personally engage in the battle for the good. Even Marxism proves to be but a modern, secular expression of the same spirit, enacting the same drama: original paradise (primitive communism), the fall (temptation of property and profit), the struggle between the good (working class) and the bad (parasitic exploiters), the arrival of the true prophet (in the form of the trinity, Marx/Engels/Lenin), the great battle (class war, revolution), the final judgment (return of the means of production to the creative working masses), and the final victory of the good (the happy communist utopia).

---

*The message of Mani (third century A.D.), another Persian prophet, may also be seen as a later edition of Zarathustrianism. Mani, who posed a serious threat to emerging Christianity, taught that good and evil are hopelessly mixed together in the world and in each soul. To liberate the sparks of Spirit from the mixture, moral action (such as abstinence from meat eating, alcohol, sex, and foul language) is demanded from each individual. "Holy ones" capable of this are to serve as teachers of others and will enter the Divine Light after death. "Auditors," on the other hand, who hear the message but cannot live it, need to be reborn until they too can enter the Divine Light. It is interesting to note that in his youth, Saint Augustine was a Manichaean auditor. Even though this church father became an enemy of Manichaeanism, his ideas remain influenced by these doctrines. During the Middle Ages Manichaeanism reared its head again in southern France with the Cathars (Greek *katharikos* = the pure ones). It took a Crusade and an Inquisition to crush them. Nonetheless, the ideas of the Cathars live on in many streams of the psychic-occult underground.

❧ THE EARTH RUNS WELL ❧

Suppose we are missionaries and we happen upon one of these ash-covered, long-haired Shaivite sadhus, sitting in the shade of one of those mighty fig trees. Suppose we try to lay this grandiose drama before his mind and tell him that this is Reality. If he would answer at all, he might smile and shake his head. "My dear friend, what you call Reality is but one of the infinite illusions flooding finite minds. And if the masses believe this doctrine, then it is simply mass illusion, mass insanity. What appears as history is but part of the eternal turning of the wheel of samsara, the endless cycle of joys and sorrows; it is the lila (game, play) of Shiva. How can there be a beginning or an end, or even a final perfection? Everything is perfect already, anyway. The earth runs well as it runs. He who has eyes, can see!"

Somewhere in his rambling lectures, the rather unorthodox Indian guru Bhagwan Shree Rajneesh (Osho) claimed that there are basically two religions in the world and that the Iranian Plateau is the dividing line between them. Indeed, west of the divide, the diverse Judeo-Christian-Islamic confessions dominate, while east of the divide, the worldview of Hinduism-Buddhism-Jainism-Taoism holds sway. On the one side, good and evil are seen as irreconcilable opposites, calling for a strenuous effort to root out the evil pole. On the other side, the absolute opposition of good and evil makes no ultimate sense, being but a reflection of the state of the isolated ego, which sees all threats to its continuity as evil. The inflated ego, even when it wears an altruistic mask as a national, group, racial, or family ego, is bound to see its existence as a merciless struggle against death, darkness, and obliteration. From its perspective, everything is wrong with the world. But the real Self is not the limited ego. According to the Hindus, the true Self, identical with Shiva, rests eternally in total Being, Consciousness, and Bliss (Sat-Chit-Anand). Once freed from our ego prison, whether one is incarnated in a physical body or not (Shaivite philosophy considers even that to be an illusion, for our being is eternal), then everything is as it is—that is, everything is Shiva.

This is easily said, but difficult to realize. Ramakrishna (1834–1886), the Bengali saint and ecstatic devotee of Kali, once told this story to illustrate the divine nature of all existence:[3]

The Master said: "Everything that exists is God." The pupil understood it literally, but not in the true spirit. While passing through the street, he met with an elephant. The driver (mahut) shouted aloud from his high place, "Move away, move away!" The pupil argued in his mind, "Why should I move away? I am God, so is the elephant also God. What fear has God of Himself?" Thinking thus, he did not move. At last the elephant took him up by his trunk, and dashed him aside. He was severely hurt, and going back to his Master, he related the whole adventure. The Master said, "All right, you are God. The elephant is God also, but God in the shape of the elephant-driver was warning you also from above. Why did you not pay heed to his warnings?"

All is Shiva; all is God. But each form, each appearance has its own power, its own character, its own potential. When one is not enmeshed and attached to the fascinating dance of Maya and her countless forms of illusion, then one can realize this. Then sinner and saint, good and evil are equally part of Being.

From such a perspective, all appearances are but the child's game that the greater Self plays for its own entertainment. In this game, it can take on any role and any state of being. Thus God can put on the mask of the Savior, the good shepherd, Mother Mary, the Great Goddess, the Ahura Mazda, the Good God; but he can just as well wear the mask of a murderous Bhairava or a frenzied Kali, and thus, by the drama of confusion and suffering, show those who have also violated their dharma, the way to Benares, where the fires of purification burn and the waters of cleansing flow. This is how Shiva can be the "devil" and still be worshipped with loving devotion, just as Ramakrishna worshipped black Kali as his "loving Mother," or, in Mahayana and Vajrayana Buddhism, Buddha can appear as a bug-eyed, fire-breathing demon and still be honored by the devout. These terrible appearances are only mirrors placed in front of the mad, illusion-driven ego. For Shaivites, all the wonderful, terrible, and awesome images that magically make up our reality are but facets of the one Self.

For the devotees of Shiva, the ultimate goal is not just to be good, to heap up the merits of good karma and go to heaven—though there is nothing to speak against such worthy aspirations; it is self-understood that one follows the path of virtue. For the Shaivites the goal is to see through the divine masks and recognize the Self; the goal is moksha, liberation from the bondage of finite existence, the release from the incessant wheel of illusion, samsara. Or as Allama Prabhu, the south Indian mystical poet of the tenth century, puts it:[4]

Feed the poor
tell the truth
make water-places
for the thirsty
and build tanks for a town—
You may go to heaven
after death, but you'll get nowhere
near the truth of Our Lord.
And the man who knows Our Lord,
He gets no results.

⛤ THE RIGHTEOUS BATTLE ⛤

Ever since the great Persian magus cast his spell, the occidental cultures have taken desperate, heroic efforts to rid the world of evil, sickness, and pain, to ban or even kill the terrifying "old serpent." This deeply rooted sentiment is perhaps the single most important motor for the ideology of progress and for the scientific drive to wipe out hunger, poverty, disease, and even death itself. Again, our sadhu would shake his head: How, in the world of appearance, can the good and pure exist without its dialectical opposite? How can "chosen ones" exist, if there are no "damned ones"? What is a puritan, without a sinner? What is the day without the night? The existence of one conjures the other. The opposites are halves of the whole. For that reason, "evil" is ever present in the world as long as the "good," the "chosen ones," are constantly fighting against it. In Indian mythology this dialectical necessity is expressed as the ceaseless struggle of the good devas against the vile asuras. Woe to the soul that is caught up in this struggle and has forgotten that it is but maya and lila.

It is all too easy to get caught up in it and to identify with the good (it flatters the ego), while seeing the bad in the other, the stranger, the outsider, or misfit. Sometimes such a discovery of evil literally forces itself upon the beholder. How must the Christians have felt when drunken, howling Vikings, who wore horns on their helmets and worshipped that one-eyed devil, Odin, descended from their dragon ships to pillage, rape, and burn their peaceful villages? They probably felt much the same way that the peaceful Californian citizens feel when Hell's Angels roar into town for a weekend party!

There is always somebody to play the devil's role. In the Late Middle Ages, it might have been the Gypsies, for example. Suddenly these colorful, dark-complexioned, vagabond people who told fortunes, prayed to the "devil" and the moon, and cheated the honest peasant, appeared in Europe. "Wherever they pass, it was believed, children die and the animals get sick. In their wake, they leave a smell of sulfur, an undertow of hell. They have been sent by the devil."[5] (Actually, the Roma or Rom, as the Gypsies call themselves, are a migrant tribe of Indian untouchable musicians and jugglers. They are related to the Dom, the untouchables who guard the sacred funeral fire of Benares.)

But one need not look even that far to find the henchmen of the devil. They are found within one's own ranks. Especially women, "by nature weaker," fall prey to the guile of the wicked one. Only think of the witches, those wortcunning hags, midwives, and nymphs, who met in heaths, uninhabited moors, or on the top of wild mountains, to intoxicate themselves with salves and to celebrate lewd orgies in honor of a stinking buck (Old English *buc* = he-goat, stag), with an ice cold phallus.[6] Such sinister, spell-brewing devil worshippers could never be tolerated by Daksha's or Zarathustra's spiritual descendents, the officials of civil society, the upholders of Church and State. Indeed, the so-called witches still celebrated an archaic fertility rite and paid tribute to the old shamanistic horned god, who lived in Celtic lore as Cernunnos, lord of the animals, and in the Mediterranean lore as Pan, the nature spirit. Commonly, the horned god or "devil" was called *Bogy* or bogey man, an appellation related to the *bock* of the central European witches. That "buck" and "bock" refer to the he-goat is a significant linguistic convergence, for they are equally related to the Slavic *bogu*, meaning a god, and the old Indian *bhaga* (lord, the giver), which we know in such words as *Bhagavad* or *Bhagavan*.

Periodically, when the pillaging hordes of heathens from the East—the Huns, the Mongols, the Magyars, the Turks, or most recently the atheistic Bolsheviks—swept over Europe, there was no doubt the devil was on the loose, trying to undo Christianity. They were seen as the hordes of Gog and Magog that the Bible had prophesied would appear at the End of Time. For the Puritan settlers of Massachusetts, the devil was in the redskins, "those tawny snakes and children of Satan," as the Calvinistic preacher Cotton Mather characterized them when calling for their eradication.[7] Such examples could easily fill an entire book.

However, it was not only the stranger or the nonconformist in one's own ranks one had to be on guard against, but the evil tempter was apt to slither into one's very own soul if one lost vigilance. He could appear as sexual desire, as undercurrents of jealousy, greed, fear, or cowardice, and would have to be purged by confession, self-castigation, and prayer as the Christians prescribe; or by absolute submission under God's will, as Islam demands; or by the most careful observance of ritual purity, as orthodox Judaism prescribes.

With this in view, it is no surprise that Bhagwan Shree Rajneesh (Osho), who taught a clever mix of Shaivite Tantra and humanistic psychology, was nearly killed by the puritanical, fundamentalist Christians that surrounded his rural commune, Rajneeshpuram, in Antilopeville, Oregon. The commune was founded in August 1981. Bhagwan lived there until November 14, 1985, when United States marshals deported him for violation of the U.S. immigration laws. How dare he teach his belated flower children that they should not resist temptation or repress their desires, but live them out, while dedicating them to God. He preached that only after the burning desire for sex, power, money, drugs, or pleasure has been allowed to exhaust itself, can Shiva be realized and the overwhelming primordial drive be sublimated and transformed into spiritual wisdom. This primordial energy is identified as the kundalini-serpent slumbering in the lower guts. When the touch of the spirit awakens it, it begins to rise, changing slowly from a reptile into a goddess as it unites with consciousness in ultimate bliss. Whoever fights this old serpent, turning its very power against itself in order to repress the desires of the organism, is bound to fail. Forever will he stand in fear of it, like a bird mesmerized by an approaching snake; he will remain frustrated, dissatisfied, aggressive, with no peace of mind. In repressing them, forbidden desires can never be overcome and purified but will continue to exert a fatal fascination.

Further Rajneesh taught his followers, the orange-clad "Neo-Sannyasins," that anyone who is busy repressing her own shakti-power will not stop with herself. On the contrary, it is always easier to locate the enemy at the other end of the index finger. When a number of like-minded repressors get together, the likely result is a whole system of repression. A new church, sect, political party, or movement, complete with laws, prescriptions, taboos, suspicious priests and functionaries, and an inevitable shadow of corruption and hypocrisy will make its debut.

Rajneesh advised his followers not to do that, but to let the kundalini-serpent rise, and to accept and love the dark, fear-inducing shadow that lurks in the darkest dungeon of the soul, for he too is Shiva! He counseled Daksha—we all are Daksha, for we are the creators of our own universe—to accept the uncanny, frightening rebel who dared make claim on our youngest, most lovely daughter, as our proper son-in-law. After all, she, who is the symbolic image of our soul, has long given her heart to him. Fairy tales show that the prince (the symbolic image of our Self) does not necessarily appear in silks and satins, but often as a stranger clothed in a bear's rough hide. Only when he is accepted can there be peace in the kingdom of our soul, as well as in the external world.

Indeed, Rajneesh must have been crazy to preach such a message in God's own country, where the fires of a puritan, Zarathustrian spirit burn brightly and where presidents contemplate "star wars" against "empires of evil" or lead crusades against an "axis of evil." In the community churches around Rajneeshpuram, the prayers for the lost souls never ceased, while billboards were erected on the highway leading to the demonic community with the warning from Dante's Inferno: "Let all who enter, abandon all hope."

It is doubtful that the former philosophy professor from Pune (India) knew much about the place where he was. Certainly he was unaware of what anthropologists call the "cultural construction of reality" of the society in which he was agitating. He must not have watched too many Westerns, those mystery dramas of the American Way of Life, where the good guy, dressed in white, guns down the swarthy bad guy at high noon and restores order. (In pluralistic India things might not have gone so far. Of course, there are tensions when money and power are involved, or when a Muslim injures a holy cow, but who would get upset about the kundalini rising?) Eventually the scene in Oregon became so heavy, so bizarre, that nervous Neo-Sannyasins became paranoid. They collected guns for self-defense. Inner tensions split the commune, and they themselves, despite themselves, were caught up in the old dualism of "we versus them." Finally, the bald-headed guru was apprehended. U.S. marshals paraded him in chains, bound like the devil, across the television screen, the modern public pillory for offenders. After his devotees paid his bail and sprung him out of prison, he mumbled into his beard that "America is not a democracy but a hypocrisy," and left for good.

◈

Worldviews or "cultural constructions of reality" are not just a matter of belief; they affect and form the "reality" in which one finds oneself. When Zarathustra declared total war on the old gods—especially the lord of the animals (Sharva)—and tried to ban them into the abyss forever, things took a different turn in Nature also. The minds of Zarathustrian priests, sharpened on the whetstone of dualistic conceptualization to a razor's edge, dissected the organic unity of life into a good half and a bad half. The *Avesta*, the holy scriptures of the Zarathustrians, sunders the children of Mother Earth into clean and unclean creatures, into useful ones and pests. It is a division that, to the chagrin of ecologists, affects our thoughts and acts to this day. The plants and animals serving the herdspeople and farmers, the cattle, sheep, and dogs, the fruit and grain, were considered good, useful, and pure creatures of Ahura Mazda. On the other hand, weeds and useless plants, predators such as wolves and bears, creepy and crawly things such as snakes, frogs, worms, spiders, and crop pests, as well as those abominations that feed on cadavers such as flies, maggots, or ants, were considered to be ahrimanic, evil and impure. Persian magi (priests) dressed in white gowns and face masks like those of our laboratory scientists made it an act of piety, pleasing to God, to kill thousands of such pests every day. Of course, in those days, such wanton destruction of life could not cause too much environmental damage. Today, however, the conceptual paradigm bequeathed to us by the old prophet, coupled with our chemical arsenals of pesticides, herbicides, and fungicides, has devastating effects.

Such fanaticism is hardly possible for the Shiva-conscious Hindu, nor for the Jain or the Buddhist, for every living creature, even the smallest bug, has the right to live, and in its life to work out a bit of its karma on its long path toward ultimate God-realization (or, in the case of the Buddhist, on its way to nirvana). In Ganesha's temples even rats and mice are fed and adored, and at certain times of the month, Hindu housewives sprinkle rice flour on the floor for the ants.

It was the contact with the spirit of India, where the lord of the animals still holds sway in people's hearts, that gave the Western ecology movement during the 1960s a major impulse. The idea of ahimsa, "live and let live," entered the popular imagination. It was finally realized—at least among a few—that every little weed and each tiny worm or bug have their meaningful place in the whole of Nature. Each one is a vital link in the chain of life (human life included). It was realized that the cruel war against Nature, coupled with an exploitative economic system that wastes resources and overproduces unneeded goods, is on a dead-end road.

In Shaivite eyes, the battle against Nature is a battle against our Self. And it is time to learn to accept the unloved part of creation and to metamorphose it with our love. It is time for Daksha to invite the seemingly uncouth Shiva to the great sacrificial feast that is Life. Will the princess with the golden ball, the princess of our soul, be able to kiss the ugly cold frog and watch it turn into a handsome, shiny prince, or will the sclerotic, intellectualistic goat-head of Daksha, with its rigid morality, prevail?

Note: All that precedes has been written in full awareness that the author himself unwittingly falls into a dualistic view of things: the "good" monist, on one hand, the "bad" dualist, on the other hand. Such is the nature of living in a conditional world, where the gods and the demons churn the primordial ocean. And sometimes it is hard to tell the difference between the two. What more can be said than that Shiva dwells in all, and to reach him, one must go beyond the rending duality?

> *Suppose you cut a tall bamboo in two;*
> *make the bottom piece a woman,*
> *the headpiece a man;*
> *rub them together till they kindle:*
> *tell me now,*
> *the fire that's born,*
> *is it male or female*
> *O Ramanatha?*
>
> DEVARA DASIMAYA,
> WEAVER AND SOUTH INDIAN SHAIVITE POET,
> TENTH CENTURY

11

TANTRA:
THE SERPENT'S PATH

———— ൦൮ഠ ————

The sensual pleasure women provide,
the joy of wine, the taste of meat:
It's the undoing of fools,
but for the wise, the pathway to salvation.

KALARNAVA TANTRA

Lovers should be pure of heart
And only think of love,
For Love is no sin, but virtue!
Love makes the bad good,
and the good better.
Love makes truly chaste.

MONTANGAGOL,
OCCITAN TROUBADOUR

It is never easy for the guardians of an old order. During the time that corresponds to the European Middle Ages, the Brahmins beheld the strange plants sprouting from the fertile soils of the Indian mind. After gestating for a thousand years, indigenous cults emerged that bore little resemblance to the venerable Vedic sacrificial ceremonies of old. What times were these, when tradition was trampled, rules of caste ignored, when untouchables received initiation, and women were given sacred mantras! Bhaktis, forgetting their everyday duties, swarmed the land, raving about God's love, while other heretics claimed that Shiva had revealed to them the "fifth Veda," the rules and regulations called *tantra* (warp, weavings), Where would this lead to? Had not the false doctrines of the Buddhists and Jains caused enough problems? The Brahmins could only speak of the emergence of a dark age.

At this juncture of history, Brahmanism and its eclipsing gods were going through a major crisis. Magical, theurgic chants and offerings were no longer the single, infallible bridge to the gods. A new metaphor of divine love defined the relation between God and man. God and the Soul loved each other like Shiva and Devi, or Krishna and Radha, in an eternal honeymoon, according to the heretics. Playing his enchanted flute, Krishna lures the lovely milkmaids (the souls) from their husbands' (the worldly concerns) beds and makes intimate, tender love to them. In such a way, God loves us totally and personally, and we may love him back in complete devotion. We may love him as best we can imagine it: as a man loves a woman or a woman loves a man, or as a mother loves her child or as a child loves its mother. We can take baby Krishna in our arms and cuddle him, or we can become babies suckling at Mother Kali's breasts. We can receive God's love like a temple prostitute or like a lover at a secret rendezvous. (Convergent sentiments are evident in Christianity, from the devotion of Mary Magdalene to the sensual cantatas of Johann Sebastian Bach, in which the soul is the yearning bride of Jesus.)

The devotional (bhakti) movement eventually gained respectability. Tantrism, however, especially the so-called "left-handed" tantrism, still upsets many an orthodox *pandit* or swami, for in its ritual context, all kinds of age-old taboos and prescriptions (such as injunctions against eating meat, drinking alcohol, or indulging in nonprocreative sex) are deliberately violated. Whoever knows Hindu Puritanism's panic fear of ritual pollution will understand this anxiety. It was not so long ago that untouchables had to ring little bells when they walked down the street, lest the touch of their shadow or a hint of their breath pollute a higher-caste Hindu How shocking the idea that in tantric rites, it is precisely the pariah woman, the street sweeper or washer maiden that is the preferred sexual partner and is to be honored as the Goddess herself. How shocking, the practices of abnormal sex (including its anal and oral variations), coupled with the eating of meat and the drinking of wine. Does not the commandment of ahimsa (non-injury) preclude the killing of animals, and does not the consumption of spirituous liquors dull the sensible, ethereal nerves that take lifetimes of clean living to develop?

Indeed, that is so. Even the Tantrists know that. But is it not proverbial that forbidden fruits taste the sweetest and excite the most? Like flies drawn to rotten meat, the souls of this confused, materialistic age are drawn to just such forbidden, crude pleasures. It is precisely here, at the focal point of modern man's obsessions, interests, and fascinations that the Tantrist master has a handle by which to grasp the lost soul and pull him toward salvation. The old, venerable rituals, the commandments and ceremonies simply do not interest the human being of the Kali Yuga anymore. If religious exercises are done at all these days, they are, more often than not, performed listlessly, automatically, or out of a sense of duty or social expectation. What really excites the fervor, on the other hand, is not the sattvic, or divine concerns, but sex, the stomach, external appearance, and personal power. Instead of condemning and repressing these *tamasic* (dark, nonspiritual) drives and enchantments from the start, Tantra tries to sanctify them, weave them into ritual, dedicate them to Shiva and, thus, take the first steps on the long path toward Self-recognition.

That, in a nutshell, is what most Tantrist masters today try to do. Bhagwan Shree Rajneesh is perhaps the best-known recent heterodox Tantrist. In a genial manner, he dressed his Tantrism in concepts he borrowed from the new humanistic, transpersonal psychology (transactional analysis, Gestalt therapy, human potential movement, etc.) and from Western occultists such as G. I. Gurdjieff and Wilhelm Reich. But despite their bright new clothes, his teachings became as upsetting to the Western establishment as they were to the orthodox Hindus. His Neo-Sannyas movement ended in disaster. Back in Pune, Hindu militants from the Radhtriya Swayamsevak Sangh (RSS) threatened to assassinate him. Generally, though, most Indians consider him to be a clown or charlatan at best, and a swindler and con artist at worst. Serious students of the tantric tradition, however, respectfully refer to Shree Rajneesh as "Acharya," (Teacher).

Despite their notoriety, the Tantrist masters continue to propagate their method as the only one suited to the Kali Yuga. Renunciations and self-denial might have been the proper way to salvation during the preceding world age, just as in the one before that, it was the sacrificial ceremony. But none of those work anymore. And just as the Vedas were the proper scriptures during the first age (Krita Yuga), the Upanishads during the second age (Treta Yuga), and the Puranas during the third age (Dvapara Yuga), so the unorthodox Tantras, or Agamas, are the trail-blazing writings of this dark, chaotic age (Kali Yuga).

ੴ THE HERESY OF THE AGAMAS ੴ

The basic message of classical Hinduism is that, despite the multidimensionality of appearances and ever-changing phenomena, despite the endless number of gods, there is really one, and only one, reality. This singular reality is indivisible *(advaita)*. The infinite diversity is but deceptive appearance. The world is a gaily woven veil of illusion that hides the One (be it called God, Shiva, Self, Vishnu, Brahman, or whatever), a veil that fools the unenlightened soul and leads it into ever new activity (karma). The souls are caught in this deception, like flies in a spider's web. The hallucination of being separate individuals causes them to seek advantage over others, to secure pleasure and power, and to try to avoid death. But all their mad effort just entangles them all the more in a never-ending cycle of births and deaths, each generating new hopes and new suffering.

It is only a resolute "No!" in answer to the restless pursuit of fleeting happiness, power, and hope that allows the human being to escape the monstrous fantasy prison of existence. It is only through self-denial and asceticism that he may escape the binding chain of deeds (karma). Like a turtle withdrawing its head and limbs into its shell, the wise man has to withdraw his five senses from the bewitching dance of Maya. His spirit must become as still as a lake on a windless day. It must become a dustless mirror reflecting the One, the Purusha, while merging with him. Even though the seeker might still be clothed in mortal flesh, such recognition and merging with God is possible. Then he will be a delivered soul *(jivanmukta)*. His separate ego will have vanished and he will make no new karma. Only remnants of his old karma *(prarabdha karma)* remain to be sloughed off. He is like an old civil servant with no pending duties, counting the days toward his retirement.

Such yearning for deliverance was quite foreign to the life-affirming Aryan nomads when they entered India, that "continent of Circe."[1] Was it the humid jungle, the monsoon, or the wiles of the natives that eroded their primitive optimism? Escape from the world of illusion and merger with the One became the goal of Patanjali's yoga, as much as of the teachings of the arch-anchorite Shankaracharya,* not to mention of the Buddhists and Jains. This is the often cited "Indian escapism," the flight from reality, with which Western scholars often patronizingly finish the phrase, "The trouble with India is . . . !"

Tantrism, however, has none of this. Like India itself, it bubbles over with a joyous life affirmation that no visitor to the subcontinent will have failed to notice. Tantrism has no quarrel with the monistic (advaitin) arguments of the world-denying monks. It agrees that all is One, all is Shiva. But that "All" includes also the grand "illusion" and the "world." How could it not? The carnival of illusion is but Shiva's game and pastime (lila), the spontaneous outflow of his limitless energy (shakti). The Tantrist does not seek to escape this cosmic masquerade ball, but to accept it, to enjoy it. This enjoyment, however, is not possible as long as one clings defensively to one's separate ego identity. But when one has learned not to separate I and Other, good and evil, wisdom and stupidity, then the divine opens up. The jivanmukta, the released soul, accepts all and loves all as her Self (Shiva). Love, not renunciation, frees the soul! Everything is divine and worthy of worship, though there is no compulsion to worship it.

In the orthodox, advaitin view of things, the All-Spirit (Purusha), whose nature is considered to be masculine, is in a state of constant contemplative rest. Nature *(prakriti)*, on the other hand, is like a seductive woman, the dancing courtesan of the world illusion, enveloping him in hallucinations. Much like a Saint Paul, the arch-conservative advaitin monk Shankaracharya utters the dire warning, "Beware! The gateway to hell is the woman! She stands between the soul and God (Shiva) realization!"[2]

The Tantrist seeker finds such a statement preposterous. Is not every woman the goddess? Do not people exclaim, when a girl is born, that Devi has entered the house? Is material wealth not a blessing of Lakshmi, one of God's Shaktis? Are not music, art, poetry, and fine scholarship gifts of the goddess Sarasvati? Is a good, wholesome meal not the blessing of Annapurna? Why demean these blessings? Richness

---

*The great sage Shankaracharya (788–820 A.D.) was, as his name indicates, a great devotee of Lord Shiva. He is the formulator of Hinduistic monism (Vedanta) and founder of the orange-clad order of monks, the Sannyasi. His Vedanta is based on the idea of *advaita* or nondualism, from which it follows that the soul *(atma)* and the All-Spirit (Brahman) are identical, whereas the apparent multiplicity of beings is but illusion (maya). To this day, his doctrine is celebrated as the "crown of all teachings." He himself is taken as an incarnation of Shiva, and is said to have been born supernaturally of a Brahmin's widow.

(artha) and sensual pleasures (kama) do not necessarily constitute a hindrance to a correct conduct of life (dharma) or to salvation (moksha). They are, rather, gifts of Shiva's Shakti, to be accepted with gratitude.

On the other hand, sickness, war, poverty, and hunger are also the play of Shiva's Shaktis. Shitala, the goddess of smallpox who rides a gray donkey; Dhumavati, the ugly widow in gray rags; Bhairavi, the ogress who teaches humankind to

Bhoga—the joyful game of existence

fear; and, of course, bloodthirsty Kali—all are honored as Shiva's Shaktis. To despair at their presence and to curse creation as unjust and the world as a torture chamber betrays lack of understanding. For the worshipper of Shiva-Shakti, they, too, are the divine Mother.

The Irish Celts believed that only the hero who had the courage to sleep with an ugly old hag could become the king. If he was capable of making love to her without reserve, she would transform into the most lovely maiden that walked the earth, for she was none other than the ancient, ever young soul of the Emerald Isle herself. But only the clarity of a royal mind would be able to pierce her ugly veils and see through her essence. In the same manner, the seeker *(sadhaka)* must learn to love these terrible Shaktis and see through their magic. To call the world bad and to reject it, amounts to rejecting Shiva—and thereby, rejecting one's own true Self.

For the austere monk of orthodox persuasion, pleasure *(bhukti)* and liberation *(mukti)* are opposites, as are worldly experience *(bhoga)* and self-discipline *(yoga)*, active engagement *(pravritti)* and quiet withdrawal *(nivritti)*, or stupidity *(avidya)* and wisdom *(vidya)*. The one is to be sought out, the other to be avoided. The Tantras teach, however, that we need both: We need wisdom to achieve enlightenment, but innocence to pass through this mortal world. Everything has its role in God's play. Why, otherwise, would there even be a creation?

The grand game of life is like a child's game. While playing hide and seek, the child strives to tap itself "free" on the home base. In a similar manner, the religious seeker tries all means to achieve liberation. But

212 Tantra: The Serpent's Path

what happens when all players are "free"? The fun ends and, after a short rest, a new game starts.

The neurotic child cannot fully enjoy the game. It has ego problems, taking winning and losing all too seriously. It feels hurt, angry, insulted, and reacts by sulking or cheating. How different are the adults in the game of life? Most have forgotten the true nature of both the game and its player and have become disillusioned, disappointed, desperate, hopeless, or fear-filled. Through its rituals, Tantra tries to lead the seeker back to a proper understanding and reveal the true nature of this illusive world of Maya—the bliss of her dance—and the enjoyer of this dance, the Self (Shiva). It tries to teach us that all we see and all we experience is our Self.

But, alas, how difficult this is for the mind to accept. The intellect surgically divides the whole into self and other and tries to avoid, suppress, or block out what is felt to be unpleasant. Transcendence of the mind or ego, however, does not imply that one does not notice the "other" anymore, that one avoids the unpleasant and ugly by sticking one's head into the sand like an ostrich. On the contrary, one is still completely aware of it, but no longer as an "other" (*Tat twam asi* = That is you).

Accepting one's sexuality, for example, does not turn one into a sex maniac or porno freak, but implies that from then on, sex is seen as something holy (part of the whole) and the partner as a sacred being. The man becomes Shiva and the woman Devi. Shit, sweat, piss, menstrual blood, semen, any bodily excretions remind the defensive ego of its creature likeness and are handled euphemistically. Acceptance, however, does not imply that one does not wash and stay clean. Feces are filthy, but not unholy. Members of the Aghori sect demonstratively smear themselves with filth and go as far as to call urine "holy water."* Vipers and poisonous spiders, too, are aspects of the Self, but again that does not imply that one should not pay them proper respect and keep clear of them. The untouchables and lepers (in the West, the bums, drug addicts, derelicts, and AIDS-infected) are Shiva also, but that fact is no invitation to unnecessarily involve oneself with them. The enlightened one's spirit is like the sun, whose warmth and light touch all—the tender flower as much as the dung pile—without discrimination. Her spirit is like the fire; it feeds on all sorts of refuse, but it remains pure.

The goal of the tantric rites and exercises is to overcome the fear

---

* Urine is also commonly used as a remedy in traditional Indian medicine.

and rigidity of the ego, to unblock the frozen energies and let them flow afresh in the divine, blissful game of being. All the energy (shakti) comes from the Self (Shiva), not from the ego or mind.

Even the awful demons of Indian mythology know that. In order to get what they want, they pray to Shiva and chastise their egos. Piece by piece, they cut the flesh from their bones, sacrificing it to Shiva until they are mere skeletons. This voluntary self-castigation automatically sets creative energy free, which enables them to temporarily dominate the three worlds. But despite their self-imposed sufferings and austerities, they remain demons, for they refuse to sacrifice themselves entirely to Shiva, the higher Self. Instead, they use the power gained to enhance their own individuality and to dominate the "other."

☙ OVERCOMING THE EGO ❧

The struggle against egoism *(ahamkara)* is the hardest battle a human being has to fight. In a sense, it is the only battle. The ego dwarf has the nasty habit of seeing everything exclusively in relation to itself and, at the same time, it projects itself on all other things, distorting and discoloring them. Because of its distortion of reality, it entangles itself increasingly in error, loneliness, and fear. The spontaneous play of God's lila becomes deadly serious; it turns ever more into a sheer horror trip. It is at that point that Shiva has forgotten his true nature, drifting as a filthy, crazed madman through the wilderness of existence. *Ecce Homo!*

We all personally know this wretch, who hallucinates that his Sati is dead, that his shakti (God's divine energy) has abandoned him. What should the poor fool do to find himself and his one and only beloved Shakti, so that he may be Mahadev again, united with her in Being, Consciousness, and Bliss (satchidananda)? What does Shiva in the Indian mythology do?

At first, he errs about the dark pine forest where he stumbles upon the neglected, love-starved wives of the rishis. He is so opposite to their rigidly self-controlled, austere husbands that he becomes an object of fascination and lust for them. Who are these women, but the unsatisfied, repressed, denied desires lingering in the dark recesses of the soul (the pine forest). Only a madman would dare satisfy them! But he *is* a madman, and thus, without second thoughts, rushing in where angels fear to tread, he is able to violate all restrictive conventions and social etiquette (symbolized by the rishis) and fulfill the wives' urgent desires.

This disregard of the conventional norm, necessary for coming to terms with one's hidden, frustrated desires, is the first step of tantric initiation. There is no way around it. All the filth and nastiness that has been locked away and chained to the dank, dark dungeon walls of our unconscious must be confronted. As our psychoanalysts have found out, these captives represent quantities of energy. They are immortal shaktis, which, if ignored, will one day emerge as furies and erinyes, as destructive compulsions and perversions. Many a would-be saint has been undone by their rage. Before any spiritual progress is possible, the repressed needs and desires must be lived out and exhausted, like a fire that exhausts its fuel or like seeds sprouting on rocky ground that exhaust their reserves. It was for this reason that the Tantrist master Bhagwan Shree Rajneesh let his "patients" spend themselves in mad "sex orgies" (as the yellow press referred to it) and in wild psychodramas before meditation began.

Before the madness of total rationalism took hold of the Western world, merry seasonal festivals (whose roots go to ancient heathen times), carnivals, and Mardi Gras fulfilled the same function. During the buffoonery and merrymaking, the devil was given his due. Let the priest and the man of reason shudder: People wrapped themselves in furs or colorful costumes, wore masks and horns; they exposed themselves indecently, drank excessively, teased old maids and virgins, and produced the next crop of babies. In this way, all kinds of psychic complexes and kinky notions were dissipated, removing potential disruptions of the harmonious flow of social life, while at the same time, so it was believed, helping nature maintain the fertility of the fields and the animals.*

After the crazed, ithyphallic Shiva fulfills the frustrated desires of the rishis' wives, the hermits curse him to lose his phallus. At that, he comes to his senses and wanders beyond the dark pine forests, up the slopes of the mountains. There, on higher ground, in the high icy desert, where the air is pure and crystalline, he sinks into quiet meditation.

---

*The ethnographic record shows that such safety valves were nearly universal. The Iroquois, for example, believed that all desires and wishes that surface in dreams should be made public and fulfilled. Only then would both society and nature remain in a state of harmony. A guessing game for finding out such secret wishes developed. Once guessed, they were enacted, even if this implied a sex orgy or the burning and rebuilding of the village.

From the tantric point of view, this indicates that the sadhaka, the student of Tantra, has raised his spirit above the carnival of sensual and worldly desires, as well as beyond false piety, and now engages in the yogic effort of transforming his drives. On all levels of being—physical, mental, and spiritual—he has tied himself into the yoke of yoga. Accompanying his spiritual exercises are the difficult body postures of hatha yoga, breathing exercises (pranayama), and special hand positions (mudras). In this manner, knots and tensions in body and soul are eliminated and the shakti energy flows more freely.

There are three kinds of meditation *(dhyana)* that the seeker practices:

1. Concentration *(savikalpa)* on one point. Shree Rajneesh calls it "centering" and refers his students to the *Vigyana Bhairava Tantra* where Parvati poses this question: "Oh Shiva, what is your reality? What is this universe filled with wonder?" Shiva answers, by indicating 112 methods for concentrating or centering the mind on one single point.[3]
2. Bringing thinking to a standstill *(nirvikalpa)*. For modern human beings, trained from early on to constantly cerebrate, this is indeed difficult.
3. Witnessing the spontaneous free flow of the mind without interfering, censoring, guiding, or manipulating in any way. This is a kingly meditation, *raja yoga*. In the Occident, it is the fisher king, the guardian of the Holy Grail, who does this meditation. A fisher is someone whose vision reaches beyond the mirroring surface (the phenomenal world). He casts his net into deep waters from which he gains his sustenance. It is no mere coincidence that Jesus chose fishermen as his disciples.*

The meditating sadhaka unconditionally surrenders to Shiva, his true Self. He considers himself as a *shivadasya*, a slave of Shiva. Though externally he seems to be still a separate person, he is in reality already one with all. As his yoga deepens, the darkness (tamas) leaves him along with

---

*There are other parallels of Shiva's story in the Celtic Christian legend of the Holy Grail. Like Shiva, Parsifal, the future fisher king and guardian of the Grail, starts as a fool wandering the wilderness. He too becomes inadvertently guilty and is cursed. Illusive flower maidens tempt him. Finally he brings the fountain of grace to flow once again and becomes the king of the Grail castle, located in high ethereal realms above the earth.

An Indian yogi practicing meditation

Hieros gamos—tantra as the union of opposites (Nepalese print)

the blemishes of the soul. Ever more shakti flows into his consciousness.

Then one day, the meditant will open his eyes and see the most beautiful, radiant maiden standing in front of him. She, too, is covered with the ashes of bitter asceticism. She, too, has traveled a long, arduous road. Now Shankar recognizes his Parvati! Now the heavenly marriage, the hierogamy, can be celebrated. In their mutual love, all oppositions and dichotomies disappear. In bliss, Shiva and Shakti melt into one and become Ardhanarishvara, combining the masculine with the feminine.

The melding together of the God and the Goddess is the fusion of matter and consciousness, of being *(sat)* and knowing *(chit)*. The more complete the fusion, the greater is the resulting bliss *(ananda)*. Satchidananda is always present, eternal in the here and now. Shiva and Shakti are always united in bliss. They are one, just as in the mystical theology of Christianity, the Father (being), the Son (becoming), and the Holy Ghost (wisdom) are eternally one. Their separateness is only apparent, it is an illusion belonging to a state of ego existence.

☙ SHAKTI ❧

Shakti is the sea of stars revolving around the polar star. She is the warm, moist monsoon wind blowing from the south, melting the ice of Shiva's north, causing the frozen waters to flow like heavenly nectar, reviving the desiccated land and letting life's seeds sprout. Shakti is also the rich, dark womb of the earth that lies at the feet of Shiva's ethereally blue mountain. As Kuja, "the earthborn," the Mother of All is blacker than coal; but in union with Shiva, she becomes golden Gauri. Shakti is also the sea and the rivers that feed it. The pilgrim bathing in a holy river does not dip into H2O, as the scientist sees it, but into the living stream of divine energy. Though sewage, industrial wastes, or cadavers are dumped into the river, Shakti remains ever pure, virginal. Her serpentine nature is reflected in the flow of the water.

Everything in southern India, where Shakti arose as a pure virgin *(kumari)* from the foaming surf, carries her signature: steaming, lush jungles; the luminescent fresh green of young rice; the ever present cobras and vipers; the stone carvings of mythical serpents (nagas) set under mighty trees under which peasants and cattle seek shelter from the sun. Here, Nagaraja, the lord of the serpents and Manasa, the goddess of snakes hold court as the stewards of the Goddess. Numerous naga temples bear witness to the fact. Not far from Cape Cormorin, in the famous temple of Nagarcoil, Nagaraja, the five-headed king of the snake folk—flanked by Shiva, Krishna, and Jain Tirthankaras—reigns supreme. The temple's sanctum sanctorum is a simple wooden building thatched with palm fronds and set into a swamp full of cobras.

It is commonly believed that Shakti lives as a snake at the root of sacred trees, or at springs and wells. Similarly, she lives in each individual, coiled tightly at the base of the spine. When this inner shakti serpent awakens, it slowly winds its way upward in the direction of the dome of the skull where, in the human microcosm, Shiva meditates in the cool heights. Again, in a similar way, the Virgin, after having stepped out of the sea at Kanyakumari, moves north, traversing sacred India, on her way to Mount Kailash.

According to south Indian tradition, it was at Suchindrum, not far from the sea, where young Parvati performed her severe penances to win the heart of the one she loved. The divine wedding took place at the edge of the inhabitable world, on the shore where

Shakti in the form of a serpent goddess

the Gulf of Bengal meets the Arabian Sea. It is indeed an uncanny, mysterious place. The sea is a translucent emerald green, constantly churning and boiling, the whitecaps running parallel to the shoreline. It is the only place in India where one can see the full moon and the sun at the same time, peering like two titanic eyes over the rim of the world. Once, a simple monk, a devotee of Ramakrishna, swam out into the dangerous waters in order to meditate on the OM on an outlying rock. By the time he finished his meditation he was enlightened, and he returned to shore as a great philosopher and reformer who brought the Vedanta to the World Parliament of Religions in Chicago, in 1893. His name was Swami Vivekananda.

The rocky beach of Kanyakumari is permeated by veins of red, yellow, white, black, green, and brown sands. For the pilgrims who come here for blessings and darshana, these sands are remnants of Parvati's wedding feast. The legend tells that Devi Kumari (the Virgin Goddess) was terribly disappointed when the long-awaited groom did not show up at the auspicious hour the astrologers had determined for the ceremony. As the favorable hour passed, she gave vent to her feelings by exclaiming, "Woe me! All these fine foods, these cakes and colored rice, may they turn into stone and sand!" Ever since, each pilgrim takes a handful of the colorful sand with him, as his portion of the wedding feast.

As Parvati waited, dressed in her finery—in a red and golden sari, adorned with sparkling earrings and bangles, decorated with fresh blossoms and jewels, her face painted with white sandalwood paste—she shone out so brightly that the skippers and boatmen who passed the Cape were struck with awe and wonder. Much like the boatmen on the Rhine when they pass the Lorelei combing her golden hair, their ships dashed onto the cliffs. To this day, when a ship sinks in the turbulent waters of the Cape, it is said that the helmsman was blinded by the sight of Devi Kumari's sparkling nose ring.

As she waited there in her radiant glory, an asura spied her out and desired to possess her on the spot. Brahma's boon had made him near invincible. Nobody except a virgin would be able to kill him. At the sight of her beauty, he forgot this condition and, literally, lost his head.

At long last, the tardy groom and his reveling troop appeared. After the wedding ritual, they rode northward on a milk white bull. At every single step of the way, temples, shrines, holy lakes, and other auspicious places appeared in their tracks.

Another legend tells that, with each step, Devi shed more of her ser-

pentine nature. The image of the primordial reptile
slowly transforming into the divine woman might
seem odd at first, but it is an archetypal picture of
the transformation that occurs when the soul
becomes one with the spirit, when the marriage of
the Anima and the Animus is being consummated.
Christian mythology, too, begins with the woman,
Eve, who is under the sway of the clever serpent,
and culminates with the image of the star-crowned
Queen of the Heavens who stands sovereign above

Naga

the serpent. In the Middle Ages, this archetypal theme found expression
with the innocent princess who is rescued from the clutches of the lind-
worm by the brave knight, Saint George. (Sometimes the transformation seems to reverse itself, as, for example, when the years of marriage
drag on and the once pretty young thing turns into a fire-breathing
house dragon that drives the poor husband into the local pub for
refuge.)

When Shakti is united with Shiva, she is a radiant, gentle goddess;
but when she is separated from him, she turns into a terrible, destructive fury. She is the endless Ouroboros, the dragon biting its own tail,
symbolizing the cycle of samsara. As such, she is Mahamaya, the great
illusion, the fascinating, treacherous mirage of an endless chain of birth,
suffering, and death, of time and space, and of a separately existing ego.

In all her aspects, whether that of the innocent virgin, the gentle
mother, or the raging beast, Shakti devotees find her worthy of worship.
Any trouble that might beset the soul, any fear, need, or sorrow can be

The cobra—guardian of Shiva's lingam

placed at her feet. For there is no power greater than hers, no one can deal with these things more effectively than she. She is both the source and the deliverance from all disaster, be it drought, flood, or earthquake in the macrocosm, or be it madness, cancer, AIDS, or whatever terrifies the individual microcosm. She appears in the form of dark, unpredictable drives, aggressions, and passions that enmesh the frail human soul like a boa constrictor its prey. There is no running or hiding to escape her. For this reason, her devotees try to unite her with Lord Shiva, that she might become peaceful and friendly. For this reason, the lingam is placed into the yoni, bound there with spells, and worshipped so that her power might be beneficial. In the light of Shiva's consciousness, she becomes beautiful. The image of Vishnu resting calmly on the world serpent, or of Krishna dancing freely on its jeweled head, tells the same truth, namely, that all Being rests upon the creative-destructive dual nature of Shakti.

Sigmund Freud was on the path to a similar realization. He labeled the all-permeating energy *libido* and understood, also, that one cannot merely suppress it. Surely the old master from Vienna looked deeply into the mysteries. His beard was long; but that of Tantra is much longer and older. The Tantrists believe that the science of the serpent power and its mastery were revealed personally by Shiva himself. This "science" allows one to transform the shimmering, rainbow-colored scales (of multifold illusion) into wisdom, the poisonous fangs (of life's terrors) into bliss, the hissing, split tongue (of dualism) into unity, and the periodical shedding of skin (of incarnations and discarnations) into realization of eternal Being. In order to achieve this metamorphosis, the Tantrists start at the lowest, crudest, rudest animal level: feeding and breeding. In the same way, the alchemist of old started with feces and rot in order to make gold; and the gardener uses urine, dung, and compost to bring forth the most delicate, nectar-filled flowers and sweet fruits. Nobody can start at the goal and bypass the frightening shakti serpent. In the following folktale, which is frequently told in the south of India, we shall see how a virtuous merchant had to find this out the hard way:

Manasa Devi, India's Lady of the Serpents, is a personification of Shakti. According to legend, Shiva, on one of his sojourns on earth, begat her with a mortal woman. As Shiva's daughter, Manasa believed she had the right to live as a goddess among gods on Mount Kailash. But Parvati would not hear of it and drove the ophidian stepdaughter back down to earth. But Manasa still had an unquenchable desire to be recognized as a divinity and be worshipped by all human beings. She was especially infatuated with a rich young merchant named Chanda. She thirsted for his devotion. Chanda, however, was not impressed by the serpent woman, for he worshipped Shiva, and only Shiva. Enraged by his rejection, she devastated his gardens and orchards and, when that did not help, she bit and killed many of his friends. Still, he paid her no heed. Once, by the power of her illusion, she appeared to him as the most ravishing maiden he had ever seen. Though happily married, he instantly fell in love and wanted her.

Manasa Devi—
the snake goddess

"You may have me," she told him, revealing her split tongue, "but only if you worship me as a goddess!" This price was more than he was willing to pay.

Another time, as he sailed the high seas in his merchant ship laden with valuable trade goods, Manasa conjured up a terrific storm. The vessel sank, the crew drowned, and Chanda was just about to go under the waves himself, when the snake-goddess appeared, floating above the tempest on a lotus throne, and offered to save him if he prayed to her. But the merchant would rather lose his life than his virtue. Though Manasa was deeply disappointed, she saved him anyway, by causing a large wave to sweep him ashore. But now she was vexed! Stealthily, she lay in wait for his sons, and sinking her venomous fangs into their heels, she killed them, spitefully, one by one. The sixth and last son, however, was on guard and had himself a snakeproof steel building built in which he and his new bride would live. The goddess, in turn, threatened the builder, telling him in a dream that she would wipe out his entire family if he did not leave a hole big enough for a cobra to slide through. On the wedding night, as the sixth son lay asleep with his bride in his arms, Manasa Devi entered the steel house and killed him.

Unbeknown to him, Chanda's wife and his mother secretly worshipped the snake goddess. Now that the last son had died an untimely death, they openly begged and pleaded with the unyielding merchant to accept Manasa's divinity before another disaster would strike the family. Their sighs and sobs softened his heart enough that he apathetically flung a wilted flower at Manasa's picture as he turned to walk away. But even this miniscule amount of worship made the snake goddess happy. Immediately, she raised all six sons from the dead. (As we know from the Aesculapian healers, a snake's poison is also medicine!) Ever since that time, Manasa Devi has been venerated by human beings as a protectress against snakebites and worshipped as Vishahara, the destroyer of poison.

⠵ THE PATHWAY OF THE ⠭ KUNDALINI SERPENT

In the great macrocosm, the jewel-crowned, thousand-headed world serpent rests deep in the waters underneath the three roots of the world tree, or at the base of the world mountain. In a similar way, the kundalini serpent lies curled tightly, its head hanging downward, at the root chakra *(muladhara chakra)* between the anus and sexus in the human microcosm. Her slumbering energies are enough to satisfy the crude, animal needs of eating and digesting, reproduction and defense. For the God seeker, the yogi or tantric sadhaka, this does not suffice. He tries to awaken the dangerous serpent and let it rise, sending its energy upward through all ethereal organs (chakras) and vitalizing every level of being, until it unites with Shiva in the highest center.

In order to arouse the snake, it must be touched with the breath of life *(prana)*, which flows through the body in invisible, ethereal channels *(nadi)*. The two main channels are the moon channel *(ida)* and the sun channel *(pingala)*, whose doorways are the left and right nostrils and which meander around the spinal cord, much like the Aesculapian

The nadis and chakras

serpents around the staff of Hermes. Unfortunately, the filth of our bad habits and the encrustations of our old karma block these channels so that they must be cleaned and cleared. This is achieved by *hatha yoga* exercises, involving correct breathing (pranayama), body postures *(asanas)*, mantra chanting, and gestures (mudras). Many a perplexed tourist will have observed and perhaps photographed the "human pretzels" sitting along the Ganges, breathing alternatively through one and then the other nostril. They are clearing their ida and pingala!

Touched by the vital breath, the awakening reptile raises its head. The muladhara chakra, imagined meditatively as a red lotus blossom with four petals, starts to vibrate and open up. Gradually, as the exercises intensify, the serpent moves up the spinal cord *(sushumna)* on its way to the thousand-petaled, royal purple *sahasrara* lotus chakra. As it winds from root to crown, the snake passes five other chakras, causing them to vibrate and radiate. On its journey, the arch-reptile climbs the ladder of the elements and transverses the abodes of the gods, which make up the microcosm as well as the macrocosm.

The root chakra belongs to the element Earth and is the realm of the god of beginnings, the Creator, Brahma. It is also the doorway to the labyrinth of the body and of the cosmos, which stubborn Ganesha guards. It represents an archaic level of consciousness, dull, stubborn, and sluggish. Imagination places a yellow square (the Earth element) enclosing a downward-pointing triangle (yoni) in the middle of the four red lotus petals of this chakra. In the middle of the triangle sits a lingam, around which a snake twists in eight loops. The snake's jaws are tightly clamped over the opening of the sushumna channel.

If the snake is enlivened enough to overcome the inertia of the lowest realm, it can rise to the "favorite place," the *svadhishthana* chakra. On this rung of the ladder, an orange-yellow lotus with six petals blooms. A white crescent moon is in the middle of the lotus, holding a seed *(bija)*. This center of ethereal energy, located in the proximity of the genitals, belongs to the element Water and represents the realm of Vishnu. Consciousness on this level is akin to sexual bliss.

If the serpent is fed even more life breath, it will enter the "jeweled city," the *manipura* chakra, located in the region of the navel. Its element is Fire.

Sahasrara

Ajna Chakra

Visuddha Chakra

Anahata Chakra

Manipura Chakra

Svadisthana Chakra

Muladhara Chakra

When its ten smoke-colored lotus petals unfold, one beholds Rudra riding a bull. The type of consciousness associated with this center is akin to hunger and digestion, expressing itself in bullish self-assertion, greed, and aggression. A conqueror like Napoleon, an aggressive businessperson, or a Western cattle baron pull their force out of this chakra.

The pilgrim who is not seduced by the tremendous power that the "jeweled city" might bestow can goad her magical snake to higher levels. She can reach the heart center, the *anahata* chakra, from which mystical sounds arise, even though it is "untouched," that is, the sound is not the result of two objects striking together. In its core, one finds a reddish-golden twelve-petaled lotus. As it opens its petals, one sees a six-pointed "Solomon's seal," in whose center Ishvara, Shiva as the personal Lord and God, enthrones. The corresponding element is Air and the associated level of consciousness is that of a philosophical and compassionate temperament, at home with symbolism and imagination.

Whoever remains unattached to the wonders revealed by the heart chakra and is not taken in by a desire for the magical powers (siddhi) it conveys, may guide the kundalini serpent higher, into the "place of purity," the *vishuddha* chakra, located in the region of the larynx. At this level, the four lower elements are distilled into their quintessence, into pure ether (akasha). In the middle of the sixteen lilac-colored lotus petals sits enthroned the half-silver, half-golden Sada-Shiva. The mystic, whose spiritual ear can perceive the holy syllable OM, draws his power out of this chakra.

If the shakti serpent rises even higher, it arrives at the "center of command," the *ajna* chakra, which blooms as a two-petaled white lotus between the eyes at the root of the nose. In this sphere reigns the "highest" Shiva, the Parama-Shiva. Here, the cleansing fire of Mahadev's third eye reduces all sins to ashes and all seeds of old karma to cinders. Here, far beyond the elemental world, the seeker may see God "face to face." It is the highest level of consciousness before reaching nirvana.

When the serpent power finally surges to the roof of the skull and floods the thousand-petaled sahasrara chakra, all oppositions, names, and forms melt into the original, primal, uncreated unity. What could one possibly say about it? Buddha, whose strangely tufted hair is not a coiffure at all, but a symbol of the flowering sahasrara, just smiles an enigmatic smile that is reminiscent of the smile of the Sphinx or the Mona Lisa.

This system of chakras, for Westerners so abstruse and complicated, integrates all levels of being, both macrocosmically and microcosmically, into one grandiose scheme. In that sense, it is similar to the system of planetary signatures and correspondences of the medieval and Renaissance philosophers and alchemists of Europe, or to the Taoist Chinese system of elements, organs, and seasons.[4] Such systems are holistic, relating the external to the internal, the human being to nature, the body to the soul, and the microcosm to the macrocosm. Since all the cosmological realms—the elements, the spirits, demons, and god—are located in the body, they become attainable to the initiate. Like a musician with her tuning fork, the Tantrist master can use powerful mantras, mystical syllables, gestures, and rituals to set this or that string vibrating. Starting at the bottom of the scale, he can tune each one and cause it to sound, until his entire universe is a harmonious symphony.

The caduceus ("the staff of Hermes")— the ancient Greek version of the kundalini

The mystical correspondences are found everywhere, in the geography of the land as well as in the body or in the sacred architecture. In this way, the Subcontinent is a divine body: sacred Bharata. Its head *(sahasrara)* is composed of the high Himalayas and its feet are the southern tip of Tamil Nadu. Places of pilgrimage in between these poles represent the mystical lotus blossoms, each having their corresponding element and residing deity. The Ganges, the Jamuna, and the mystical (invisible) Sarasvati are the three streams, representing the ida, pingala, and sushumna. Prayaga (now Allahabad), a famous place of pilgrimage a few miles upstream from Varanasi, is the confluence of these three divine rivers, the ajna chakra, where they merge just as they do in the microcosm, at the root of the nose.

The theme replicates itself in sacred architecture. The stone temple represents the body with its seven ethereal centers. The core of the structure, the innermost sanctuary *(garbhagrha)* where God reveals his presence in the lingam and yoni, is associated with the heart chakra *(anahata)*. The gateway to the temple, guarded by Ganesha, represents the root chakra. Then, at ground level, follow the "favorite place" and the "jeweled city." The higher centers rise vertically above the inner sanctuary (heart chakra) up the tower, the dome of which represents the

The sacred geography of India—holy places as chakras

thousand-petaled sahasrara lotus. In a concrete way, thus, each temple is a sacred body and each body is a temple.[5] With its wide plains and then the sudden rise of the Himalayas, the sacred land of Bharat becomes itself a giant temple.

The path a worshipper takes in the temple is like that of the kundalini serpent through the chakras. At the threshold, she respectfully presses her forehead to the ground, or at least touches it with her right hand. In so doing, she touches the feet of the deity, much as she would honor elders or teachers by touching their feet. Then she moves toward the inner sanctum, the equivalent of the heart chakra, where her spirit soars upward into higher planes. In this way, common folk who cannot find the way to their heart chakra through meditative exercises, do so externally by visiting a temple or going on a pilgrimage.

⚛ RETURNING TO ONENESS ⚛

The outpouring of shakti, symbolized by the flow of Ganga's waters from heavenly heights into abysmal depths, is the process of becoming, unfolding (pravritti)*, creation, multiplication, evolution, and fertility; it

is a sacrifice, ultimately culminating in exhaustion, confusion, rigidity, illusion, and death. The yogi, searching for his Self, is in every sense odd, a contrary and a renunciant. He wants to stop the cascading river of creative energy and force it to flow in the opposite direction back to its source, to Shiva. He wants to reverse Ganga, that is, the flow of breath, of thought, of speech, and of the white and red seed (seminal and menstrual emissions). He wants to unite Shakti again with Shiva and prevent her outpouring, because only then will the dizzying wheel of suffering (samsara) be overcome and the unity of satchitananda be maintained.

Kali—the destroyer of illusion—manifesting herself during a tantric ritual

With the awakening of the kundalini, the energy moves again from the dull, dark, lower regions upward toward its origin. In the process, semen, words, deeds, and breath are reabsorbed and returned in order to be reunited with the unmoved observer beyond name, beyond form, and beyond mind. Some babas drive a little plug into their penis, showing they have stopped the shedding of seed. Others

---

Pravritti is a Sanskrit concept that has no direct English equivalent. It includes the ideas of opening, engaging, progressing, being active, flowing forth.

The yab-yum icon (Tibetan)

become *muni*,* refusing to speak, while others might let their fingernails grow through their hands, indicating that they have stopped doing. Still others practice holding their breath for extended periods of time, perhaps even letting their disciples bury them alive for a number of days as proof of their mastery.

Other yogis, closer to the tantric tradition, unite in sexual rituals with a yogini.† Imitating the lingam and yoni, they let the erected penis rest blissfully but motionlessly in the vagina. The semen must not be ejaculated. Instead, it must rise, shooting as energy up the spinal cord (sushumna), where it explodes the roof of the skull, causing the thousand-petaled lotus to burst into radiant blossom.

Breathing plays a major role in the yogi's meditations. He learns to equate the outflowing and the inflowing breath with the rhythm of day and night, light and dark. As the meditation deepens, the exhaling and inhaling become the rhythm of summer and winter, life and death, of the light, pleasant ages (yugas) and the heavy, dark ages. Finally the realization dawns that a universe disappears every time it is drawn back in. In between the breaths, there are pauses of rest *(pralaya)*. Here, at this very point of quiescence, sits Shankar. Here the human being touches the unconditioned void, the timeless primal state, Shiva himself, who is beyond creation and destruction. This is the goal into which the yogi wants to be absorbed, like a drop in the ocean, for he has realized that wishes make for disappointments and that the very seed that generates life makes death possible.

The old Vedic sacrifices were deliberate acts of creation. By the magic power of chants, spells, theurgic gestures, and libations, the priests conjured the conditions they deemed favorable and necessary.

---

*Sanskrit *muni* = silent hermit
†Sanskrit *yogini* = female yogi, sorceress

The gods were coerced into giving children and cows, rich harvests, good weather, victory, success, and well-being. But then, slowly, the vigorous optimism of the Aryans seemed to vanish, giving way to the insight that everything that comes into being must go out of being again. The grandiose work set in motion by Daksha's horse sacrifice was bound to be undone again by the opponent force, by Rudra, the God of destruction. Why, then, reasoned the later thinkers of the Upanishads, continue this senseless carousel? Why not rest beyond the wearying cycles of doing and undoing?

Sri Yantra—the tantric mandala

Such reflections provided the soil for the terrible asceticism to flourish. Even now, the one who has chosen the harsh taskmaster of yoga and renunciation (*sannyas*), commands respect. Not wasting his shakti energy, by closing the door to the outflow of seed, word, or deed, he becomes laden with potential power. If such pent-up force is released in the form of a curse, it is terrible indeed! Did not the single look of the sage Kapila suffice to reduce the sixty thousand sons of Sagara to ashes on the spot? On the other hand, the blessing of such a penitent will find unconditional fulfillment. The ordinary man or woman, harried by the daily cares of life, can only worship such an ascetic as a god, for he has become godlike. Even the celestials fear his might. His accumulated power might suffice to knock them off their heavenly thrones. Therefore, they try every means possible to distract him, tempting him with wordly fame, riches, power or, what proves more effective, with seductive, passionate, heavenly maidens who cause him to spill his seed and involve him again in the cycles of life and death.

To many of the orthodox giants of renunciation, who have withstood the lures and temptations of woman and world, the Tantrists are but shameless heretics, for they seem to deny the need of such self-martyrdom. The Tantrists proclaim that an enlightened soul can remain in samadhi, experiencing the blissful union of Shiva and Shakti, and still be fully involved in the world. He can talk, sing, dance, make love, think, eat, and drink as it pleases him. His actions create no new karma, for he is not attached. There is no one there to be attached. The ego, which otherwise would entangle itself, has been dissolved into Shiva. He is "God-realized." Never abandoning the highest bliss, never losing total samadhi, Mahadev descends into his universe, which is his pastime and game (lila). In so doing, he takes on infinite forms. He is you, he is I, he is the cop and the robber, he is this stone and that cow. Enlightenment, according to the Tantrists, accepts all. It accepts all wishes, passions, words, and deeds, but lets them be pure and without problem, lets them partake of the whole, makes them holy.

12

THE SAINT, THE HERO, AND THE BEAST

Till you've earned
knowledge of good and evil
it is
lust's body
site of rage
ambush of greed,
house of passion
fence of pride
mask of envy.
Till you know and lose this knowing
you've no way of knowing
my Lord white as jasmine.

MAHADEVIYAKKA,
SOUTH INDIAN POETESS, TWELFTH CENTURY

Tantric teachings, meant to guide the human soul into the harmony and spontaneity of God-realization, are recorded in the form of dialogues between the two cosmic lovers, Shiva and Devi. Some of these writings fly on the wings of sublime spirituality, while others degenerate into vile, sinister black magic. An aura of dubiousness clings to the many Tantrist gurus, as well. The Tantrist master seems to unabashedly contradict himself. At one time he might say this and, at another time, that—an inconsistency that is bound to ruffle the logician. However,

231

the guru is not necessarily as illogical as he first seems; neither is he a liar. Each soul is different, and everyone is enmeshed in the spider web of illusion in a distinct way; hence a variety of methods are needed.

Basically, there are two paths available to the Tantrist devotee of Shivta-Shakti. There is the proper, "right-handed" path *(dakshin-marga)* and the secret, "left-handed" path *(vamarga)*. While the right-handed Tantrists interpret the five forbidden things (the five M's: *madya* = wine, *mamsa* = meat, *matsya* = fish, *mudra* = magical gesture, and *maithuna* = coitus) in a purely symbolic manner, the left-handed devotees take them quite literally.

The followers of the left-handed path, the Kaulikas, who use the *Kaula Upanishad* as their sacred text, teach abominations that make the hair of the orthodox Hindu stand on end. Claiming that the injunctions of the holy Vedas no longer suffice in this dark, materialistic age, they propose that the very temptations that lead the soul like a moth to the flame of destruction must be used to lure the soul to liberation. It is written in the *Kaulnava Tantra:*[1] "The Lord of Tears (Rudra) has shown in the leftist doctrine that spiritual advancement is best achieved by means of those very things which are the cause of man's downfall."

Tantric taboo-breakers meet in secret circles, hidden from the public eye, "like the sweet juice in the rough coconut," in order to ritually indulge in alcohol, drugs, and dishes of fish and meat—and to practice magical postures of copulation. Sex is experienced in a sacred, not a profane context, for otherwise, "any animal in rut would become enlightened!" During the ceremony, the man is none other than Shiva and the woman is none other than Parvati. Their naked bodies are transmuted into the temple in which all the gods of the universe and all the spheres of heaven are contained. The Kaulikas experience themselves in a totally sanctified, divine state before they return as normal mortals back to the everyday world. Once returned to the triviality and hustle bustle of daily existence, they conform to the social norms like any other citizens. Deep inside of the soul, however, glows the wondrous knowledge of their true, divine, magical nature. They are initiates into divine mysteries.

There are reports of debauched, degraded Tantrist sects that do not shrink from perversion, gore, and murder, claiming that the terrifying goddess of this age, Kali, craves blood. There are reports of secret meetings under the cloak of the night, in cemeteries and at burning ghats that bring to mind the blackest masses of Satanists. Some tantric texts, like the Buddhist *Guhyasamaja Tantra,* are totally repulsive if interpreted literally: A diet of human flesh, excrement, urine, menstrual blood, and semen is prescribed for the sadhaka. The men should learn to kill without a tinge of conscience, use any woman freely for their carnal pleasure, and mock those who cling to conventional moral prescriptions. Interpreted correctly, these injunctions are meant as shock therapy to free seekers from their moral and social conditioning, to expose its arbitrary nature, to free the mind from mistaking its programming for "reality," and thus, lay bare the deeper ground of being, revealing the One hidden underneath the veils of good/evil, right/wrong, pure/impure, and male/female.

It is easy to see how dangerous such eccentric paths can be, how they could lead to complete physical, moral, and mental disaster. Especially for Westerners, such a path can turn into a poisonous fascination. There are reports that quite a few of the Neo-Sannyasi of Bhagwan Shree Rajneesh, having undone their social conditioning and overcome their inhibitions, have slid into criminal activity, insanity, drug abuse, or spiritual vacuum. But even in Asia one comes upon mental wrecks who lost their senses when, during tantric initiation, their minds balked at having to swallow their own feces or to engage in some unspeakable perversion. The energy liberated by removing inhibitions lashed back at them. Shakti unchained turned into an ogress and took possession of them, for they were not strong enough to guide this force into the right channels. Psychoanalytically, one might say that the unleashed libidinal energy flooded and swamped their psyche. The archaic, archetypal forces they conjured but could not master, took hold of them and now feed on them like vampires.

Tantra is obviously not to be taken lightly. Basically there are three ways to approach this secret knowledge, corresponding to the three types of human beings, types that are a reflection of the three basic principles or qualities (gunas) that pervade and constitute the universe. First of all, there are those who are permeated by light, spiritual qualities (sattva); they are the "holy ones," the *divya*. Second, there are the men and women of deed and action, filled with the dynamic quality of lively animation (rajas); they are the "heroes," the *vira*. Finally, there are the commoners, the followers of the herd, the *pashu*, whose sluggish, dull nature (tamas) puts them under the sway of their desires and fears and whose life runs in boring routine. For each type, Tantra must, perforce, have a different meaning.

❧ THE RITUALS ❧

The divya, the holy man of God, has no need of external ritual. He knows that the wine (madya), "which makes drunken to the point of falling," is but the flow of shakti energy back to the center of being, causing the devotee to become inebriated with bliss, and dumb and unsteady on his feet in matters concerning the "world." The meal of meat (mamsa) indicates the unreserved offering of one's own body, one's flesh and blood to the Lord. The fish (matsya) represents the five senses, which dart about in the ocean of the sensory world.* These are offered to Shiva. For the divya, the magical gestures (mudra) are but the spontaneous, natural demeanor of doing the right thing at the right time. The sexual union (maithuna) indicates the bliss of successful yoga, the union of thought and action, of inside and outside, of spirit and soul, of Shiva and Shakti. The saints, who have achieved all this, have no need to perform special rituals. They have no need to try to transform the blind sexual drive by means of the symbolism made available through tantric lore. They have no need to imagine the passage of the kundalini snake and the unfolding of her lotus buds, for they are already in full bloom, overflowing and open to the cosmos.

The man of action, the hero (vira), has left his faintheartedness and fears behind, while at the same time maintaining his virtues. But since he does not have the wisdom of the divya, he sees neither the arbitrary nature of social conditioning nor the cultural construction of reality and cannot grasp the subtle esoteric secrets. In order to understand the mysteries, he must be given concrete *(pakka)*, down-to-earth points of reference. He must directly confront the apparently repulsive and tabooed aspects of existence. He must look them in the eye, accept and integrate them into the whole, so that they might become wholesome and holy. For the vira, the hero, the forbidden five M's consist very concretely of the experience of drinking wine, eating fish and meat (sometimes urine and feces), taking on magic postures, and engaging in intimate intercourse.

Neither the path of the divya, nor that of the vira is fitting for the "man of the herd," the pashu, whose first striving is his security and the satisfaction of his needs and desires. He is much too bound up with his

---

*The fish can also be interpreted as the streams of energy—the ida, pingala, and sushumna—which have been led to their confluence.

drives to fathom the sublime spirituality of all things. The direct physical enjoyment of the forbidden M's would only cruelly confuse him or leave him addicted to them. Thus, for the pashu the tantric ritual is not much different from the ordinary worship service, the puja. In devotion he offers coconut juice or cow's milk, which stands for wine; he offers white beans, ginger, sesame, salt, or garlic, which stands for meat; he offers red radish, red sesame seed, or eggplant in place of fish; he sprinkles roasted grains and seeds as mudra; while his childlike submission at the lotus feet of the Goddess betokens the maithuna. In doing so, he believes that the gods will be pleased and will bless him. There is no reason to doubt the effectiveness of his service, for by means of his symbolic gestures, the archetypes, the gods dwelling in his soul, are truly moved and become responsive.

Thus, it is actually only the heroes who engage in the genuine tantric rite. They will have prepared themselves for a long time through yoga exercises and meditation. In some schools, only husband and wife participate as maithuna partners, but more traditionally, a very young woman, a virgin or a prostitute, becomes the Goddess at "Shiva's wedding." As in all sacred rites, the participants purify themselves by bathing. The secret place is decorated with flowers and candles and perfumed with incense. The bodies are rubbed with musk, sandalwood, cinnamon, camphor, and other enlivening essences. The participants eat fish to generate the red, rajasic power (commonly associated with the woman's menstrual blood) and meat to invigorate the white soma of the male fluid. Step by step, the man transmutes into Shiva and the woman into Parvati. With fragrant smoke, flowers, sacred words, and morsels of food, they serve and worship each other.

During puja, the ordinary devotional service, as it is celebrated daily at the temples and home altars, the sleeping goddess is awakened by the devotees with song and music, the clanging of bells and cymbals, and the blowing of conch shells. By virtue of the power of imagination, the living image residing deep in the soul is projected onto the stone idol or icon, which becomes animated with the living divine presence. This externalized archetype is greeted reverently with folded hands, graciously welcomed and worshipped. The devotees treat its numinous presence like a beloved and honored guest. They bathe its image in water and fragrances, feed it choice tidbits of food, garland it with flowers, and entertain it with song and dance. Then, after a certain time, after it has blessed the devotees with a glimpse of higher reality, it returns to its divine origin. The same thing happens during a tantric ritual, only, instead of using a lifeless picture or a stone statue, the divine manifests itself in the living bodies of the participants. The foods and wine are thus not enjoyed by ordinary mortals, but by the divine pair themselves, by Shiva and Parvati.

Food and sex are basic to survival. They are of such fundamental concern that all societies surround them with a tight network of prescriptions and proscriptions. Deliberate violation of social conventions regarding food and sex is portentous for both society and the individual. Violation blasts open the image people normally have of themselves and of the world, and allows a temporary manifestation of the awesome void beyond time, norm, and ego. The Tantrist guru, as an initiator, uses such shock techniques to let the individual glimpse the divine ground of all existence. The use of alcohol and of psychedelic herbal substances *(aushadhi)* intensifies this process, as does the total nakedness of the body, for clothes are part of the personality's masks.

A jar of aphrodisiacal and consciousness-changing substances is frequently offered as "food" to the kundalini serpent, by ceremonially placing it in the middle of a mystical geometric design *(yantra)* drawn on the floor. With the help of these substances, the naked pair levitates into ever higher realms. The steps of transformation into the god and goddess are punctuated by ritualized hand gestures or mudras.* The mudras can perhaps be understood by comparing them to the spontaneous gestures people flash at each other in our own society: the raised hand, its palm opened outwardly, indicates happy surprise or signals a greeting to a friend; the balling of the hand to make a fist indicates a concentration of potential power; the flicking of the middle-finger or the making of a "fig" counters the "evil eye" or wards off a curse; the pointing of the index finger indicates something or releases a directed flow of energy. Such spontaneous, partially instinctive, partially culturally conditioned hand movements can pierce the psyche profoundly. Some such gestures highlight those special moments when everything comes together effortlessly and harmoniously, as for example, when the French chef curves his index finger and thumb to form an "O," while smacking his lips, at the very moment

---

*According to the ethnobotanists Claudia Müller-Ebeling and Christian Rätsch, mudras can also be understood as the energizing, roasted aphrodisiacal seeds (poppy, cardamon, pine, hemp, datura, or anis) that the lovers hand each other. See Claudia Müller-Ebeling and Christian Rätsch, *Isoldens Liebestrank* (München: Kindler Verlag, 1986), 32.

he has given his exquisite chef d'oevre just the right pinch of spices.

Each chakra on the body of the goddess, starting with her yoni (vulva), the fiery seat of shakti, is gently and reverently touched, while holy mantras are spoken for each part. During the ceremony the man draws a yantra with rice flour on the ground. It consists of abstract geometrical lines that represent all the gods and energies pervading the universe. Squares represent the earth, circles stand for the heavens, triangles pointing upward signify masculine energies, whereas triangles pointing downward indicate feminine energies. Now Shiva sits himself in lotus posture in the middle of the yantra. The goddess worships his linga, and then slips her yoni over the erect member, as the *hieròs gámos,* the celebration of the sacred marriage, takes place. Thus united, face to face, without hasty, animalistic movements, without passion, in total meditative nonactivity and not wasting energy, they experience the primordial Unity, the satchitananada, out of which everything is born and into which everything returns.

During this union, the fiery shakti power starts to rise. At first it is but a thin flicker of a flame. As it is fanned by prana-breath and as it passes the chakras, it gains in intensity, until the whole body is a conflagration, a funeral pyre for the ego. Finally, the entire universe transforms into an ocean of fire, consuming all created forms. And now, the soma, which had been held in the cup of the crescent moon that decorates Shiva's hair, starts to melt, slowly releasing drops of nectar. The gentle dribble of heavenly fluid becomes a trickle, then a stream, and finally a mighty torrent that plunges into the ocean of fire, cooling it and at last extinguishing it.

Now the holy ceremony, which only true heroes can complete, is finished. The sadhakas have experienced their indwelling divinity, without denying their "lower animal instincts"; they were carried to the throne of God and overcame the polarities that rend the world.

❧ TANTRIC INFLUENCE ☙

The cult of tantric love challenged Brahmanic orthodoxy at the same time that the courtly romance of the knights and their chosen ladies flourished in Europe and that Omar Khaiyam composed his love lyrics. Was it mere coincidence? Was it an auspicious constellation of stars, the *Zeitgeist,* cultural diffusion, or a sudden flowering out of the collective unconscious?

In contrast to conservative Hinduism, the tantric ritual respects neither race, caste, nor sexual differences. The tantric texts, the Agamas, could be read by women as well as men, untouchables as well as twice-born Hindus, by heretics (i.e., Buddhists) as well as by the orthodox. This is not to say that race, sex discrimination, or caste were abolished. In everyday society they continued to play their role as always. It was merely recognized that they were irrelevant in relation to opening up to the divine, eternal Self. Being beyond such social barriers, it is easy to understand how tantric rites could spread as far as Ceylon, Cambodia, China, Japan, and even to the far north of Siberia.*

The temple sculptures of Konarak and the Shaivite temples of Khajuraho, whose lively in coitu representations elicit the constant clicking of tourist cameras, bear witness to the vitality of tantric inspiration in India.

The hearty traveler who manages to visit one of those nearly inaccessible cloisters perched on the rock ledges on the Himalayan roof of the world, can discover ancient paintings and sculptures, covered by layers of soot from centuries of burning butter lamps. The faded paintings, whose quality equals that of the finest of Western medieval art, reveal intertwined couples, locked in love's embrace. Somehow, these delicate erotic *yab-yum* (mother-father) figures do not seem to fit the dark, cold monastery halls and the litany-chanting, celibate monks. Here in Tibet, Shiva and Parvati have transformed into the Buddha and Prajna-Paramita, the goddess of supreme wisdom, or into the thousand-armed, thousand-eyed bodhisattva of compassion, Avilokiteshvara (the lord who looks down in compassion) and his female consort, the savioress, Tara.

Avilokiteshvara, the highest bodhisattva, the meditation-Buddha (Dhyanaibodhisattva) of our times, refused to enter nirvana because of his compassion for all the suffering creatures. He vowed to remain in the sea of illusion (samsara) until all were saved. Since his own separate identity had long been extinguished, like a candle burned out, he can take on any form (at least, according to the followers of the diamond vehicle, the *Vajrayana*.) Thus he can appear as Vishnu to the Vaishnavas, as Shiva to the Shaivites, as Jesus to the Christians. In Tibet he is worshipped in the incarnation of His Holiness, the Dalai Lama.

Since a bodhisattva is "empty" or "void" *(shunya)*, that is, free

---

*The influence of tantric philosophy was evident even in Siberia in the early twentieth century in the teachings of Grigorij J. Rasputin.

from residual, old karma, the three worlds become his free game, his lila. He is no longer attached, therefore he can pass through virtue and vice, poverty and wealth, and suffering and joy without a snag. A future Buddha, having achieved this evenness of mind, will not be thrown off course by the five forbidden fruits, the five M's. He can indulge freely in them, but does not need to, for he sees through their empty nature. There is no ego involved, no mirror upon which the dust can settle.

All duality is overcome in the embrace of yab-yum: nirvana and samsara are one! The infinite void *(mahashunya)* and the infinite energy of shakti balance each other out, melding together into the great bliss of "suchness, of "just-so-ness" *(tathata)*. This blissful state of nonseparateness finds expression in the ever present Buddhist mantra *Om Mani Padme Hum* (the jewel in the lotus blossom). In its tantric interpretation, the jewel or thunderbolt (vajra) is the linga resting in the yoni, which is frequently symbolized as a lotus (padma). Enlightenment occurs when the linga is brought to rest in the yoni.*

Nowadays, Tantrism has come into vogue in the industrialized societies of the West. It is no longer the secret passion of a curious handful of anthropologists and Indologists. As the social norms and traditional patterns of behavior reel under the blows of supertechnology, as social roles become ever harder to define, due to the chaotic changes induced by numerous factors (economic, environmental, informational, etc.), more and more people have great difficulty finding out who they are, why they are here, what is expected of them, in short, what kind of universe is it in which they live. Parents and grandparents—the role models in traditional society—cannot provide answers, for they themselves cannot keep up with the changes. Their store of experience becomes as quickly irrelevant as yesterday's newspaper headlines. Surely, for many there is at present enough food to eat, plenty of stylish clothes to wear, and nonstop media entertainment; but when it comes to finding out the purpose of life, the proper role behavior, or the right way to handle the drives and emotions, Babylonian confusion reigns.

This state of norm confusion is especially true in the relation between the sexes. Seldom have men and woman been as alienated from each

---

*As Shiva, in the form of bodhisattva Avilokiteshvara, traveled further north, he changed his gender. Emphasizing his gentle, compassionate nature, he became the heavenly Virgin of the Chinese, the beloved goddess of mercy, Kwan-yin (Japanese Kwannon).

other as in today's "urban singles" society. Despite liberalizing the laws concerning marriage and divorce, free relationships, abortion, prostitution, homosexuality, and pornography, the industrialized societies are ever more at odds with human sexuality and emotion. The liberalization has shifted the racing engine into a higher gear: The abreaction of accumulated frustration has merely become more frantic, more zesty (Erica Jong's "zipless fuck"), more commercialized, and more expensive. But the participants give less of themselves and are lonelier than before. However, in the final analysis, economic growth (and the associated exploitation of the environment and resources) can only move with the motor of programmed dissatisfaction and frustration of the natural drives: Only the unsatisfied are driven to consume so desperately, in order to make up for the deficits of an empty life. Increased frustration translates into more sales. Whoever is loved needs less candy and sweets, new cars and the latest fad clothes. Whoever has gotten a glimpse of her cosmic self needs not to bolster her bruised ego with status symbols and conspicuous consumption. It follows, like night follows day, that those who live contrary to cosmic harmony (dharma) will feel afraid and lost in a hostile, aggressive environment. Then one's energies and wealth are poured into arming and fortifying oneself. On a larger, collective scale, this becomes the biggest of big business. Cannons and rockets become ersatz lingas. On the personal level, even sex becomes a weapon of the cornered ego.

In such a setting it is no wonder that many glossy books on the subject of Tantrism fill the book shops. The many seminars on tantric sexuality are but a symptom of the yearning of love-starved souls, of those wounded and maimed in the war of the sexes. Tantra becomes interesting, for it promises reaching the divine ground of Being, not by the exclusion of the basic carnal level, but by its inclusion in the loving union of the sexes.

13
POLLEN DUST AND ASHES

———— ❦ ————

Take these flowers, take my song:
You, sitting on a tiger's skin,
unshakable in your meditation,
your eyes, red and heavy from hemp's fumes,
turned inwards, seeing all,
all that was, that is and that which will not be.
Your tears, Rudra, garland my neck;
all one hundred and eight of them
I have caressed.
For you are the last before Nirvana,
you, the greatest joy, giver of life,
terrible enemy of all evil.

NEPALESE DEVOTIONAL SONG,

FIFTEENTH CENTURY

Every moment the mortal human being ought to sing Shiva's praises in his heart.[1] But there are certain times of the day when chanting the Lord's name and performing *Har puja* (Shiva worship) is especially auspicious. Such times are at sunrise, noon, and sunset. Of the seven days of the week, it is on Monday (Somavara), the day of the moon, that he draws nearest to his devotees.

The Hindus still observe the cycle of the old Indo-European double month, starting with the fourteen days of the "dark," waning moon and continuing with the fourteen days of the "light," waxing moon.

241

During this span, it is always the evening of the thirteenth and all of the fourteenth day, that belong principally to Shiva. Especially when the full moon rounds out, one finds Mahadev in a good mood, easy to please, and therefore with a willing ear for one's concerns. Then it is Pradosha Vrata, a time for staying awake and fasting.[2]

An old legend tells of a hermit who taught a banished queen and her two sons, who were hiding in the forest, the secret of the proper observation of this watch. He exhorted the two princes to fast the preceding day, take a bath in the river before sunrise, and then worship the five family gods, namely, Shiva, Parvati, Ganesha, Skanda, and Nandi. The water with which the idols are bathed should be placed into a magic circle, a mandala, drawn on the floor. This water they should drink the following morning, after having kept vigil throughout the night. All the while, hymns to Shiva-Mrityunjaya, "the conqueror of death," should be sung and the forehead smeared with three stripes of ashes.

After the princes had celebrated the Pradosha Vrata eight times in this manner, they had accumulated enough merit to win back their kingdom and eventually enter Shiva's heaven. One of the young men was blessed with a drink of the nectar of immortality and the other won the hand of one of the most beautiful heavenly princesses. When other people became aware of their success, they too began to worship Shiva on those auspicious days of the month in exactly the same manner. Even the gods began worshipping thus.

Such a festival on the eve of the full moon was not just thought up abstractly by the priests and politicians who were eager to fill the calendar. Rather, it is based on a finely tuned perception of a cosmological-biological event, namely, the interplay of electromagnetic and "ethereal" forces of the moon, the sun, and the earth. Any naturally sensitive person, as well as those who have developed their "antennae" through meditation, a meatless diet, and abstinence from alcohol, will be able to notice the special quality of this time, the increase in energy and vitality. Exact scientific experiments, as well as old-fashioned peasant wisdom and farmer's rules concerning the best times to sow and plant, confirm that during this time, starting on the eve of the full moon, seeds germinate and sprout with special vigor.[3] At this time, worms, mollusks, amphibians, fish, reptiles, and insects are more lively and sexually active. Barn animals become restless and go more readily into heat. Human beings, not excepted, suffer sleeplessness, vivid dreams, increased sexual desire, poetic flights, and heightened aggressiveness (as police statistics prove).

In all of this, the third eye (the pineal body, that remnant of the archaic reptilian brain) plays a role. It registers the increasing light intensity of the moonlit night (and probably other factors, such as lunar gravity) and, in turn, induces the endocrine glands to work harder. The biorhythms, tied to lunar cycles, evolved in our phylogenetic biography long before the conscious, reflective ego. Using these rhythms in connection with meditative techniques, occultists are able cross beyond the threshold of normal ego-consciousness.

Especially on the approach of the full moon, it is easiest to kindle fantasy and induce love-magic. The moon, eroticism, and the power of imagination are linked. To this day, one considers poets, lovers, and madmen as moonstruck, or lunatic. All this brings us back to Shiva's third eye. By burning the god of the sex drive with its glare, he transformed the animal drive into spiritual fertility, into the power of the world-engendering, creative imagination. At the conclusion of the full moon celebration, the devotees rub ashes over their foreheads. The connection with Eros is shown in another legend, which tells that on that day, Shiva and Parvati, swooning in the afterglow of lovemaking, are in an especially good mood and will fulfill any wish asked of them. This festival, anchored in cosmological-biological rhythms, was also celebrated by our Indo-European ancestors, especially by the Celts, whose lore has so much in common with the Vedic Aryans.[4] It was the original "Friday" of the double month, or fortnight, on which the Celts fasted and sacrificed to the gods. Germanic tribes, such as the Anglo-Saxons, dedicated the day to Freya, the goddess of love, vegetation, and divination. The Catholic Church took over the ancient custom of Friday fasting, but severed it from its cosmic context and applied it to the seven-day week. Now, "Friday the thirteenth" has degenerated into a vague superstition as a day to exercise special caution.

Every day of the Hindu double month is dedicated to, and reflects the nature of, a certain divinity. (For a long time, even in the Christian West, the days reflected the nature of the god for which they were named. Even now in Catholic regions, the saints provide each day of the year with a unique quality.) Thus, the fourth day of the waxing moon belongs to elephant-headed Ganesha, the sixth to his brother, Skanda, and the eighth to Durga. Each day is, as well, a meditative step toward Shiva-realization, as it leads from ordinary waking consciousness to dream consciousness, then to deep-sleep consciousness, and finally, breaking through to the "fourth state," or superconsciousness. Thus, in Shiva-raja yoga, the days progress from new moon to full moon in the following manner:[5]

First day: everyday waking consciousness (new moon)

Second day: waking dreaming

Third day: waking deep sleep

Fourth day: waking superconsciousness (Ganesha's day)

Fifth day: dreaming everyday consciousness

Sixth day: dreaming dreaming (Skanda's day)

Seventh day: dreaming deep sleep

Eighth day: dreaming superconsciousness (Durga's day)

Ninth day: catatonic everyday consciousness

Tenth day: catatonic dreaming

Eleventh day: catatonic deep sleep

Twelfth day: catatonic superconsciousness

Thirteenth day: superconscious everyday consciousness (Shiva's day)

Fourteenth day: superconscious dreaming

To the casual observer, these steps seem to be but another of the prescientific systems of ordering time. To the yogi, however, they indicate steps leading into the depths of the macrocosmic, as well as microcosmic, being. On the thirteenth day of the waxing moon, the macrocosmic "superconscious level" of being comes closest to our everyday, mundane consciousness. On this blessed day, it is easiest to experience the flash of white light in front of the spiritual eye. The feeling is that of awakening out of deep catatonic sleep and being immersed in a radiant ocean of light. In order to reach this point, one has to go with nature, following the lead of the moon.*

---

*The full moon after equinox is instrumental in determining the date of Easter each year. This is one case where awareness of the synchronicity of lunar rhythms and states of spiritual consciousness has been maintained in the West. Thus, at the time of Christ's resurrection, plant life grows more vigorously than at most other times of the year.

✌ LINGAM PUJA ✌

By worshipping the lingam/yoni, human beings connect themselves with the divine ground of being. The ancient ritual helps them come closer, step by step, to their own divine nature. At the same time, Ishvara (God in his personal form) approaches the soul of each worshipper, step by step, until that fleeting glimpse of divine truth (darshana) is possible. In this way, Shiva worships Shiva.

In preparation for the puja, the devotees take a bath and wear freshly washed clothes, preferably of natural fibers like silk or cotton. After rinsing their feet, they enter the meditation room singing hymns. Sitting in front of the lingam, they blow the conch, rings bells, and call upon God to seat himself on the throne. A libation of five holy fluids *(panchamrit abhishek)* is gently poured over the lingam, as an expression of veneration. The libation consists of Ganges water, honey water, sugarcane juice, or of one of the sacred gifts of the cow: milk, yogurt, or rendered butter (ghee). Seawater, coconut milk, fragrant oils, rose water, and other such precious liquids are also acceptable. It should be noted, though, that each liquid has its special merit. For example, washing the lingam with cow's milk (never water buffalo's milk!) moves God to grant children, and washing it with ghee opens heaven's doors.

The pouring of the essence upon the lingam is accompanied by singing Shiva's name 108 times, or 1008 times. Finally, the Lord is rinsed in pure Ganges water, smeared with cooling sandalwood paste, and decked with flowers. It is believed that the water and sandalwood cool the lingam, which is ever hot and inflamed because Shiva has a fiery eye and is chafing from having drunk the poison. In some temples, cooling liquid constantly drops from a perforated copper pot onto the feverish lingam.

During the ceremony, the Lord is constantly entertained by singing, the offerings of water and fire *(arati)*, and the invitation to taste the slices of coconut meat, sweets, and fruits.

His nose is pleased by the smell of sweet incense and camphor. Like a great king, he is fanned with a fan of yak-tail

Harpuja

hair, which is cooling and drives the flies away. As the puja comes to its climax, it swells to a crescendo of clanging bells and cymbals and the blowing of conch shells. Finally, white ashes *(vibhuti)* are rubbed on the foreheads of the pious, and fruits, sweets, and bits of coconut are distributed and eaten as *prashad* (blessed food), in a manner similar to the bread and wine taken by Christians after the celebration of the Eucharist. In this manner, the Hindu believer has a daily experience of the Lord's presence.

☙ SHIVA'S FLOWER GARDEN ❧

In a deep, esoteric sense, the soul is God's garden of delight. The flowers with which one honors his sign, the lingam, are but externalizations of what grows in the inner garden. They are the thoughts and dreams, wishes and hopes, virtues and vices all of us hold. The lingam puja demands that one take only the freshest, most beautiful blossoms, preferably those grown by one's own toil. They must not be stolen or begged for, nor should their fragrance be inhaled, for that is the food upon which the gandharvas, the angels, subsist. Flowers grown in one's own garden equal Vedic horse sacrifices in moving the favor of the gods.

Since "those born of bud and stem" are living beings incarnated in the cycle of samsara, their dedication is a genuine sacrifice. In every plant, all the deities are present: Brahma lives in the roots, Vishnu in leaf and stem, and Shiva in flower and seed. Pollen and seed mark the end of the plant's life cycle and belong, consequently, to the God of dissolution. They are, in a sense, the fire and ashes of the vegetable kingdom. They are consigned to Shiva so that they may rest in him before a new cycle of life, a new season, causes them to reincarnate.

In the European Middle Ages, each flower had a mystical significance. For example, the rose spoke of the five red wounds of the Savior, the lily of the immaculate Virgin's purity, and the violet of the soul's humility. Similarly, Hindu folklore attributes special meaning to each and every flower. Nothing is arbitrary; each species has its definite purpose and time at which it is to be offered. The system is so complicated that one must almost be born a Hindu to understand it. Very generally, one offers white blossoms to achieve peace and quiet for they have light, positive (sattvic) qualities. Red flowers give strength and provide energy for any undertaking, for they have a rajasic (active) nature. Dark flowers are tamasic and help realize dark desires and negative passions, such as revenge and destruction of foes. Yellow flowers fulfill the wish for food and are offered during famine.

Holy scriptures, like the *Shiva Dharma Samgraha*, give exact directions regarding the use of flowers. If, for example, one places an indigo blossom *(Indigofera enneaphylla;* Sanskrit *nilivrksha)* on the lingam, many obscure wishes come true. A garland of sweet-smelling oleander *(Nerium oleander;* Sanskrit *karavir),* which may only be offered in the dark of the night, opens the treasury of the god of wealth. As the saying goes:

> *No enemy as great as sin;*
> *Nor friend as good as devoutness;*
> *No god as great as Rudra;*
> *No flower as good as Karavir.*

The white, funnel-shaped flowers of the thorn apple (datura) sound the trumpet of salvation. With a red lotus one conquers kingdoms, with the white lotus one becomes a ruler, and with a blue lotus, given with a pure heart, one opens the gates to Shiva's heaven. The lilac blooms of the giant milkweed *(Calotropis gigantea;* Sanskrit *arkah)* replace a course with Dale Carnegie, for their effect is one of "making friends and influencing people." The earnest swain who pleases God with jasmine blossoms *(Jasminum grandiflorum;* Sanskrit *jati)* will be able to marry the damsel of his dreams within six months. Separated families can be reunited when they decorate the lingam with the bright red flowering sprigs from the asok tree *(Saraca asoka;* Sanskrit *ashokah)* The flowers of the chaste tree *(Vitex negunda;* Sanskrit *nirgundi)* free one from servitude. (Christian monks used this plant to free themselves from the bondage of carnal desire). One is cured of jaundice when one places sweet flag *(Acorus calamus;* Sanskrit *vaca)* on the lingam. Whoever desires horse, oxen, or work elephants should offer Shiva musk rose *(Rosa moschata;* Sanskrit *kubjaka).* Whoever wants her enemies wasted, can offer camphor laurel *(Cinnamomum camphora;* Sanskrit *kapur).*[6] The list of plants and their application can be extended indefinitely but, since our purpose is not a study of ethno-botany, we shall stop here.

It must only be added that Mahadev is pleased by most plants, but not by all. Especially taboo are the mendacious trio of flowers that, at the beginning of time, bore false witness on behalf of Brahma, who claimed to have found the end of the infinite column of fire. Recall how

Vishnu and Brahma, quarreling as to who was the greatest between them, decided to find the end of the great column of fire that suddenly descended into their middle. Vishnu, diving into the depth, admitted he could not find the bottom of the fiery column, which was Shiva's fire lingam. Brahma, however, lied, claiming to have found the top. He coerced three flowers to bear false witness in his behalf. The three floral culprits in question are the white fragrant blooms of the spiny screw pine *(Pandanus odoratissimus;* Sanskrit *ketaki),* the bandhuk *(Pentapetes phoenicea;* Hindi *dopahariya),* and the bitter, thorny vervaine, called *ganiyari (Premna integrifolia;* Sanskrit *agnimanthah).*

Naturally, one could not expect these plants to sincerely carry one's wishes to Shiva. If one uses them, one is bound to remain stuck in whatever hell one finds oneself in. The pandanus or screw pine flower has, nonetheless, a most wonderful fragrance, so that to this day, women like to put a sprig of it in their hair. Its essential oil is used to perfume soaps, shampoos, and hair oil, and its fragrance belongs, along with patchouli and jasmine, to the typical odors of India. Although the plant raised his ire, even Shiva cannot resist its magical scent. On his wedding night, Shivratri, he put a flowering sprig of pandanus in his matted hair. On that sacred night in February, it is acceptable to worship him with this flower, but only then.

There are other plants, such as neem *(Azidirachta indica),* white roses, and some kinds of jasmine and mimosas that are equally unacceptable to Shiva. The flower of the century plant *(Agave americana;* Hindi *kantala)* is also unsuited for worship, for it resembles the screw pine. The red hibiscus is never offered to Shiva, but instead to Kali, for it symbolizes her angry, bloodshot eyes. Shiva does not like dill. In India as in Europe, dill is considered a remedy against ecstasy, including the ecstasy of love. Does this account for his dislike of the plant, or is it that he is afraid of being henpecked by Parvati? In any case, there was a curious custom in peasant Europe by which women sought to obtain the upper hand in marriage. During the wedding ceremony, the bride secretly carried mustard and dill seeds with her and whispered the following magical words:

> *Husband, I've got mustard and dill,*
> *You must obey my every will.*

Not only the kinds of flowers and the time of day to offer them are ritually prescribed, but also the seasons and months to use them. Thus, during the month of Jyeshtha (May/June), the lingam should be washed with buttermilk and worshipped with lotus blossoms in order to achieve happiness. In the preceding month of Vaishakha (April/May), one may acquire the merit of a horse sacrifice by washing the Lord's member in clarified butter and decorating it with the white blooms of the *mandara (Nyctanthes arbortristis)*. If one worships the lingam during the spring month of Chaitra (March/April) with the flowering risps of the kusha grass *(Desmostachya bipinnata),* one becomes wealthy. During the month of Phalguna (February/March), one can claim half of Indra's throne by honoring Shankara with perfumed water and the flowers of a kind of mimosa *(drona)*. During the cool month of Margha (January/February), one may fly in the wagon of the sun and the moon if one places the flowers of the wood apple, or bel, tree on the Lord's member. The highest social rank awaits him who worships with the thorn apple (datura) during Pausha (December/January). One shall cross the three worlds like a streak of lightning and arrive at Shivalok, "Shiva's heaven," when one offers him indigo blossoms during the month of Margashirsha (November/December). Whoever washes the lingam with milk and decorates it with jasmine at Karttika (October/November) will be blessed with a darshan of Mahadev. A light in the celestial chariot bearing the banner of the peacock awaits the devotee who offers the giant milkweed *(Calotropis giganta)* at Ashwina (September/October). During the preceding month of Bhadrapada (August/September), a ride in the chariot bearing the banner of the swan is assured for those who offer silver sprigs of a common weed of the amaranthus family *(Achyranthes aspera)*. Those who but for a meal a day fast during Shravana (July/August) and give oleander blossoms, will be rewarded with a thousand cows. And, finally, if one offers sandalwood flowers during Ashadha (June/July) and bathes in the river during the dark of the moon, one will reach the realm of Brahma one day.[7]

The preceding by no means exhausts the endless elaboration of India's esoteric plant lore. Not only flowers, grasses, herbs, and shrubs cross-relate to all gods, planets, seasons, and times of day, but there is even a spiritual science of the leaves of these plants, telling when and how they are to be used in Shiva's worship. We can safely ignore them but for one: the bel or bilva leaf.

❧ BEL: SHIVA'S TRIUNE LEAF ❧

Western visitors to an Indian temple might have noticed a cloverlike leaf resting on a Shiva lingam and, if they thought anything at all, they might have supposed the wind blew it there. It is, however, a very special leaf, purposely placed. It belongs to the bel, bilva, or wood apple tree *(Aegle marmelos)*, called in Sanskrit the *shriphala,* the "tree rich in fruit." Like orange and lemon, it belongs to the citrus family and has, indeed, a large green, orange-sized fruit with a very hard, woody rind. Its orange marrow is made into a refreshing sherbet, which no miserable globetrotter, suffering from the "Bombay bomber blues" (dysentery, diarrhea) should ignore. It is an effective remedy for loose bowels of any kind, as well as for piles.

Because Shiva loves this tree more than any other (the sacred fig tree, or pipal, belongs to Vishnu), it is frequently planted next to Shaivite shrines. One of Shiva's 1008 names is Bilvadandin, "carrier of the wood-apple staff." As part of their morning ablutions, believers splash some river water (which they carry in small brass pots used for ritual purposes) on the tree's roots while chanting mantras. Others honor the tree with rice, orange powder, *(sindur),* or by lighting small butter lamps at its trunk. Women might hug the trunk, wrap red string around it clockwise, or braid a few of its trifoliate leaves into their tresses, in order that their wishes be fulfilled and their husbands stay strong and healthy. In order not to anger Shiva, the tree is never felled and its wood is never burned. (However, if it is absolutely necessary for some reason to chop it down, to do it one hires a Muslim, who is hell bound, anyway!)

The main thing about the tree is its threefold leaf. Like the clover of Saint Patrick, it is the symbol of the triune God, the threefold nature of the universe, the three gunas, the trinity of creation, sustenance, and dissolution. An oath sworn on such a leaf is equivalent to our swearing on a Bible. Because of its cooling nature, it is placed on Shiva's hot lingam. Sometimes the cooling is augmented by writing the word *Ram* (God) with sandalwood paste on it.

The three-leaved bilva or bel plant (Aegle marmelos)

⚛ Bangeri Baba ⚛

Shiva-Aushadhishvara is the lord of herbs and consciousness-changing drugs. Hemp (*Cannabis*) and thorn apple are his favorites. He is the only god of the entire pantheon who is constantly "high." In many folktales (puranas) he appears as a "lord of fools" (Bholanath) who is easy to please, who can't say no, and who often gets into trouble because of his habit of getting stoned. In this aspect, he plays the role of the divine trickster, much like Coyote of the American Indian or Rabbit of African lore. Bhagwan Shree Rajneesh, in his lectures on the *Vigyana Bhairava Tantra,* calls Shiva the original hippie.[8] The *Bhagavata Purana* tells that, in order to save a worshipper out of the clutches of a demon, he "assumed half the body of Parvati, fastened up his matted hair, rubbed his body over with ashes, ate a large quantity of hemp, swallow-wort* and thorn apple; and wearing a Brahmanical thread composed of white snakes, clad in an elephant's hide, with a necklace of beads and a garland of skulls, riding upon Nandi, accompanied by ghosts, goblins, specters, witches, imps, sprites and evil spirits, Bholonath came forth.

Bhang—Shiva's holy plant

On his forehead was the moon; he placed the Ganges on his head and his eyes were very red."[9]

The tales told by storytellers about this disheveled trickster, whose eyes are always red because he smokes too much hemp, fill the evening hours in the villages with much merriment. It is said that he is lazy, does not shave, stinks like an old billy goat, and just can't get himself positively motivated. He is so addicted that he even hocked Parvati's wedding dowry—her jewels and golden ring—in order to buy himself more dope.

---

*What is referred to as the swallow-wort is generally taken to be a milkweed, an asclepiadaceae with white, sticky juice, which, because of its Avestan name *haoma* and its ritual use by the Parsees, is believed to be the Vedic soma. However, as this plant has no psychedelic properties whatsoever, the "swallow-wort" could conceivably refer to opium, which also produces a milky sap.

However, we should not feel too sorry for her, for in part, she is also to blame. After they were married, Shiva continued his habit of rambling through the forests and mountains, being gone from home for long stretches of time. The new bride felt quite neglected. Since she was versed in the magic of herb lore, she decided to brew him a drink from the flowering tops of the female hemp plant. That did the trick! After having taken a couple of draughts, he looked at her and suddenly realized that there was no woman more beautiful than she and no place as fine as the simple hut that was their home.

Another version of the same story tells of Parvati as an overworked housewife with two squalling brats hanging onto her, and a lazy husband. Not only was he slothful, but always hungry. Constantly he nagged her to cook him something, even though the larder was usually empty. Finally, she simply cooked him a batch of bhang (hemp leaves), and although he might have become totally indolent, at least he was satisfied and left her in peace.

Another story tells of a sensitive Shiva who became a drunkard because he took the curse of his father-in-law, Daksha, too much to heart. But, however he acquired his bad habits, Parvati still loves him and tenderly calls him her *bhola,* her dear fool.

Shiva's devotees, the sadhus, roam about the Subcontinent in *imitatio dei.* Like their master, they cover themselves in ashes, avoid work, let their hair grow long and matted and bleach it yellow with lye, smoke immense quantities of ganja and thorn apple, and refer to their Lord as "Bhangeri Baba." It is easy to understand that the modern Indian government is not on best terms with them. The sadhus take the drug in order to "lift off" and see the world from a philosophical perspective, and as an aid to meditation. They claim it is an important help in maintaining brahmacharya (sexual abstinence), which is so important in accumulating shakti power.

The "madness," the constant state of being "high" of Shiva and his devotees can be interpreted in another manner. It is the drunkenness with the divine spirit, the ecstasy of his presence. Shiva fills his followers with "holy madness." As though pouring away putrid water, he empties their minds of mundane common sense, and, in turn, fills them to the marrow of their bones with heavenly ambrosia, with the joy of liberation.[10] The devotee is a liberated soul, but in the eyes of those caught in the endless cycle of illusion, the wheel of samsara, he appears to be a madman *(pittar),* a hysteric, a drunk, or a mental case. How is the ordinary citizen of the world to understand the utterances of such a pittar? His words sound as absurd as the statements of the dervish to the orthodox Muslim, or as the poems of the Dadaist poet to the ears of the European bourgeoisie. Emily Dickinson expressed this illusive paradox by writing:

> *Much madness is divinest Sense*
> *To a discerning Eye—*
> *Much sense—the starkest Madness—*
> *'Tis the Majority*
> *In this, as All, prevail—*
> *Assent—and you are sane—*
> *Demur—you're straightway dangerous—*
> *And handled with a Chain.*[11]

One of the great Shaivite saints of Tamil Nadu, Manikkavacakar (ninth century A.D.), who was repudiated for his weeping, laughing, rolling on the ground, and incoherent babbling, sings out:

> *Though the world mocked me*
> *calling me "demon,"*
> *I abandoned shame.*
> *The local people's despising talk*
> *my mind bent*
> *into ornaments of praise.*[12]

Ecstatically, this ecstatic poet and upholder of Shaivite philosophy proclaims:

> *We're not subject to anyone.*
> *We don't fear anything.*
> *We've joined His devotees.*
> *We'll dive (into the sea of bliss) again and again*
> *And cavort there with His devotees.*[13]

The madness and intoxication of the Shaivites (especially in south India) is one of having completely fallen in love *(prema-bhakti)* with Shiva, the lover of souls. The divine fool sees no problem of sustaining his flight of soul with song and dance and, possibly, underscoring it with drugs. Why, otherwise, would Shiva-Aushadhishvara have given human beings songs and magical herbs? Is it not so that they help break down the prison walls of our rigid, ossified minds? In the guise of a guru, Shiva appeared to Manikkavacakar in the port city of Perunturai and made him his *bhakta* (devotee of the yoga of divine love):

> *While unperishing love melted my bones,*
> *I cried,*
> *I shouted again and again,*
> *Louder than the waves of the billowing sea,*
> *I became confused,*
> *I fell,*
> *I rolled,*
> *I wailed.*
> *Bewildered like a madman,*
> *intoxicated like a crazy drunk,*
> *so that people were puzzled*
> *and those who heard wondered.*
> *Wild as a rutting elephant which cannot be mounted,*
> *I could not contain myself.*[14]

Apart from the outbursts of Pentecostalism, such God-drunkenness remains rather suspect in Western cultures. Already the Old Testament, the cornerstone of our Zarathustrian, Judeo-Christian worldview, rejects inebriation and ecstasy as a form of worthy worship. They smack too much of the drunken religious orgies of the Canaanites, the Baal, and Mother Goddess worshipping enemies of the Chosen People. Again and again, the call is made for sobriety and moderation. Loss of self-control is feared. A drunken man is beside himself, without being in God.[15] Despite the debaucheries of Dionysian bacchants, despite licentious Saturnalias and the Hilaria,* ancient Greece and Rome ranked the *logos* (reason, logic, ordered speech) and *ratio* (reason, computation) higher than "divine madness." The infamous "bread and circuses" were spectacles designed to control the masses, rather than expressions of religious fervor. Christianity

---

*Saturnalia = a licentious, orgiastic Roman festival in December in honor of Saturn. Hilaria = a "hilarious" festival in honor of the goddess Cybele, held at the vernal equinox to celebrate the renewal of life on earth, symbolized by the resurrection of the youthful god Attis.

has continued this emphasis on sobriety, and saints have always had to beware that their rapture not be taken for demonic possession. Saint Paul (Galatians 5: 12) warns against drinking and feasting, telling his flock that those who indulge will not inherit the kingdom of God.

The murderous persecution of witches at the close of the Middle Ages was basically a crusade against remnants of an ecstatic nature religion that also used consciousness-changing drugs (witches' salves). The French Revolution, marking the victory of the rational Enlightenment over archaic authorities, went even as far as putting up a statue of the "Goddess of Reason" on one of the Parisian *places*. It signals the attempt to establish the rule of the rational intellect once and for all. It is a major marking point of what the famous German sociologist Max Weber called the *Entzauberung der Welt* (the demythologization of the world). The current "war on drugs" is entirely in line with this cultural tradition. Alcohol might be permitted, might even be necessary to occasionally let steam off, but moderation is the citizen's first duty. She is reminded to mind her P's and Q's (pints and quarts of alcohol). Life is proverbially serious.

Given the complexity and speed of the modern technological civilization, we can only agree that, apart from uppers (drugs such as coffee or tobacco) and downers (such as barbiturates or alcohol), psychedelic substances have no place in our cultural cosmos. They would, indeed, subversively undermine it. In a largely agrarian society like India, however, drugs like hemp and thorn apple are fully integrated. Though their use is generally not approved of for young people or those in the full of life, these psychedelics are readily available for the world-renouncers (sannyasins), the holy vagabonds (sadhus), and the old, who are preparing their souls for the journey beyond.

❧ SHIVA'S GARDEN OF MADNESS ❧

Let us subject the plants that play such an important role in the cult of Shiva to a little closer scrutiny. First of all there is hemp *(Cannabis indica),* the seed of which Shiva, at the beginning of creation, personally planted into the soil. Ever since, it has had a long history as a useful fiber plant and as one of the chief remedies of Ayurvedic medicine. The Shaivites, who are above all interested in its consciousness-changing potential, refer to it as *subjee* (vegetable), *vijaya* (victory), *unmatti* (madness), *siddhi* (magic power, since it is used to heighten paranormal faculties such as telepathy, levitation, invisibility, seeing spirits, reading thoughts, and other such things that the rational citizen of modern materialistic civilization places into the realm of fable or psychiatry), Harshini's weed (Harshini is the god of the funeral rites), Shivapriya or Shankarpriya (Shiva's beloved), Shivamuli (Shiva's root), *angaj* (cream of the body), and many other colorful names. Already in the Brahmanas, written some 2800 years ago, the sacred entheogenic plant is referred to as Vijaya (Victory) or as Indracarana (the food of Indra, the constantly inebriated god of thunder).[16] Most familiar to Westerners is the name *charas,* referring to the plant's resin mixed with pollen, which Muslim merchants smoke as "hashish" in their water pipes, and which is trafficked all over the globe by criminal organizations such as the notorious "Bande Française," or by various "liberation movements."

The Hindus prefer bhang, a simple concoction of leaves and female flowers of the dioecious plant species. These are finely minced, mixed with yogurt, spiced with black pepper, and drank as a liquid, or rolled into marble-sized balls and eaten. At major social events such as Shaivite holidays, at weddings or funerals, two or three such bhang balls are taken with a glass of water or hot, sugared, milky tea *(chai).* During the wedding festival, the bride and the bridegroom are taken to be the living incarnation of Shiva and Parvati. Like Shiva at his own wedding, the groom arrives with a dancing, singing, jesting following of friends and relatives, coming to fetch his bride. The drug helps all participants to elevate their minds into a sacred reality, so that the event becomes a re-enactment of the original divine wedding.

Bhang can be baked into sweets *(mithai)* or drunk with buttermilk or fruit juices *(sherbet),* or prepared as a refreshing summer drink called *thandai.* The ingredients—including spices, nuts, and chicory seeds *(kasni)*—must always be ground and stirred in the auspicious clockwise direction, in correspondence with the movement of the sun, before they are mixed, together with bhang, into milk or rose water. Such a drink is commonly compared to the stream of ambrosia that gushes as a jet from Shiva's topknot. It is Ganga, the heavenly river, which floods the soul with colorful pictures. A folk saying from Bihar draws the connection:[17]

> *Ganga and Bhanga are sisters*
> *Who live in Gangadhara**

---

*Shiva, as the upholder of Ganga

Ganga will give you wisdom,
Bhanga will show you the way to heaven.

Before taking a drink, the brew is dedicated to Shankar by lifting it to the forehead and invoking his name. Having thus been consecrated, it is received back from God as *prashada,* as an "agent of God's grace."

Ganja is the name given to the better quality of hemp flowers, which are often baked into sweet pastries or smoked in hollow clay pipes called *chilam* or *chillum*. The holy men and women, the yoginis, may indulge in smoking this herb as much as they want to, for hav-

Intoxicated Shiva with chilam

ing broken all social bonds of family, region, or caste, they no longer belong to the world, but entirely to Shiva. As a sign of their status, they walk about naked or dressed in simple red or orange wraps, the color of the flames of the funeral pyre. Smoking hemp is also condoned with very old men, the poorest of peasants, and the untouchables on the bottom of society. Anyone else who indulges is looked at askance. Chronic *ganja-wallahs* enjoy about the same degree of respect as the chronic alcoholics or junkies do in Western society, and the Indians are quite upset when their youth imitate the hippies.

Chilam—an attribute of Shiva

Sadhus and sadhvis (female sadhus), however, no longer live in the world of mortals. As they wander from one holy place to the next, they live in "dream time."* At every step, they witness the deeds and wonders of the living gods. The chilam accompanies their journey through a "mythological" universe. Generally they smoke twice a day, once "when the crows are cawing," in the morning hours just after the mandatory bath and the round of begging, and once in the evening hours. The sadhus smoke the pure dried herb, without any admixture of tobacco or other substances.

The chilam, their only possession apart from beads, a begging

---

*This is a frame of mind similar to that which Australian Aborigines call *altjira*.

bowl, and a sleeping blanket, is honored as a Shiva lingam. Some chilams are very simple tubes of red, baked clay; others, like the black clay pipes from Manali, are decorated with magical designs and runes. Some show a cobra wrapped eight times around the stem, a sign of shakti energy rising through the chakras.

More often than not, smoking the chilam is a social, not a private affair. Sitting under the sheltering branches of a pipal or banyan tree, or on a river bank, the holy man or woman will share the ritual with other sadhus, devotees, or even foreigners. Casually talking, telling witty stories, profound parables, or even jokes, he will wait until the "vibrations" are just right *(shanti)*. Then he'll pull the magic funnel out of its bag. He might stroke it, maybe even talk to it, or put it to his lips like a horn and blow a long sustained, steady tone. Like a shaman, with his spirit caller, he invites the helping spirits and gods to participate.

Now the magic weed is stuffed into the pipe. Before lighting it, the sadhu might growl like a wild animal or a demon. Sometimes it is lit with two matches, one for Shiva and one for Shakti. The fire hits the dry herb like lightning from Shiva's third eye. The flame is Kali reducing the world to ashes, for the enjoyment of Shiva. The red glow in the funnel is Shakti; it is the funeral pyre of Manikarnika, Shiva's favorite dancing ground in Benares.

Just before taking the first long draught, the sadhu shouts *"Bom Shankar!" "Bom, bom Bholanath!"* or simply, *"Bom! Bom!"** These invocations have their equivalent in Western cultures, when we raise our glasses of spirituous liquors with the toast of "Cheers" or "To your health!" In both cases, the hope is expressed that the impending change of mood and consciousness may take a good turn. For the Indians, "bom, bom" (or "bam, bam") signifies the bleating of a goat. Why that? It is the "bah, bahs" of the goat-headed cocreator or demiurge Daksha. He represents the unintelligent, mundane rationality that is, compared to the higher universal wisdom, but the stupid bleating of a hardheaded, sclerotic animal. Ever since Shiva-Rudra destroyed the self-satisfied sacrifice of Daksha and placed a goat's head on him, this archpriest has been praying to Shiva continuously in his monotone "bom, bom," and has been rewarded with grace.

---

*Shankar = Shiva in his peaceful, gentle form. Bolanath (Hindi, *bhola* =simple, innocent, dumb; *nath* = lord, protector) is an aspect of Shiva who is uncomplicated, who cannot say no, and who fulfills every wish of his devotees.

Now the smoking funnel circulates in the auspicious clockwise direction among the participants. When one receives the pipe, one lifts it with both hands to one's forehead, pressing it on the third eye (ajna chakra), while calling out "Bom Shankar," or a similar invocation. At this moment the mind must be absolutely centered; nothing must distract it from its essence, from Shiva. It is not an ordinary mortal who raises the chilam, but it is Shiva himself, dedicating it to himself. And now, fully concentrated, he takes a strong, steady

Daksha

toke. What fills his lungs and then permeates his whole body from head to toe is not the smoke from a burning weed, but heavenly ether (prana). The tourist, who thinks of "smoke" or, for that matter, who bothers to think at all, will inevitably start to cough. Coughing, however, is not considered to be a good omen: it reveals disharmony or perhaps a bad conscience. In that case, the resulting visions might be confused or distorted; Shiva might appear as an unpredictable Rudra or even as a wild, paranoid, maniacal Bhairava.

For the genuine sadhu, however, such problems do not exist. He sucks *prana* into his being, holds it for a long time, and then releases it in an even, steady stream. One or two such draughts suffice to "arrive," to enter the sacred realm. Now he is Shiva! He is Narayana, "God in human form."* *Shivoham* (I am Shiva) is no longer an empty formula. The breath he releases becomes the very life-breath of creation. He looks at his World and loves it. She is his dancing Shakti. He is pure consciousness. He has pierced the veil of illusion and is no longer attached. Nothing more needs to be said, nothing to be done, nothing to be thought. In his total awareness, everything is blessed, everything is eternal. And now, they may come to him, his children, the villagers, the young and old, the animals too. Full of respect and full of trust, they lay their hopes and wishes, their worries and sorrows at his feet. Since he is Shiva, and since they have approached him with pure hearts, their wishes will be fulfilled, in miraculous, unforeseen ways.

---

*OM *namo narayana,* "Hail God in human form"—with these words sadhus greet each other when their paths cross.

◈ SACRED ASHES ◈

Smoking the chilam constitutes a dissolving, an annihilation, a process of dying. In this little pyre circulating form hand to hand, the manifold veils, shells, and husks enveloping our being catch flame. The rotting cadavers of past misdemeanors, the corpses of past deeds (karma) are turned into snow-white ashes. The cold, rigid, unkind, illusionary world of Daksha dissolves in the smoke and is returned to an unfixed, floating, nonrigid, youthful state. The mental complexes barricading the "super-sensual" world are shattered, and the demonic hordes accompanying Shiva dance and frolic in front of the eyes of the initiate. They are but etheric images of the spirits of nature. Suddenly, the dead appear also, and the gods! In a deeper state of samadhi (religious trance; absorption in the ultimate reality), all these "supernatural" beings disappear, making way for unspeakable "suchness" (or tathata, as the Buddhists call it). Now Shankar sits in total absorption in absolute bliss, consciousness, and being (satchitananda) on Kailash, the mountain of pure snow, the mountain of white ash, the mountain of salvation.

Somehow, imperceptibly at first, the snow softens and starts to melt. Single droplets form trickles, and these in turn become crystal-clear, bubbling mountain streams. Now Ganga spills down Mahadeva's matted locks. As a mighty stream she reaches the earth and inundates the underworld. Her touch revives the bones of the dead and raises the doomed sons of Sagara, who were cremated by the fierce fire of an ascetic's eye, back to life. Kama, the lust for existence and the joy of the lila of life, is resurrected. Thus the sadhu returns to the world. After the chilam is cold and the meditation has come to an end, he may dab his forehead with some of the chilam's ashes, or taste them, placing them on his tongue as *prashad*. The grayish white powder is said to be one of the best medicines, a heal-all. The *Tirujnanasambandar* declares:

> *The holy ash, which gives back to us our life,*
> *The holy ash, which brings salvation,*
> *What has one to fear, whose forehead is dabbed with white ash?*

Some sorcerers empty the remains of the smoked pipe into a polished coconut bowl or a bit of a skull. They then scry these ashes, much as the tea leaf reader "reads" the leaves at the bottom of the teacup. The different shapes and shades of the flakes and globules, which roll like tiny rudrakshas in the bowl, turn into faces and beings—dwarfs, goblins, giants, landscapes, and events—becoming alive, only to fall into gray formlessness again. Pure white ash indicates used-up karma; dark, incompletely burned rests indicate the fateful seeds of unredeemed karma, springing into external reality, seeking further salvation.

The ritual is concluded with a scrupulous cleaning of the pipe. It constitutes a purification, analogous to the meticulous cleaning rituals Hindus perform on their bodies after such activities as eating, excreting, sleeping, or having sexual intercourse. Ceremoniously, the chilam's owner pulls a strip of cloth through the funnel. While his neighbor holds the other end of the strip, he moves the chilam rhythmically, hypnotically, back and forth, polishing it until it is shiny. Other sadhus simply take a handful of grass and clean the pipe without much ado. Finally, the clean chilam, the cloth strip, the coconut shell, and the stone that serves as a stopper to prevent the ganja from falling out at the bottom, are carefully stored in their proper bag. To the anthropologist it becomes obvious that the chilam and its container are, as far as their ritual importance and sanctity are concerned, on a par with the medicine pipe and medicine bag of the American Indians, and with similar magical paraphernalia of shamans everywhere. One senses the great antiquity of these things.

The place value of ashes in Shaivite mythology comes to expression in the following statements from the *Brahmanda Purana*. After the jealous and embittered hermits of the pine forest had cursed the youthful, virile Shiva, along with their seemingly unfaithful wives, they practiced even harder austerities. But all their self-torture did not help them, for they got ever further from the right path and became ever more dissatisfied and confused. At long last, their father Brahma admonished them to swallow their foolish pride and to worship Shivas's linga. They bathed, and then rubbed their bodies with ashes until they looked bleached white, like ghosts. Now Shiva appeared to the penitents, telling them:[18]

> I am Agni and Devi is Soma. The ashes are my seed, and I bear my seed on my Body. I am Agni, the maker of Soma and I am Soma who takes refuge in Agni. When the universe is burned by my fire, and reduced to ashes, I establish my seed in ashes and sprinkle all creatures.

As the rishis calmed down and completed their penance, he explained further:

The supreme purification of this entire universe is to be accomplished by ashes; I place my seed in ashes and sprinkle creatures with it. One who has done that which is to be done by fire will master the three times. By means of ashes, my seed, one is released from all sins. When ashes illuminate anything brightly and make it fragrant, from that moment on it is called "ash" and ashes alone remain from all evils. . . .

Therefore, illustrious ones, ashes are known as my seed, and I bear my own seed upon my body as is my custom. Henceforth, ashes will be used for protection against inauspicious people, and in the houses where women give birth. And one who has purified his soul by bathing in ashes, conquered his anger, and subdued his senses will come into my presence and never be reborn again.[19]

Once upon a time, many, many years ago, the great rishi Mankanaka cut his finger on a blade of kusha grass. His tapas (the heat generated by ascetic exercises) had been so strong that his blood had clarified. What flowed from the cut was no longer red blood, but a clear greenish juice, like plant sap. The sage became so happy that he danced for joy, and everybody who saw him started to dance, until all creatures of the forest were dancing. Then, a young Brahmin, a stranger, came along and asked: "Why all this excitement?"

"Don't you see, worthy Brahmin," jubilated the rishi, "green sap is flowing in my veins! How formidable my penance has been!"

The stranger just laughed. Taking a blade of *kusha* grass, he also scratched his skin. Ash, white and pure as driven snow, came trickling out. Mankanaka, recognizing his Lord, fell on his knees.

The Occident is quite familiar with the mystery of ashes. The ancient Greeks performed magic with the ashes of sacrificial animals. For the alchemists, ashes belonged to Saturn, the oldest of the planetary gods, he who marks the periphery of the visible world. Though his cruel scythe spells death, in his sack he carried the seeds of the future. The alchemists reinterpreted the inscription *I.N.R.I.* above Christ's cross as *Igne natura renovatur integra* (Nature is completely renewed by fire); with that, Golgotha, the mount of salvation, becomes a mount of ashes. In the athanor, the oven used for transmutation, the alchemists "calcinated" the "black raven" into the "white dove." In some European fairy tales, such as Cinderella, the heroine (representing the human soul) has to be humbled by ashes and cinders before she is ready to become the bride of the prince (the symbol of the spirit).

The Christmas season especially bears within it the holy mystery of the ashes. Like the Phoenix, the mythical Egyptian bird that consumes itself in flames and is reborn from the ashes, the Christ Child is born each year again in the darkest night of the year, amid the snows (ashes) blowing fiercely from the north. Along with the spirit-child comes Santa Claus, traditionally an old, haggard man dressed in fiery red like the Indian sannyasi, carrying a sack of apples and nuts, the seeds of future life. In Lusatia (Lausitz), in Slavic central Germany, he appears as a rider on a white horse, carrying a sack of ashes.

In the Scandinavian North at this time of the winter solstice, the yule log is burned. Its ashes were considered holy and were made into medicine for house, barn, and field. And finally, there remains with us the Ash Wednesday custom, when after the buffoonery of Mardi Gras the priests preach penance and dab ashes on the head of the believers. An Indian sadhu would have no difficulty understanding this custom.

By now, the implementers of the rational Enlightenment have successfully wiped away most of the cobwebs of such old "superstition." Apart from sentimental value or satisfaction of the intellectual curiosity of folklorists, they have little place in the modern world. And yet, the colorful imagery of myth, ritual, and fairy tale are the food of the soul, and as such a human birthright. It is no wonder that during the 1960s and '70s, when cheap jet transportation made it possible, the youth of the industrialized world flocked to India, gorging on the smorgasbord of religious imagery and ritual. The sadhus, being beyond the rules and taboos of caste, class, or race, did not have to worry about ritual pollution in dealing with these mlechhas, these unclean foreigners. As the hippies and flower children streamed over the Kyber Pass and poured into Bharat (India), many natives thought they might be refugees from drought and famine, and freely fed and sheltered them according to the Vedic rule: "Treat the guest as God!"

In some way, the Indian peasants were not wrong in their assumption. Indeed, the young travelers were fugitives—refugees from a spiritual drought. They were starved for meaning; their schools and colleges taught them only scientific agnosticism and philosophical nihilism. Now they sat hungrily at the feet of gurus or joined the roaming sadhus. Along with smatterings of Hinduism, they learned the ritual of the chilam. Under the guidance of the sadhus, they learned to elicit totally different dimensions from the illegal herb than those they were used to from puffing a marihuana joint. The joint, which had entered the scene in the States via black jazz musicians and Mexican *braceros* (migrant workers), was capable of taking some of the hard edges off the technological nightmare and opening the ears to the sound of cool jazz or good rock and roll. The chilam, however was different. It opened the door to Shiva.

❧ THE SHADOW OF THE NIGHT ❧

Another plant plays an important role in the cult of Shiva. It is called the thorn apple, devil's trumpet, or jimson weed; it is one of the most poisonous plants known. The Indians call this nightshade Shivashekhara (Shiva's crown) or dhatura (from Sanskrit *dhat* = gift), a term that Linnaeus borrowed as the scientific nomenclature for the genus *Datura*. A few seeds from the thorny apple or a morsel of its rank-smelling foliage in the smoking mixture can send the mind of the sadhu cruising through his body or through the astral world. For the uninitiated, it confuses the senses and is apt to throw the autonomic nervous system into a spin. It can turn a man into a raving satyr and a woman into a nymphomaniac, but it can just as easily terminate life. For Shiva, the master of poisons, the drinker of the Halahala, the conqueror of death (Mrityunjaya) this herb poses as little a problem as it did to his Thracian counterpart, the god of inebriation, Dionysos, whose locks were also adorned with the perfumey, white, trumpet-shaped flowers.

At their major festivals, Shaivites take a few seeds of dhatura together with bhang, in order to join the ghosts, goblins, and elemental spirits in their riotous abandon. Anyone who has experienced a celebration such as Shiva's Night (Shivratri) in Mahadev's city on the Ganges, will inevitably think of descriptions of the Dionysian hosts, the satyrs, nymphs, and frenzied maenads who, according to some authors, used thorn apple to spike their wine.[20] It is possible that

Thorn apple (dhatura)—
another sacred plant of Shiva

Shiva and Kali are historically connected with Dionysos and his mother—legend has it that the latter two traveled to India riding a white bull—and that datura was the nexus of their cults.[21] More likely, the tropane-alkaloid responsible for ancient Greek Dionysian revelry was derived from mandrake or henbane. The datura plant seems to have come from India to Europe much later with the Gypsies, whose occult powers, it is believed, are based primarily on their exact knowledge of its use. The Thugs, too, are said to ritually indulge in this nightshade in preparation for their strangling expeditions.[22]

The power of the thorn apple is not to be taken lightly. It unfetters inhibitions and gives vent to whatever is hidden in the deepest, darkest recesses of the psyche. It can be truly demonic. Many curious and careless hippies have come to a bad end after trying this treacherous drug.*

Native sorcerers treat the plant with utmost respect. The Nepali shaman *(jhankrie)* dares approach it only in the framework of an elaborate ritual. He fasts and abstains from sex before seeking out the plant, on the evening of an auspicious day, such as when the new moon (Shiva moon) reappears. He goes either totally nude or merely wraps his loins with an unstitched orange cloth, upon which are printed sacred symbols (tridents, chakras, swastikas, the OM, suns, etc.). He offers a few grains of rice, water, or beer, and lights a butter lamp. All night long, his songs laud Shiva, whose manifestation the dangerous nightshade is. As the morning dawns, he finally plucks the leaves he needs and takes them to give to his patients as medicine.

In tantric tradition the thorn apple and hemps are the Divine Couple in plant form. The dhatura is the uncontrollable Rudra; the ganja is gentle Devi.

---

*Without knowledge of exact dosages and without prior psychic catharsis, datura can be lethal. Two cases are known to the author personally. In Kovalam, Kerala, where the plant grows wild, a young Italian woman chewed a few seeds. She became so heated that she stripped and ran naked through the nearby Muslim fishing village, where the inhabitants stoned her. In her delirium, she ran off the cliffs and drowned. Another case occurred in Ladakh (West Tibet), where a young Swiss man wandered off after having chewed datura seeds. His companions found him days later in a mental hospital. His personality was permanently changed.

14

SHIVA'S FESTIVALS
AND HOLIDAYS

———— ᑯᕦᓚ ————

> *To the utterly at-one with Shiva*
> *there's no dawn,*
> *no new moon,*
> *no noonday,*
> *no equinoxes,*
> *nor sunsets,*
> *nor full moons;*
> *his front yard*
> *is the true Benares,*
> *O Ramanatha.*
>
> DEVARA DASIMAYYA,
> SOUTH INDIAN POET, TENTH CENTURY

Like Europe during its feudal period and India today, where 80 percent of the population are still rural folk, traditional peasant societies are tied to the flow of the seasons, to the annual cycle of sowing and harvesting, and to the natural rhythms of the plant and animal kingdoms. These rhythms, in turn, are tied to the movements of the heavenly bodies, the sun, the moon, and the planets. Peasant society's existential link to the rhythmic pulses of nature is mirrored in a rosary of colorful seasonal festivals, worshipping the gods that stand behind the ever recurring phenomena.[1] The dates are not set according to some abstract or utilitarian considerations (like nationalistic holidays), but flow out of the natural cosmic order themselves.

The solar and lunar cycles provide the framework for Hindu holidays. The old Indo-European double month, consisting of the waxing and waning lunation, plays a major role. The dark and light halves of the month are seen as the nights and days of the pitris, the fathers, or ancestors.

Here, we shall mainly investigate the Shaivite festivals. The many colorful birthdays of the gods *(jayanthis)*, the countless regional celebrations, and the caste-specific holidays we must leave aside, and even such great annual events as the Ramlila, celebrating Rama's victory over the ten-headed demon king Ravanna.

⁓ THE DESCENT OF THE GODDESS ⁓

The traditional Indian year starts in the spring with the waxing moon, in the second half of the month of Chaitra (March/April). It begins with a nine-day homage to the Goddess. The winter crops have just been harvested and now, for nine days and nine nights, Durga, the mother of all beings, appearing as nine Shaktis, dwells among the people. She is feasted and entertained like a visiting queen. Songs are sung, her pictures and statues are garlanded and her name is ever repeated *(japa)* in the hope that she may reveal her divine essence in darshana.

These nine days remind the worshipper of Durga's nine-day struggle with the demon Bhandasura. Ganesha's roguery had brought the demon into existence. The little rascal with the elephant head wanted to make himself a little toy monster with which to play. Out of the dust that was left of Kama after Shiva had zapped the god of lust, Ganesha kneaded a lumpy figure and breathed life into it. Quickly the new demon developed into an ambitious egomaniac. Right away, he began with the hardest austerities, which eventually gave him the power to threaten the three worlds. Nobody, except Durga, could destroy the monstrosity.

Esoterically, the terrible nine-day battle stands for the nine steps the individual soul *(jiva)* has to take on its way to realizing its higher nature (Shiva). For three of the days, the devotees worship the goddess as the wild, demon-killing, lion-riding Durga; for three more days, they worship her as Lakshmi, the provider of prosperity; for the final three days, they honor her as Sarasvati, the goddess of light, who inspires wisdom. On the tenth day, the day of her victory, the goddess leaves the world of manifestation and returns to her husband on Mount Kailash. The thrice transformed goddess represents the three major steps taken in the transformation of the human soul: It starts with the victory over demonic forces, goes on to worldly prosperity and then to the gentle wealth of wisdom, and reaches its goal in the return and unification with the Self. It is a threefold alchemy, metamorphosing step by step from the tamasic, to the rajasic, to the sattvic state of being, before regaining wholeness.

❧ FESTIVALS OF THE HOT SEASON ❧ AND THE RAINY SEASON

Now, the goddess having returned to higher regions, the month of Vaishakha (April/May) arrives. The temperature rises daily; hot, desiccating winds blow billows of fine dust over the parched land. People and animals become irritable, the monkeys languish, and the cattle hunger. Finally it is so hot that the flies and mosquitoes die off. It is understandable that, under these conditions, the "cool" goddesses, such as Ganga and the goddess of the pox, Shitala "the refreshing one," is paid homage. On the seventh day of the waxing moon, Ganga Saptami (Ganga's seventh) is celebrated with refreshing dips into the *kunds* (water tanks) and rivers. It marks the day Shiva released the headstrong goddess from his tangled locks.

During the following month of Jyeshtha (May/June), during the first ten days of the waxing fortnight, the great bathing festival of Ganga Dussehra (Ganga's tenth) is celebrated. The holy stream, now swollen with clear, fresh waters from the melting ice and snow of the high Himalayas, invites millions of bathers. Those who do not live near the Ganges sprinkle themselves and their household belongings with holy Ganges water, which can be bought in small sealed copper pots. Such pots are often kept and worshipped the whole year, much as European peasants used to keep "Easter water," to which they attributed magical and healing powers. Dussehra, the "tenth," is associated with the ten sins, which the holy dip will wash away as surely as the sins of King Sagara's sons were washed away. Some claim the bath will cleanse the sins of ten lifetimes; others specify ten sins as follows:

1. Usury
2. Theft
3. Extramarital sex
4. Bad words

5. Slander
6. Senseless prattle
7. Greed, jealousy
8. Bad thoughts concerning others
9. Useless wishing
10. Killing, murder

As Ganga passes over the land, she triumphantly rides her *makara*, which is a strange beast, a fanciful combination of dolphin, shark, and crocodile, with the legs of a goat in front and a fishtail in back. (It is associated with the constellation Capricorn in the sky.) Leading her along is the chariot of Bhagiratha, the long-suffering sage whose penance brought her from heaven. On the last of the ten days of the bathing festival, some devotees stretch garlands of red and golden-yellow flowers across the quarter-of-a-kilometer-wide stream. Others, who are more athletically inclined, swim, jubilating loudly across to the opposite bank.

Mountains of gray, billowing clouds rent open by Indra's thunderbolt release torrents of water and put an abrupt end to the hot, dusty season. The monsoon removes the tattered, dusty rags of Mother Earth and dresses her in new, verdant clothes. Every wheel track and hoof print fills with water teeming with the wriggly life of hatching mosquito larvae. The air is like a sauna. Roving sannyasins flee the rains, retreating to the monasteries (ashrams). Now, during Ashadha (June/July), women wearing their prettiest saris form processions and swing in tree

The river goddess, Ganga, on her mythical crocodile (makara)

Ganesh Chaturi—at the conclusion of the festival, the idol is dissolved in the water

swings, just like the goddess enjoys doing, as they honor Parvati.

The snake folk of the underworld have their day of honor during the month of Shravana (July/August). It is Naga Panchami (Naga's fifth). The peasants fast on this day and catch thousands of cobras, which are taken as guests of honor to the Shiva temple where they are treated with milk and showered with flowers. Mahadev, who loves these cold-blooded creatures, is very pleased. In return, he blesses the barren with issue and protects the worshippers from snakebites. All day, colorful snake dances are performed in the street, and snake charmers exhibit their art. Those who cannot manage to capture their own live specimens can buy gigantic cloth snakes or worship the nagas' images in stone, metal, or plaster. At the end of the festival, all the slithering guests are released unharmed.

Ganesh Chaturthi (Ganesha's fourth) follows on the waning fortnight during the following month of Bhadrapada. It is the official birthday of the thick-skulled elephant, renowned for his intelligence and stubbornness. As Vighneshvara, the cause and remover of all hindrances and obstacles, he is everyone's concern and is, consequently, enthusiastically feted with music, mountains of rich sweets, and street processions of his garishly decorated plaster-of-paris idol. This is the day when everyone is careful not to look at the moon, for Ganesha cursed it for laughing at him. As the visiting deity leaves the world of manifestation, the colorful statues are sunk into the tanks and rivers to dissolve.

During the same month, on the third day of the waxing moon, on Haritalika Tij, Hindu wives fast and pray for their husbands that they may live long and stay healthy. The Brahmins, known for their hearty appetites much as our portly Western monks and parsons, are invited to sumptuous meals on this day, while the women who serve them may not even take a drink of water. The intention is to remind the womenfolk of the austerities of Parvati, which she undertook in order to win Shiva as her husband.

ᙦ FESTIVALS OF THE FALL SEASON ᙤ

During the month of Ashwina (September/October), as the sun's arch noticeably diminishes, the Hindus remember their departed. In the waning half of the moon, *shraddhas,* rites for the deceased, are performed and the dead are fed in order that they may become benevolent ancestors (pitri), instead of turning into wicked ghosts (pisachas).

Then, after the dark of the moon has passed and its light starts to wax anew, worshippers celebrate Navaratra, "the nine nights of the Goddess," the counterpart to her spring festival. Once again the great Mother of Creation descends from her lofty throne to spend nine days and nine nights with her devotees. Like any young bride living far from her childhood home with her husband, she desires to see old friends and family once again. Shiva, being a kind husband, allows her thrice three days. He would get too lonely if she stayed away any longer. Indian households receive her correspondingly like a married daughter and spoil her with devotion, good food, and song.

For the celebration, artists will have fashioned stately plaster statues of the Goddess and her lion and painted them with glowing colors. Dressed in fine silks, garlanded with flowers, she will be serenaded, incensed, and fanned. On the tenth day, after she has decapitated the buffalo demon, the masses pour into the streets to accompany her as she leaves the external world once again. Kin groups, guilds, and groups of friends throng to the river or tank where the statue is sunk into the water. It seems that these hundreds of veritable works of iconographical art, reminiscent of classical sculptures, ought not just be dissolved in a watery grave but should find a place in museums or as home decorations. But, to the Indian, it is absurd to hang on to the dead, external form when the spirit inhabiting it has long departed.

The appearance and transfiguration of the Great Goddess during the fall harvest season is an archetypal motive in traditional peasant societies. Not so long ago, Christians celebrated Mary's ascension to heaven

Women worshipping a tree during the fall festival

at the August full moon. Now the Ascension is fixed on August 15 in the ecclesiastical calendar. In rural areas of the Alps, women still bundle seven or nine magical and medical herbs, which they have gathered for the year's use, and bring them to church for the blessing. In much the same manner, Indian women dedicate a bundle of nine herbs *(nava-patrika)* to Durga.[2] Ancient Mediterranean cultures also celebrated the departure of the vegetation goddess in the fall, when Persephone repaired to the underworld to be united with her black husband, Pluto, only to reappear in the spring.

Twenty days later, on the dark moon of the month Karttika (October/November), the Goddess is honored as Lakshmi in a festival of lights. Thousands of butter lamps are set afloat in the river, sparkling like the stars in the sky. On the very next day, the first day of the waxing moon, the Goddess is worshipped in her world-nourishing manifestation of Annapurna, on the festival of Annakuta, which means "mountain of food."

A very long time ago, the wise rishi Vyasa walked the narrow lanes of Varanasi, begging for his daily food. The citizens must not have been especially generous, for his stomach was constantly growling with hunger. Grumpy, as rishis tend to be, he placed a curse on the city. For three generations, he doomed the inhabitants to be without wisdom, wealth, or salvation. Lord Shiva, who loves his city, was not at all pleased by this turn of events. Quickly, he took on the form of a Varanasi householder and Parvati appeared as his matronly wife. When the disgruntled sage passed with his horde of disciples yelling, as beggars do to this day, "Ma, anna do!" (Mother, give me food), Parvati invited the whole troop into her house and dished up a delicious mess of rice, lentils, and curd. At that, Vyasa completely forgot his curse and just shook his head, mumbling, "What a wonderful city where one finds liberation, while, at the same time, being able to eat the tastiest of foods!"

Ever since, Annapurna manifests in the thousands of housewives who gladly fill the bowls of the many sannyasi, sadhus, sadhvis, poor widows, and sometimes even stranded hippies who make their daily rounds. The festival of Annapurna is part of the overall harvest festival and is celebrated by piling up mountains of rice, pigeon peas *(dal* , and other pulses in the courtyards of the temples.

The next full moon, falling on the last day of the month of Karttika, is the day celebrating Shiva's manifestation as a column of fire (*tejo-lingam*). This blazing pillar, radiating the eternal light of truth through-out the universe, is the very one that appeared when Vishnu and Brahma were battering each other's egos in the battle of their relative importance. The light of this primal lingam shines on in the sun, the moon, the stars, in lightning and fire, as well as in the glow that fills all souls. The Tamils are convinced that the original manifestation of this column of light occurred on the red hill of Arunachala, near Tiruvannamalai. It was here that the maiden Parvati sat in bark cloth and practiced austerities that were to melt Shiva's heart. And it was here where Saint Maharishi Ramana, whom the peasants regard as an incarnation of Lord Shiva, had his hermitage.[3] Every year at this time, devotees fill a hollow on the sum-mit with butter, oil, camphor, and other offerings, and light it. The fire of this "spiritual beacon" burns up to three months and is visible for up to sixteen miles. Anyone who sees it is freed from future births into the world of samsara, for this light drives away the darkness of ignorance.[4]

After Karttika, the cooler season, pleasing to the European tourist, begins. The first important festival in this winter season, at least in Varanasi, is Bhairava's eight days, falling on the first eight days of the waning moon of Margashirsha (November/December). Pilgrimages are the expression of obeisance to this terrible lord during this time. Only on the last day of the festival (Bhairavashtami) is his face revealed to his devotees in his temple and a chain of silver skulls placed around his neck.

The winter sun reaches its lowest point during the month of Pausha (December/January), as it moves through the constellation of Capricorn, which is identical with the fabulous chimera Makara, who serves as Ganga's vehicle. It follows that devout Hindus bathe at this time in the Ganges, despite the nippy air. In south India, the Arudra fes-tival honors Shiva-Nataraja, the lord of dancers, at this season.

❧ FESTIVALS OF SPRING ❧

Processions of scrubbed, combed, and neatly dressed school children welcome the goddess of light and learning, Sarasvati, and her swan, on the fifth day of the waxing moon in the month of Margha (January/February). It is the first spring festival, like Our Lady's Candlemas (once the festival of the Celtic goddess of light, Brigit), with which it is connected by ancient Indo-European roots.

Now it is not long until Shivratri, the night of Shiva, sets everyone in motion. It marks the night of the new moon on the fourteenth day of Phalguna (February/March), on which Shiva and Parvati were married. Mahadev is in such a good mood on that night that he will fulfill any wish, as long as the devotee does not eat or drink anything and stays awake the whole night, washing the lingam every three hours, first with milk, then with yogurt, then with clarified butter, and finally, with honey water, all the while chanting *Om Namah Shivaya*. Placing thorn apple or wood apple (bel) leaves on the lingam will please the Lord more than heaping gold and diamonds upon it. Feeding Brahmins and beggars after the watch is part of the worship.

In Varanasi, the bathing ghats are jammed with hundreds of thousands of eager bathers on Shivratri. After the dip, they squeeze through the narrow alleys to get to the Golden Temple, to experience darshana with the Lord, who is never closer than on that day. To accrue merits, young men run at jog trot the twenty-five miles of the famous pilgrim route, the Panch-kroshi Road. (*Panch kroshi* refers to the five elemental shells that surround the city, in analogy to the five elemental "bodies" that clothe the human soul.) Shortly after midnight one hears them running, chanting Shiva's name, as their shadows hush through the dark.

At about 3:30 A.M. all the temple bells are clanging wildly. The thronging masses, meanwhile, have turned, with the help of bhang and datura, into ghosts, goblins, sprites, animals, and beasts that make up Shiva's reveling company. The magic, lunatic world of Shiva wipes out the mundane, everyday reality. The Muslims, in the meantime, hide anxiously behind the walls of their ghetto, as the frenzy of the pagans peaks out. Among the crowds, joining the procession, as Shiva goes to pick up his bride, are hundreds of fierce Shiv Sena warriors, swinging iron tridents. All kinds of miracles occur on this night: the sick are healed, saints levitate or walk on water, and some fly magically across the Ganges and receive divine revelations.

During the three days leading to Shivratri, the greatest classical musicians meet for a Drupad Mela. Years of practice and yogalike discipline have turned the artists themselves into finely tuned instruments. Because they have diminished their egos, Shiva himself can play and improvise through them for his own pleasure and joy. Divinities can incarnate into the sound forms and communicate with the listeners. The patter of the *pakhavaj* hand drums becomes the sound of Nataraja's dancing feet.

The *Mahabharata* tells how the celebration of Shiva's night came about:[5]

One day, a wise man visited the court of King Chitraghanu. Finding the king fasting, he became curious and wanted to know the reason for his abstinence from food and water. The noble king, whose mind was so clear that he could remember his previous lives, told him the following story:

"Once, in my former life, I was a hunter, a pariah, living on the outskirts of Varanasi. In order to feed my wife and children, I had to kill animals and birds and sell them on the market.

"One day, as I was ranging the jungle far from the city, night overtook me. In order to escape the prowling wild animals and other dangers of the night, I climbed up a tree, which happened to be a bel tree, and tied my game into one of the branches. Though fatigued, it was impossible to even think of sleep. I was very hungry and thirsty. As I thought of my poor family, which was starving and did not know what had happened to me, teardrops rolled down my cheeks and fell to the ground. To pass the time, I plucked the trifoliate leaves and let them float down. Finally, as the new morning dawned, I could climb down and go home. On the way, I sold the deer I had shot the day before and bought some food to take to my family. On the way, I met a poor beggar. I fed him even before I myself had eaten anything.

"Many years passed and I had long forgotten the incident, when, one day, two angels came to me. Even though I was an outcaste, they carried me to Shiva's abode, and then I realized what had come to pass that night. Without my having known it, that very night was Shiva's wedding night. Unintentionally, I had honored the three-eyed God with my fasting and waking. Underneath the bel tree, there had been a Shiva lingam, which I had inadvertently washed with my salty tears and decorated with bel leaves I had mindlessly plucked. Through these acts, I earned enough merit that I could enjoy the bliss of Shiva's heaven for many, many years. Having to take care of remaining karma, I had to come back. Thus, incarnated as a king, this is my last incarnation."

The wise man was moved by the wonderful story. Wherever he went, he told others about it, and that is how the observance of Shivratri came about. By now, the learned scholars have understood that the story is a parable: The dangerous jungle in which the archer got lost was his mind, and the wild beasts that threatened him in that long, dark night were his passions, drives, and desires. The fact that the hunter lived near Varanasi makes him out to be a yogi, for Varanasi stands for the ajna chakra, the third eye, upon which yogis learn to concentrate. It is the place where the three energy streams (ida, pingala, sushumna) flow into one. His climbing into the crown of the bel tree signifies the rise of the kundalini up the spine. The deer he had shot and tied securely into the branches stands for the unsteady intellect tied and calmed by the bonds of yoga. The tears he shed for his wife and children are the compassion and love a yogi has for all creatures still caught in the wheel of suffering (samsara). The threefold bel leaves, which he picked during the night, also stand for the three streams of energy, the combination of the force of the sun, the moon, and the fire, focusing on the chakra on the forehead. The rising sun, after the long, dark night, is but a symbol of the dawning of full enlightenment, the flaring up of the crown chakra (sahasrara), the daybreak of the "fourth state of consciousness" (turiya). This new, total awareness allowed the hunter to recognize that there was a Shiva lingam at the foot of the tree. He had a vision of the truth (darshana) before turning back to the world to do his duties (dharma). The beggar whom he met on the path was none other than his everyday earthly self, the mortal human being of this one, unique incarnation. The food he was able to give to the beggar and bring to feed his family was spiritual food. It was derived from the yogic transformation of old karma, old sympathies and antipathies that the arrows of his meditation had shot down. But a tiny morsel had been left uneaten, betokening that there was still a bit of karma left. In order to take care of it, he had to incarnate just one more time, as king Chitrabhanu, before he could completely enter the Lord.

Shortly after Shiva's night, the third great spring festival is celebrated. It is the Holi festival, falling on the next full moon, which marks the transition from Phalguna (February/March) to Chaitra (March/April). It is in line with other old Indo-European spring celebrations, like Laetare Sunday, when the winter demon is driven out or burned as an effigy of straw and rags, wood and pitch, on a public fire. For the worshippers of Vishnu, this joyous day recalls Krishna's killing of the child-devouring witch, Holika. The story, somewhat reminiscent of Hansel and Gretel, tells of an arrogant king, who demands from his subjects that they worship him and only him. His only son, however, continues to be devoted to Vishnu. The angry king hires the witch Holika to do the boy in. The old hag, fireproof due to her black magic, grabs the child and jumps into the fire with him. As the boy cries to

Shiva incinerates Kama, who disturbed his meditation

God, a miracle happens: the fireproof witch burns, while he remains unscathed. Every year at Holi, she burns anew.*

The Shaivites interpret the spring fire in a different manner. For them it is the flame shooting from Shiva's third eye, which incinerates the lecherous god of carnal passion who arrives with the spring. Swamis, intent on sublimating their passions, interpret the image as the dissolving of desires and egoism in the heat generated by yogic exercises. For the common people, it is just the highlight of a colorful carnival. Day by day, as the celebration approaches, the tension and excitement mount. Boys, unable to await the time, start squirting each other with red paint and snitching old boards and branches to put on the growing pile of combustibles. Finally, on the night of the full moon, a Brahmin walks seven times around the Holika and then lights the bonfire.

That night and into the next morning all hell breaks loose. Youths with eyes red from drugs and sleeplessness race through the streets, pelting everyone and everything in sight with bags and balloons filled with

---

*Some versions of the story tell how the demon witch Putana tried to give baby Krishna suck from her poison breast. Indeed, he sucked so hard, that he sucked her very life out of her. Her lifeless remains were burned in the Holi fire.

*Holi—the festival of colors—
in the morning*

orange and red colors. It looks as though it has rained blood. It is a fool's paradise, punctuated by hilarious laughter, the blaring out of the grossest obscenities, and by pranks and tomfoolery. The fools hug and kiss, or fight with each other. No one who dares to step out on the street is excepted or respected; not even the constables, Brahmins, or landlords are spared. Women tend to hide in the houses and watch at a safe distance, from behind the curtains. Tourists are advised under no circumstances to leave their hotels, for it has frequently happened that they were pelted with flying excrement and that they were pummeled, their hair pulled out, stripped naked, dumped into the river, and ridiculed. On the other hand, it is just as possible that the tourist will be given generous bear hugs, called *bhai*, (brother), and treated to some bhang and datura, which will instantly turn the world into a mad fantasia. What will happen depends mainly on the personality of the visitor—whether he is frightened and bothered or has good humor.

The Holi celebration has never lost its character of an old springtime fertility festival. Grotesquely large wooden penises with bright red glans and scrotums are set up in the streets. Sexual bravado is pronounced and demonstrated with suggestive, undulating hip movements during improvised dances. The fellows brag of their virility, promising to make their women scream with delight until they beg for mercy.

Toward noon, finally, the wild frolic ceases. The mythological beasts, the mob of goblins and horny satyrs disappear. People wash their red stains off and dress in fresh clothes. In the afternoon, the men, dressed in fresh, white *dhotis* or pajamas, and the women in their finest saris, promenade the streets. Friends visit each other, embrace three times, kindly smear red powder on each other's foreheads, and exchange smiles and sweet milk can-

Holi—the following afternoon

dies (burfi). Masters bow to their servants and gurus to their pupils in order to receive the red powder from their hands on their forehead. The atmosphere is relaxed and friendly as at no other time of year, for the buffoonery acts like a catharsis, providing a vent for all the stored-up frustrations that accumulate like old dust on furniture.

During this holiday in Varanasi, Shiva's idol in the Golden Temple gets to wear a golden mask. In the evening and the next day, many people go to worship the sixty-four yoginis, the sorceresses who attend Durga.

⊰ KUMBHA MELA ⊱

Every twelve years, the planet Jupiter passes through the constellation of the water carrier, Aquarius, who empties his pitcher upon the earth. At this time, millions of worshippers congregate at one of four auspicious places for the Kumbha Mela, the "fair of the pitcher," Hinduism's greatest festival. Halfway in between the major melas are the Ardha-Kumbha Melas the "half pitcher fairs."

The pitcher in question is none other than the famous jar containing the nectar of immortality, which the gods and demons churned, in common toil, from the depth of the Milk Ocean. As the devas and asuras struggled for the pitcher, four drops of the precious liquid spilled and fell to the earth. The places where they fell became *thirthas*, fords, leading to the other side, to the higher worlds. One drop touched the feet of the Himalayas, at a place now called Hardwar (Doorway to God). It was at this very place that the rishi Bhagiratha forced Ganga to descend to earth by virtue of his strong asceticism. Another precious drop fell at Prayaga (today's Allahabad), where the three streams, the Ganges, the Jamuna, and the mythical, invisible Sarasvati flow together. A third drop came down near the city of Ujjain, where a lingam of light also manifested, and the fourth one dropped at Nasik, on the Godavari River.

Every twelve years, masses of people, millions strong, congregate at one of these sites to celebrate for one whole month. A procession, as colorful and bizarre as if it sprang from the canvas of a surrealist or a Hieronymus Bosch, opens the mela. Naked babas, carrying tridents, have the honor of leading the huge parade. Following them are various sadhus, holy men, god-possessed fakirs, yoginis, ash-and-sack-cloth penitents, and gurus in palanquins, or on horse, camel, or elephant. They are eager to take the holy dip, perform ablutions, give evidence of their siddhi power, have darshan, or offer to their ancestors (shraddha) on these astrologically auspicious days.

The crowds are so huge that there is danger of being trampled if a panic breaks out. In 1954, the onrush was such that some five hundred people were trampled to death. During a half-mela, at Hardwar in 1986, some fifty pilgrims met their deaths. Besides the energies generated by such masses, problems of health and hygiene give the authorities headaches, for it is all too easy for cholera, dysentery, or some other contagious disease to break out. Nowadays, medical centers are set up to inoculate the visitors.

The most violent mela must have been at Hardwar early in the nineteenth century, before the British were in firm control of northern India. Armed with their iron tridents, the nagas (naked babas) fought with other sannyasi orders for the right to lead the procession. Reports tell of some eighteen thousand holy men who were disembodied in the bloody battle. But ever since then, no monk, be he ever so learned or devout, has questioned the right of these wild, naked Rudras to take first place!

Whatever may happen, the atmosphere of a mela is so strong that anyone who has experienced one will not forget it for a lifetime. The colorful chaos blows the rigid concepts of the mind to pieces, in terms of what is possible and what is not. One meets holy men who, many years ago, thrust an arm into the air, shouting, "For Shiva!" and have never taken it down. Now it sticks out like a bird's claw, rigidly frozen into position. Others might have sworn to stand on one leg for the rest of their lives, dedicating this deed to Mahadev, the chief of yogis. Then there are those who sit on nails, thorns, or glowing coals. One baba carries a boulder suspended from his scrotum. Next to walking skeletons who subsist on leaves, water, or merely air, might be a guru fat enough to top the Guiness Book of Records, hoisted up onto a comfortable litter by sweating devotees. The smells of wafting incense, burning hemp leaves, the bluish smoke of dried cow pies used as cooking fuel, the din of songs, chants, prayers, bells, conch shells, mooing cattle, the talking, clanging, and clattering, are part of the overall atmosphere that constitutes the transforming power of a mela. Overwhelmed, one can but mutter, "Shiva, Lord, have mercy!"

NOTES

Chapter 1

1. Charles Wesley, "Hark! The Herald Angels Sing" (1739).
2. Nirad C. Chaudhuri, *Hinduism, A Religion To Live By* (Oxford: Oxford University Press, 1979), 240.
3. Hansferdinand Döbler, *Die Germanen, Legende und Wirklichkeit von A bis Z* (Barcelona: Prisma Verlag, 1975), 215.
4. Karl Jettmar, "Skythen und Haschisch," in *Rausch und Realität,* vol. 2 (Hamburg: Rohwohlt Verlag, 1982), 531.
5. Heinrich Zimmer, *Philosophie und Religion Indiens* (Frankfurt am Main: Suhrkamp Taschenbuch, 1973), 450.
6. Alain Daniélou, *Shiva et Dionysos* (Paris: Librairie Artheme Fayard, 1979), 32.
7. A. L. Basham, *The Wonder that Was India* (Calcutta and New Delhi: Rupa Paperback, 1967), 358.
8. Basavanna, in *Speaking of Siva,* translated with an introduction by A. K. Ramanujan (Harmondsworth, England: Penguin Classics, 1979), 19.
9. Ibid, p. 69.
10. Bhagwan Shree Rajneesh, *The Book of Secrets,* vol. 2 (London: Rashneesh Foundation, Thames & Hudson, 1974).

Chapter 2

1. U. P. Arora, *Motifs in Indian Mythology* (New Delhi: Indika Publishing House, 1981), 62.
2. Haralds Biezias, "Baltische Religionen," in *Germanische und Baltische Religionen* (Stuttgart: Verlag W. Kohlhammer, 1975), 340.

Chapter 3

1. T. R. Rajagopala Aiyar, *Sri Rudram and Chamakam* (Bombay: Bharatiya Vidya Bhavan, 1985), 9 ff.
2. Karl Schlesier, *Die Wölfe des Himmels* (Köln: Eugen Diederichs Verlag, 1985), 112.
3. Wolf-Dieter Storl, *Shamanism among Americans of European Origin* (Berne, Switzerland: Inaugural dissertation, University of Berne, 1974), 83 ff.
4. Erika Bourguignon, *Psychological Anthropology* (New York: Holt, Rinehart, & Winston, 1979), 233–268.
5. Mircea Eliade, *Le chamanisme et les techniques archaiques de l'extase* (Paris: Editions Payot, 1951), 430 ff.

6. H. R. Ellis Davidson, *Gods and Myths of Northern Europe* (Harmondsworth, England: Penguin, 1969), 147.
7. Sri Swami Sivananda, *Lord Shiva and His Worship* (Shivanandanagar, Uttar Pradesh: Divine Life Society, 1984), 226.
8. Nirad C. Chaudhuri, *Hinduism*, 185.
9. Hermann Lübbig, *Oldenburgische Sagen* (Oldenburg: W. Kohlhammer, 1980).
10. Eugen Jung, Swiss collector of Nepalese folktales, personal communication with author, 1986.
11. Åke V. Ström, "Germanische Religion," in *Germanische und Baltische Religionen I*(Stuttgart: W. Kohlhammer, 1975), 121.

Chapter 4

1. Ajit Mookerjee has taken the quote from the *Mundaka Upanishad* and placed it in the book *Ritual Art of India* (London: Thames and Hudson, 1985). I have taken the quote from the German translation of this book: *Rituelle Kunst Indiens* (Munich: Kösel, 1987), 154.
2. Swami Sivananda, *Lord Shiva and His Worship*, 144.
3. *Shiva Purana:* Vidyeshvara Samhita, 6.

Chapter 5

1. T. R. Majupuria and Indra Majupuria, *Pashupathinath* (Lashkar, Gwalior, India: M. Devi Lalipur Colony, 1982), 221.
2. Aiyar, *Sri Rudram and Chamakam*, 173.
3. Devdutt Pattanaik, *Shiva: An Introduction* (Mumbai: Vakils, Feffer & Simons, 1997), 23.
4. Rudolf Meyer, *Die Weisheit der Deutschen Volksmärchen* (Frankfurt am Main: Fischer Taschenbuch, 1985), 82.
5. Wolf-Dieter Storl, *Von Heilkräutern und Pflanzengottheiten* (Braunschweig: Aurum, 1997), 120.
6. Griffith's *Ramayana* i. 204; quoted in W. J. Wilkins, *Hindu Mythology* (Calcutta, Allahabad, Bombay, Delhi: Rupa, 1982), 132.
7. Eliade, *Le chamanisme*, chapter 5.
8. Wolf-Dieter Storl, *Culture and Horticulture: A Philosophy of Gardening* (San Francisco: Bio-dynamic Farming and Gardening Association, 2000), 123.
9. Heinrich Zimmer, *Philosophie und Religion Indiens* (Frankfurt am Main: Suhrkamp 1973), 192. English original, *Philosophies of India*, (New York: Bollingen Foundation, 1951).
10. Gopi Krishna, *The Dawn of a New Science* (New Delhi: Kundalini Research and Publication Trust, 1978), 60.
11. Basham, *The Wonder that Was India*, 23.
12. Wendy D. O'Flaherty, *Hindu Myths* (Harmondsworth, England: Penguin Books, 1976), 145.
13. Swami Harshananda, *Hindu Gods and Goddesses* (Mysore: Sri Ramakrishna Ashrama, 1982), 182–183.

14. Alain Daniélou, *While the Gods Play* (Rochester, Vt.: Inner Traditions, 1987), 17–19.
15. Oswald A. Erich and Richard Beitl, eds., *Wörterbuch der Deutschen Volkskunde* (Stuttgart: Alfred Körner, 1974), 247.
16. Hans Findeisen and Heino Gehrts, *Die Schamanen* (Köln: Diederichs Gelbe Reihe, 1983), 116.
17. Trevor Ravenscroft, *The Spear of Destiny* (New York: G. P. Putnam's Sons, 1973). The same theme is also mentioned in Harvey Rachlin's *Lucy's Bones, Sacred Stones and Einstein's Brain* (New York: Henry Holt, 1996).
18. Kardinal Franz König, *Der Glaube der Menschen* (Bonn: Borromäusverein, 1985), 14.
19. Rudolf John Gorsleben, *Hoch-Zeit der Menschhei.* (Leipzig: Koehler & Amelang, 1930), 475.

Chapter 6

1. Wilkins, *Hindu Mythology*, 292.
2. Pattanaik, *Shiva*, 32.
3. Harshananda, *Hindu Gods and Goddesses*, 292.
4. David Annan, "Thuggee," in *Secret Societies*, edited by Norman MacKenzie (London: Collier Books, 1967), 55–70.
5. Pattanaik, *Shiva*, 33–34.
6. Emil Nack, *Götter, Helden und Dämonen* (Wien, Heidelberg: Carl Ueberreuter, 1968), 175.

Chapter 7

1. Fred W. Clothey and J. Bruce Long, *Experiencing Siva* (New Delhi: Manohar 1983), 62.
2. Zukav, Gary. *The Dancing Wu Li Masters* (New York: Bantam Books, 1979), 217.
3. Sivananda. *Lord Shiva and His Worship*, 70.
4. Eliade, *Le chamanisme*, 169.

Chapter 8

1. The retelling of the story of Shiva's wedding is based on the compilations of Chaudhuri, *Hinduism,* 225; and Pattanaik, *Shiva,* 26–28.
2. W. J. Wilkins, *Hindu Mythology* (Calcutta, Allahabad, Bombay, New Delhi: Rupa Paperback, 1982), 335f.
3. Sri Swami Sivananda, *Hindu Fasts and Festivals* (Shivanandanagar, India: The Yogi-Vedanta Forest Academy Press, 1983), 107.
4. Alan Bleakley, *Fruits of the Moon Tree*, Chapter 7 (London: Gateway Books, 1984).
5. D. K. S. Dabu, *The Message of Zarathustra* (Bombay: New Book Company, 1959), 155.
6. Diana L. Eck, *Benares, City of Light* (London: Routledge & Kegan Paul, 1983), 140.

Chapter 9

1. C. Dimmit and J. A. B. Van Buitenen, *Classical Hindu Mythology* (New Delhi: Rupa, 1983), 216.
2. Basham, *The Wonder that Was India,* 188.
3. Ibid., 118.
4. Wendy D. O'Flaherty, *Siva: the Erotic Ascetic* (London and New York: Oxford University Press, 1981), 282.

Chapter 10

1. Ervad S. D. Bharucha, *Zoroastran Religion and Customs* (Bombay: D. B. Taraporevala Sons, 1979), 170.
2. Mircea Eliade, *Patterns in Comparative Religion* (New York: Meridian Books, 1963), 164f.
3. F. Max Mueller, trans., "The Sayings of Ramakrishna," in *A Book of India,* edited by B. N. Pandey (Calcutta, Allahabad, Bombay, New Delhi: Rupa Paperback, 1981), 321.
4. Ramanujan, *Speaking of Siva,* 167.
5. Maurice Magre, *La clef des choses cachées* (Paris: Fasquelle Edieurs, 1935). German translation, *Die Kraft des frühen Himmels* (Bad Münstereifel und Trilla: Edition Tramontane. 1985), 157.
6. Claudia Müller-Ebeling, Christian Rätsch, and Wolf-Dieter Storl, *Hexenmedizin,* 4th edition (Aarau, Switzerland: AT-Verlag, 2002), 54. American edition, *Witchcraft Medicine* (Rochester, Vt.: Inner Traditions International, 2004).
7. Storl, *Shamanism among Americans of European Origin,* 21.

Chapter 11

1. Nirad C. Chaudhuri, *The Continent of Circe* (Bombay: Jaico Publishing House, 1983).
2. Kamalakar Mishra, *Significance of the Tantric Tradition* (Varanasi: Arddhanarisvara Publications, 1981), 45.
3. Rajneesh, *The Book of the Secrets,* 1974.
4. Storl, *Von Heilkräutern und Pflanzengottheiten,* 147 f.
5. Swami Harshananda, *All about Hindu Temples* (Mysore: Sri Ramakrishna Ashram 1981), 9 ff.

Chapter 12

1. T. C. Majupuria and I. Majupuria, *Erotic Themes of Nepal* (Lashkar, Gwalior, India: S. Devi Madhoganj, 1986), 185.

Chapter 13

1. The devotional song at the beginning of the chapter is found in Hans-Georg Behr, *Von Hanf ist die Rede* (Frankfurt am Main: Zweitausendeins, 1995), 44.
2. Sivananda, *Hindu Fasts and Festivals* (Shivanandanagar: The Yoga-Vedanta Forest Academy Press, 1983), 125.
3. L. Kolisko, *Agriculture of Tomorrow* (London: Kolisko Archives, 1939), 13 ff. Also see Storl, *Culture and Horticulture,* 197f.

4. Martha Sills-Fuchs, *Wiederkehr der Kelten* (München: Knaur, 1983), 105.
5. Sivananda, *Hindu Fasts and Festivals*, 129.
6. The author is indebted for much of this information to Professor R. Rao of the Department of Botany, Benares Hindu University, Varanasi, Uttar Pradesh.
7. Majurpuria and Majupuria, *Pashupathinath*, 202 f.
8. Bhagwan Shree Rajneesh, *Das Buch der Geheimnisse* (München: Wilhelm Heyne Verlag, 1983), 84. This is a translation of the English original *The Book of Secrets* (London: Thames & Hudson, 1974).
9. W.J. Wilkins, *Hindu Mythology* (New Delhi: Rupa & Co., new ed. 1982, first ed. 1882), 279.
10. Glenn Yokum, "Madness and Devotion in Manikkavacakar's Tiruvacakam," in *Experiencing Shiva*, edited by Fred W. Clothey and Bruce Long (New Delhi: Manohar Publications, 1983), 20.
11. Arthur M. Eastman, ed., *The Norton Anthology of Poetry* (New York: W. W. Norton, 1970), 847–48.
12. Yokum, "Madness and Devotion in Manikkavacakar's Tiruvacakam," in *Experiencing Shiva*, 22.
13. Ibid., 28
14. Ibid., 20
15. Aldo Legnaro, "Ansätze zu einer Soziologie des Rausches" in *Rausch und Realität*, Bd. 1, 104.
16. Wolf-Dieter Storl, *Bom Shiva* (Solothurn, Switzerland: Nachtschatten Verlag, 2003), 15.
17. Erika Moser-Schmitt, "Soziokultureller Gebrauch von Cannabis in Indien" in *Rausch und Realität*, Bd. 2, 938.
18. O'Flaherty, *Siva, the Erotic Ascetic*, 161.
19. O'Flaherty, *Hindu Myths*, 147–149.
20. Harold A. Hansen, *Der Hexengarten* (München: Trikont-Dianus, 1983), 66.
21. Daniélou, *Shiva et Dionysos*, 112 ff.
22. Hansen, *Der Hexengarten*, 63.

Chapter 14

1. Storl, *Culture and Horticulture*, 197.
2. Swahanada, *Hindu Symbology*, 51.
3. Arthur Osborne, *Ramana Maharshi and the Path to Self-Knowledge* (Bombay: Jaico Publishing House, 1982), 40 ff.
4. Paul Brunton, *A Search in Secret India* (London: Rider, 1934), 153.
5. Sivananda, *Hindu Fasts and Festivals*, 141.

BIBLIOGRAPHY

Aiyar, T. R. Rajagopala. *Sri Rudram and Chamakam*. Bombay: Bharatiya Vidya Bhavan, 1985.

Annan, David. "Thuggee." In *Secret Societies,* edited by Norman MacKenzie. London: Collier Books, 1967.

Arora, U. P. *Motifs in Indian Mythology*. New Delhi: Indika Publishing House, 1981.

Basham, A.L. *The Wonder that Was India*. Calcutta and New Delhi: Rupa Paperback, 1967.

Behr, Hans-Georg. *Von Hanf ist die Rede*. Frankfurt am Main: Zweitausendeins, 1995.

Bharucha, Ervad S. D. *Zoroastran Religion and Customs*. Bombay: D. B. Taraporevala Sons, 1979.

Biezias, Haralds. "Baltische Religionen." In *Germanische und Baltische Religionen*. Stuttgart: Verlag W. Kohlhammer, 1975.

Bleakley, Alan. *Fruits of the Moon Tree*. London: Gateway Books, 1984.

Bourguignon, Erika. *Psychological Anthropology*. New York: Holt, Rinehart, and Winston, 1979.

Brunton, Paul. *A Search in Secret India*. London: Rider, 1934.

Chaudhuri, Nirad C. *Autobiography of an Unknown Indian*. New York: MacMillan, 1951.

———. *Hinduism, A Religion to Live By*. Oxford: Oxford University Press, 1979.

———. *The Continent of Circe*. Bombay: Jaico Publishing House, 1983.

Clothey, Fred W., and J. Bruce Long. *Experiencing Siva*. New Delhi: Ramesh Jain, Manohar Publications, 1983.

Dabu, D. K. S. *Message of Zarathustra*. Bombay: The New Book Company, 1959.

Daniélou, Alain. *Gods of Love and Ecstasy:The Traditions of Shiva and Dionysus*. Rochester, Vt.: Inner Traditions, 1992.

Davidson, H. R. Ellis. *Gods and Myths of Northern Europe*. Harmondsworth, Middlesex, England: Penguin Books, 1969.

Dimmitt, C., and J. A. B. Van Buitenen. *Classical Hindu Mythology*. New Delhi: Rupa Paperbacks, 1983.

Döbler, Hannsferdinand. *Die Germanen, Legende und Wirklichkeit von A bis Z*. Barcelona: Prisma Verlag, 1975.

Eck, Diana L. *Banaras, City of Light*. London: Routledge & Kegan Paul, 1983.

Eliade, Mircea. *Le chamanisme et les techniques archaiques de l'extase.* Paris: Editons Payot, 1953.

———. *Patterns in Comparative Religion.* New York: Meridian Books, 1963.

Erich, Oswald A., and Richard Beitl. *Wörterbuch der deutschen Volkskunde.* Stuttgart: Alfred Kröner Verlag, 1974.

Findeisen, Hans and Heino Gehrts. *Die Schamanen.* Diederichs Gelbe Reihe. Köln: Eugen Diederichs Verlag, 1983.

Gorsleben, Rudolf John. *Hoch-Zeit der Menschheit.* Leipzig: Koehler & Amelang, 1930.

Hanson, Harold A. *Der Hexengarten.* München: Trikont-Dianus Verlag, 1983.

Harshananda, Swami. *All about Hindu Temples.* Mysore: Sri Ramakrishna Ashrama, 1981.

———. *Hindu Gods and Goddesses.* Mysore: Sri Ramakrishna Ashrama, 1982.

Jettmar, Karl. "Skythen und Haschisch." In *Rausch und Realität*, Band 2. Hamburg: Rowolt Verlag, 1982.

Kolisko, L. *Agriculture of Tomorrow.* London: Kolisko Archives, 1939.

König, Kardinal Franz. *Der Glaube der Menschen.* Bonn: Verlag des Borromäusvereins, 1985.

Krishna, Gopi. *The Dawn of a New Science.* New Delhi: Kundalini Research and Publication Trust, 1978.

Legnaro, Aldo. "Ansätze zu einer Soziologie des Rausches." In *Rausch und Realität*, Band II, edited by Gisela Völger and Karin von Welck. Hamburg: Rowohlt Verlag, 1982.

Lübbig, Hermann. *Oldenburgische Sagen.* Oldenburg: Heinz Holzberg Verlag, 1980.

Magre, Maurice. *La clef des choses cachées.* Paris: Fasquelle Editeurs, 1935.

Majupuria, T. R., and Majupuria, I. *Pashupathinath.* Lashkar, Gwalior, India: M. Devi Lalipur Colony, 1982.

———. *Erotic Themes of Nepal.* Lashkar, Gwalior, India: S. Devi Madhoganj Publications, 1986.

Meyer, Rudolf. *Die Weisheit der Deutschen Volksmärchen.* Frankfurt am Main: Fischer Taschenbuch. 1985.

Mishra, Kamalakar. *Significance of the Tantric Tradition.* Varanasi, India: Arddhanarishvara Publications, 1981.

Moser-Schmitt, Erika. "Sozio-ritueller Gebrauch von Cannabis in Indien." In *Rausch und Realität*, Band II, edited by Gisela Völger and Karin von Welck. Hamburg: Rowohlt Verlag, 1982.

Nack, Emil. *Götter, Helden und Dämonen.* Wien, Heidelberg: Verlag Carl Peberreuter, 1968.

O'Flaherty, Wendy D. *Hindu Myths.* Harmondsworth, England: Penguin Books, 1976.

———. *Shiva, the Erotic Ascetic.* London and New York: Oxford University Press, 1981.

Osborne, Arthur. *Ramana Maharshi and the Path of Self-Knowledge.* Bombay: Jaico Publishing House, 1982.

Pandey, B. N. *A Book of India*. Calcutta, Allahabad, Bombay, New Delhi: Rupa & Co., 1981.

Pattanaik, Devdutt. *Shiva: An Introduction*. Mumbai: Vakils, Feffer and Simons, 1997.

Rajneesh, Bhagwan Shree. *The Book of Secrets*, vol. I. London: Thames & Hudson, 1974. Copyright of Rajneesh Foundation.

Ramanujan. A. K. *Speaking of Siva*. Harmondsworth, Middlesex: Penguin Classics, 1979.

Rätsch, Christian, and Claudia Müller-Ebeling. *Isoldens Liebestrank*. München: Kindler Verlag, 1986.

Ravenscroft, Trevor. *The Spear of Destiny*. New York: G. P. Putman's Sons, 1973.

Schlesier, Karl. *Die Wölfe des Himmels*. Köln: Eugen Diederichs Verlag, 1985.

Sills-Fuchs, M. *Wiederkehr der Kelten*. München: Knaur Taschenbuch, 1983.

Sivananda, Sri Swami. *Lord Shiva and His Worship*. Shivanandanagar, Uttar Pradesh, India: Divine Life Society, 1984.

———. *Hindu Fasts and Festivals*. Shivanandanagar, India: The Yoga Vedanta Forest Academy Press, 1983.

Storl, Wolf-Dieter. *Shamanism among Americans of European Origin*. Berne, Switzerland: Inaugural Dissertation, University of Berne, 1974.

———. *Von Heilkräutern und Pflanzengottheiten*. Braunschweig: Aurum Verlag, 1997.

———. *Culture and Horticulture*. San Francisco: Biodymanic Farming and Gardening Association, 2000.

———. *Bom Shiva*. Solothurn, Schweiz: Nachtschatten Verlag, 2003.

Ström, Ake V. "Germanische Religion." In *Germanische und Baltische Religion*. Stuttgart: Verlag W. Kohlhammer, 1975.

Swahananda, Swami. *Hindu Symbology and Other Essays*. Madras: Sri Ramakrishna Math, 1983.

Wilkins, W. J. *Hindu Mythology*. Calcutta, Allahabad, Bombay, Delhi: Rupa & Co., 1982.

Yokum, Glenn, Madness and Devotion in Manikkavacakar's Tiruvacakam." In *Experiencing Siva*, edited by Fred W. Clothey and Bruce Long. New Delhi: Manohar Publishing, 1983.

Zimmer, Heinrich. *Philosophie und Religion Indiens*. Frankfurt am Main: Suhrkamp Taschenbuch, 1973.

Zukav, Gary. *The Dancing Wu Li Masters*. New York: Bantam Books, 1979.

INDEX